The Nature of Organizations

Robert Grandford Wright

Pepperdine University

Dickenson Publishing Company, Inc.

Encino, California and Belmont, California

ISBN-0-8221-0188-2

Library of Congress Catalog Card Number: 76-47314

Printed in the United States of America

Printing (last digit): 9 8 7 6 5 4 3 2 1

Cover design by Donald A. Vaughn
of Honolulu, a close friend of the author.

To the spirit of exploring

Contents

Preface

The aim of this book is to bring about a keener sensitivity to the nature of human organizations. It was written in the belief that through a heightened awareness of the realities of organizational life, the relations between people and their structured enterprises have a better chance of being improved. To achieve a meaningful improvement in this area, we need to gain three kinds of insights. First, we need to know what can be changed, what cannot be changed, and why. Second, we need varied perspectives of these institutions if we are to acquire a respect for the high order of their complexity. And third, we must draw from organizational needs behavioral, intellectual, and philosophical implications for the challenge of leadership.

The approach to the study of organizations used here was that of an outsider looking in on their happenings. The method is similar to that used by an anthropologist to study and understand the subtleties of a tribal society. The terms *organization theory* and *organization behavior* were not accepted as titles for the book because agreement on the meaning of these phrases is rare. However, many of the passages in the book are heavily influenced by what most scholars consider part of organization theory, while others are affected by teachings attributed to organization behavior. Both realms of study throw a certain light of understanding on the nature of organizations. In addition, though all of the social disciplines—psychology, social psychology, economics, political science, and anthropology—are important to studies in this area, the approach used in this analysis emphasizes social and cultural anthropology as the means to best explain the nature of organizations in a comprehensive yet individuated way.

The design of the book follows the lines of the gestalt process of learning from overview, to detail, and back to an overview. This is done in the belief that explanations of organizations (or anything else) first require a broad-brush understanding of the subject. Then details can be learned, but this time as they relate to the overall phenomenon being studied. Finally, the general portrait of an organization is again drawn, but now with the details held firmly in place. So the book opens with an overview of the role, types, needs, and life cycle of organizations. It then narrows its attention to the details: structure, anatomy, subsystems, and culture. The focus of the book then broadens again to encompass a composite view of the overall nature and character of organizations. The reader, in this way, is encouraged to "see" an unfolding flow of relationships and interrelationships.

No writer can completely recount all of those persons who influenced his work. One can only attempt to acknowledge those who made the most pronounced and immediate mark on the development of his thinking. Fortunately, a number of persons directly or indirectly, knowingly or unknowingly, intentionally or unintentionally, touched the thoughts and feelings behind this essay. I am grateful to the following people for their personal influence in bringing the text from mind to manuscript: the late Chester I. Barnard and E. Wight Bakke, André Delbecq, Amitai Etzioni, John Gardner, Milton Gordon, Walter Goldschmidt, Robert Kahn, Daniel Katz, Louis Kaufman, Barbara Levy, and William Wolf. I am indebted to David Moore and my colleagues at Cornell University for preserving the supportive institutional setting within which most of the writing could take form. I thank Donald Vaughn, comrade and confident, for the symbolic cover design. A special note of appreciation is struck for Ann Hylton Wright and Karyn Yasulaitis for their invaluable and very special contributions. For their assistance in creatively sculpting the roughly hewn manuscript, I thank June Woodson Beeson, Dr. Jack R. Dustman of California Lutheran College, Professor Steven Kerr of Ohio State University, Janet Greenblatt, and Bernice Lifton. Any ungraceful lines that remain of course are of my doing. I am deeply grateful to each of these people for their influence on the writing. Without them, this essay would never have made its arduous way from thought to writing pad to the book you hold in your hands.

R. G. W.

1

Role of Organizations

Human interaction is seen as being, at one and the same time, a need of man and a requisite for society, . . . The individual is primarily motivated toward his own physical self-perpetuation and his symbolic self-aggrandizement, yet both of these can be achieved only through deep dependence and involvement with others.

Goldschmidt[1]

The civilization humans have shaped is dependent upon formal organization for nearly every enterprise. The zeal with which people throw themselves into intense organizational activity caused one observer, Robert Seidenburg, to summarize its influence:

Modern man has learned to accommodate himself to a world increasingly organized. The trend toward ever more explicit and consciously drawn relationships is profound and sweeping; it is marked by depth no less than by extension.[2]

The decentralization of power to a myriad of organizations, or pluralism, is unique to democratic societies. The essence of this social phenomenon is basic to all but totalitarian states. Although culture may support the basic ideal of individual freedom, the vigor of any society depends upon the strengths of its organizations. Such critics of democracy and pluralism, as José Ortega y Gasset and Wilhelm Ropke[3] warned that a multitude of weak organizations would lead to the demise of a social order. This threat to social integrity is, of course, present to some degree in all societies. However, when a society is dependent upon organizations—standing between the state and the individual for supplying nearly all of the people's needs, strong ones are indispensable. The alternative to organizational life is satirically pointed up by behavioralists Burleigh Gardiner and David Moore:

1

> The techniques, processes and structural forms of large-scale organization are here to stay, for it is the primary and basic social invention of civilization. Take away large-scale organization and you are back to living in a cave or mud hut, eating rutabagas and turnips, and discovering why the Anglo-Saxons invented all those four-letter words, as you try to shoot a racing rabbit with a bow and arrow.[4]

Though large-scale organizations may not be the "primary and basic social invention of society," surely they are "here to stay" because the large-scale responsibilities they have acquired are here to stay—and those responsibilities are growing larger. Therefore, it is not a matter of considering whether organizations are socially desirable. Rather the issue is one of making them better serve mankind, and this can be brought about only through an increased understanding of their internal arrangements.

It is this sense of the importance of understanding organizations that has enticed people from diverse fields of study to search for universally applicable principles of ordering human ventures. The study has gone beyond separate academic disciplines to attract the attention of scholars in nearly every area of the social sciences. The search for a theory of organization has created an explosion of research and analyses. Though the results often raise more questions than answers, the contributions may make management philosopher Peter Drucker's prediction come true:

> Among the major innovations of the past ten or fifteen years . . . the basically nontechnical innovations have had a greater impact . . . and have contributed more to the increase in productivity in this country, than all technical innovations. . . . In the long view of history, it is for social innovations—and not technical ones—that America may be best remembered.[5]

Research leading toward a deeper understanding of organizations continues to be a primary concern for large numbers of sociologists, social and cultural anthropologists, social psychologists, political scientists, and economists. Scholars from each of these disciplines, and from others, have contributed to the current state of knowledge on the nature and dynamics of organizations. Consequently, the field of organizational research is functionally and historically an interdisciplinary area of inquiry marked by diversity in concepts, terms, and methods of study.

Indeed, the very nature of organizations justifies diverse approaches. Like a living thing, each is a distinct entity. Each has its own physical and social environment, formal structure, established goals, and requirements for self-maintenance. An organization is a complex system continuously adjusting to reach its desired goals while striving for perpetuity and a degree of balance. Viewed another way, it is a contrived, formal grouping of people into a social system to cooperate in tasks toward specific goals.[6]

TRAITS COMMON TO ALL ORGANIZATIONS

All organizations possess within the following universal characteristics:

Common Traits

Purpose, or goals
Authority centers
Formal structure
Contrived grouping of people
   (division of labor or
    specialization)
Delegative processes

Communications systems
Incentive systems
Control systems
Strategic internal policies
Status hierarchy
Leadership roles
Informal structure

Let us consider certain general traits of all organizations. An organization is formed when some endeavor requires the efforts of more than one person for its accomplishment. This condition can arise either because the task is too big or too complicated for one person to handle. So, an organization can be as small as the coordinated efforts of two individuals or as large as the largest structure of persons imaginably engaged in cooperative interaction. Such arrangements are either the means to produce or distribute products or services or they are arenas for merely interpersonal affiliations.

An organization is a structuring of human relationships so that members can have expectations of each other. It is designed by people; therefore it has imperfections. Organizations mature and grow, partially through a designed scheme and partially in an unordered manner. The designed element of development is a rational response to internal pressures to expand and re-form relationships because of functional necessities. As an example, orderly development is achieved by the leaders of the organization when they reassess the purpose of the enterprise, reconceive the means to that end, or redesign the structure and related activities so that they fulfill the newly devised functions in an efficient manner. In contrast, unstructured change comes as a result of unordered, seemingly nonrational responses to various cultural and psychological forces on people within the enterprise.

Consider, for instance, a small business firm in which the owner/manager has carefully designed jobs so that they could be done efficiently by persons with certain individual skills and interests. This is orderly development. One senior employee, however, is permitted to do whatever he believes should be done across job descriptions, even though efficiency suffers, because he did the work that way, was loyal and now, resists restrictions. This is unstructured, *seemingly* nonrational development. Hence, to the uninitiated, the enterprise seems to be the result of a series of half-design, half topsy-turvy decisions over time. The sensitive observer, instead, looks behind arrangements that seem illogical for their cultural or psychological causes.

Support Groups

Each organization has outside support groups, or constituencies, that support it through their use, or their concern with the intended use, of the service or product offered by the enterprise. It is forced to grow, contract, or change because of the expectations of such constituencies. When the enterprise fails to respond over time to relatively minor shifts in requirements of its supporters, the forces toward change intensify, and the demands for modifications become more pronounced. In response, an organization may react through revolutionary behavior rather than through a planned evolutionary adjustment, or metamorphosis. Such abrupt change can be disruptive, causing loss of continuity, imbalances, and overcorrections. Once social relationships have been established, in a word, the emerging organization tends to be slowly "reactionistic" rather than "activistic." This means that organizations often do not act in response to foreseeable pressures for change on the horizon of time. Rather, they are apt to wait, reacting only when forces requiring change build to a clamor for immediate action.

Structural Development

An organization develops certain processes to serve as the means to sustain itself *and also* to generate a productive outflow. In a business firm the means for production and distribution are designed to fulfill these functional activities. The type of design is based upon constraints imposed by the economics of efficient resource use, and the expectations of groups served, or constituency groups. The methods of sustaining the organization include, among others, incentives to attract and retain people, authority to keep them functioning toward the endeavor's goals and to mediate role behavior, and communications to relate organizational inducements to individual rewards.[7] The same type of structural development evolves in church groups, military units, charitable enterprises, political campaigns, communes, and college fraternities and sororities. These aspects, which are common to all organizations, often are not designed along functional needs, but rather are developed pell-mell over a period of time in response to such influences as tradition, conditions in the external environment, and the attitudes of the leaders of the organization.

Flexibility of common traits. These common traits, as well as the others listed on page 3, however, are designed to function differently in different organizations. Consider, for example, the forces that bear on the design of the means through which an organization maintains its continuity. Based on its needs for self-maintenance, each enterprise has traits common to all. The design or emergence of these aspects, however, is heavily tempered by behavioral and cultural influences within the individual enterprise. For instance, in one major plant with over 2,000 workers, its leaders decided to decentralize much of their authority to the lowest production units. These units of ten to twelve members were given broad discretion to make decisions collectively on matters affecting unit production with minimum involvement from people above. Unit members could hire, schedule, reward, correct, and fire fellow members as required. Consequently, the arrangement became a tradition that influenced such factors as personnel selection, loyalty bonds, authority and status relationships, incentives, advancement, leadership, and control. The tradition was reinforced when people who found the arrangement appealing were attracted to the plant, while those who found it unsatisfactory stayed out or left the firm. In this example we see how an organization develops partially in response to influences by people in sensitive positions and by tradition. Further, the sum of such reactions produces a unique organizational character, or "personality."[8] That dimension of organization defies any explanation based exclusively on rational grounds.

Psychological Development

An organization is subject to unorderly development when its leadership is affected by popularly accepted trends in organizational design. This is natural. People, as social creatures adopt that which works well for others. These fashionable trends concern the relationships of people in group effort and can often be applied effectively. However, faddish arrangements, though appropriate in a specific situation, often fail when applied to organizations in general. Nonetheless, there is a tendency to apply, *en bloc,* arrangements effective in one setup to another that is totally different. Popularized practices momentarily successful are appealing. And leaders are no more immune to fads than the rest of us.

As examples: During the early era of industrial development, time and motion studies led the way to finer degrees of specialization than had previously been customary. Currently, many believe that work is overly specialized, that less structure is needed to reduce boredom, absenteeism, and loss of identity. Many business firms today are accepting the idea that "job enlargement," or "job expansion," is a way to enrich work. We have witnessed times when the authority to make decisions and act was tightly held at the top of the organization. Now, many major enterprises are emphasizing the decentralization of authority down to the lower operating levels. The span of management (or ratio of subordinates to a superior) was once kept very narrow to maximize conformity, dependency, and control. Today, the trend is toward broader spans of management. Early organizations were rigidly organized, with unyielding structures similar to the formation of a traditional military unit. More recently, organization arrangements have been viewed in terms of individual members and groups; structures have been modified to recognize the vested interests and unique qualifications of some individuals.

In sum, organizations develop in a manner best described as half design, half topsy-turvy. The designed element comes from rational responses to functional needs; the spontaneous, from revolutionary overcorrections, personal biases of leaders, traditions, and arbitrary adoptions of fashionable organizational arrangements.

Is a Group an Organization?

A group, according to the dictionary and common usage, is an assemblage of individuals in whom the kind, degree, or intensity of the relationships is not clearly definable. To group is to classify. So, a group could be, among other classifications, an audience, a crowd, an assembly, a mob, a clan, or a family gathering. Though some sociologists contend that through group processes, or dynamics, a true organization emerges, the structure may be minimal as contrasted with the complex edifices discussed here. This distinction is required because a group's formation may be casual, short-lived, nebulously structured, and without coordinated responsibilities for achieving a goal. The organization, by contrast, is formed to accommodate intense interaction, of extended duration, requiring higher degrees of structure, through which joint responsibilities for goal attainment can be exercised.

An organization is more than a group. It is something more than a casual human assemblage such as a neighborhood, a social party, a college class, or even sororities and fraternities. Groups are aggregations of people who have some relationship to one another that places them into a common classification. Group members in the classification, however, may or may not interact. In contrast, an organization is a more concrete social process, with more definable boundaries, through which social interaction must take place and cooperation gains expression by striving toward goals requiring mutual effort.

Key Elements of an Organization

Examine the key elements of an organization displayed in the following example, in which the demands of a situation convert a group into a simple organization, which then reverts back to a group: Several men are idly talking while watching another man attempt to move a cumbersome crate from a loading dock to a waiting truck. When the chatting men see that the task of the worker is too difficult, they decide to help him. Each implicitly agrees to carry a share of the burden and help guide the others in maneuvering the crate safely from the dock to the vehicle. Whoever is in a position to act as a guide will direct the others and warn them of impediments to a safe move. After completing the chore, the working man returns to his tasks, the other to their idle talk.

We can readily see the *characteristics of an organization* that emerged as a result of the demands of this situation:

1. A formal organization arises when a task, because of its size or complexity, requires the efforts of more than one person. A human organization can be formed rapidly for simple tasks.
2. An organization must have consciously coordinated activities.
3. The participants accept the goal(s) of the organization.
4. A division of labor is made so that each member becomes accountable for a part of the endeavor.
5. The formal organization that emerges is a system of coordinated activities; thus, it becomes something more than the sum of its parts.
6. An organization can disband leaving no physical evidence of its existence.

A number of these elements, however, are not evident in all groups.

By summing Traits One through Four, we can state a definition of a formal organization. An organization is a *contrived open system of coordinated activities by two or more participants to achieve a common goal or goals.* Now, what implications does such a definition suggest?

MEANING OF THE DEFINITION

"Contrived"

The word *contrived* indicates that formal organizations are partially designed by people. The implication from this is that a formal social organization is a less uniform and perfect structure than are biological or physical structures.[9] *Biological structures* have, to a greater or lesser degree, the identifiable traits of specific size and shape, metabolism, movement, irritability, growth, reproduction, entropy, and, most significant as a contrasting delineation to this discussion, adaptation. *Physical structures* have identifiable traits of size, shape, and movement. They are made up of two fundamental components—matter and energy. Though under certain conditions these components are capable of interconversion, predictable changes occur along orderly lines based on principles of physics and chemistry. A *social structure* commonly is not as adaptable to environmental changes, nor as predictable in its adaptation to forces exerted on it, as are either biological or physical structures. A major principle of organic or inorganic evolution—the gradual, orderly change from one condition to another—is absent from a social structure. Thus, change is related to the capacity of an organization's leaders to perceive a need for it, and to its tolerance by both the endeavor's leaders and participants. The importance of the ability to introduce change, and certain impediments to its implementation, will be discussed in greater detail in Chapter 2.

"Open"

A social system, or organization, is an *open* structure, whereas biological and physical systems have distinct bounds that differentiate their forms from other entities. They are semiclosed systems with distinguishable physical forms. For example, semiclosed biological organisms such as human beings exchange energies with their environment to maintain themselves and to secure the nourishment to be productive, thereby continuing to sustain themselves. People require air, water, food, and certain environmental conditions to live; given these essentials, their physical structure or system is preserved.

A social system also exchanges energies with its environment. An organization requires people and a basic social environment to exist. In addition, most require capital, equipment, materials, and land. Unlike a biological organism, however, fulfillment of these requirements does not in any way ensure that the health of the organization will be preserved. People leave enterprises, even successful ones, to pursue other endeavors. They retire or are promoted—or demoted. They may become nonparticipants by electing to leave the organization temporarily or to disassociate themselves from the venture's goals through loyalties to other activities. Unlike the physical constraints of a biological organism, the structuring of human relationships changes in form. The quality of openness of a social organization permits its form to change even when it enjoys sufficient resources to sustain itself. Its openness permits changes in its composition in two ways: First, its productive capabilities change with the turnover of people; and second, its capacity to maintain its strengths internally changes as new human relationships emerge.

The openness of an organization suggests the need for a continuing reassessment of its work force requirements. This fluidity also calls for incentives to attract people to the organization, to retain them, and to induce them to accept required role behavior. Workers also need inducements to assume different role behavior and role relationships as required by the evolving organizational structure. Leaders tend to emphasize activities dealing with the assessment of needs for human resources, and with attracting people to fill such needs, often neglecting efforts to make the most of the human assets they already have. That is, often less care is given to retaining the human asset in the system, to fostering patterns of behavior and interrelations that synthesize human energies, and when required, to providing an internal culture within which acceptable behavior will be "different" behavior. Some organizations, by contract, have outstandingly successful programs to help employees to develop the capacity for growth and change. Fluor Corporation, for instance, has an ambitious program called Personnel Growth, Inc. available to its staff to identify their individual needs and to assist employees to fill requirements observed.

"System"

The definition of an organization includes the phrase "system of coordinated activities." When the activities of two or more people are coordinated, a structured pattern of expectations and behavior results. This phrase, by definition, rules out most groups as salient forms of organization. Such activities are a patterning of events or happenings, in contrast to the physical patterning of the anatomical structures of biological systems. Herein lies one of the major difficulties for the student striving to understand human organizations. A biological system such as a human being has a physiology and an anatomy; its anatomical structure can be studied, and certain explanations of its physiology (or "events") can be found even when it is not functioning. A biological organism is a composite of interacting systems whose activities are under the influences of a fixed field of chemical and physiological forces. A social system, however, is a pattern of activities governed by elements from a fluid field—or, more accurately, from two fluid fields—of forces. Some of these forces emanate from the external environment of a social system. They include influences like public attitudes, political environment, economic conditions, and social mores. The behavior of an organization is also affected by a field of forces from within itself such as the traits of its leadership, its traditions, and its culture.

Though understanding the behavior of an organization of people is an abstract process when compared with the concreteness with which physical entities can be studied, the fact that organizations are *systems* of activities suggests an approach for gaining the necessary insights. The term *system* merely defines a set of objects or people whose activities are so interrelated, and therefore integrated, that the total assumes a uniqueness. Thus, an organization is more than the sum of its parts.

A distinct character emerges as a consequence of the total endeavor's interrelated state. Therefore, one cannot acquire an understanding of the formation by attempting to reconstruct it, that is, by fragmenting it and then adding its parts. Not only is this an exercise in futility, but in the process of studying the fragments the student is also led to accept inaccuracies because of the oversimplification. The popular parable, "The Blind Men and the Elephant," serves to illustrate the confusion that can result from attempting to study an integrated entity through dissection and analysis of its individual parts.

> As you may recall, a number of blind men were asked to describe an elephant that was in their midst. One man felt the tusk, another the ear, yet another a leg, and so on. Their descriptions accurately described the elephant, but only in terms of their limited perceptions of the whole animal. One said that an elephant was like a large stone, another likened it to a winnowing fan, another said it resembled a tree. Though each described the elephant by the part he felt, none could describe the animal as it was because each man lacked the *perspective* to *perceive,* or "see" the whole.[10]

Since an organization is an integrated system of activities, it can only be viewed in total for total understanding. Without a conceptual understanding of that whole, it is impossible to acquire true comprehension. Instead, we can gain only a distorted image of organizational realities unless we are given a sufficiently broad framework within which to relate its subsystems and other interdependent elements. In the absence of this overall view of the organization, understanding— through explanation, rather than description—is impossible.

The idea of viewing an organization in total, at first brush, seems impractical and unfeasible. Such a broad perspective appears to defy true comprehension. Yet it is the only way to understand the behavior of a *specific* organization. In Chapter 7, a model will be presented to make such an exploration both more practical and feasible.

"Common Goals"

Finally, the definition requires that an organization must be examined as an entity formed *"to achieve a common goal or goals."* This presupposes that the members of the group support its objectives through their individual contributions to the overall effort. To some this means that all of the people involved in such an enterprise automatically adopt the purpose for which the organization has been formed. This can readily happen in common pursuits organized for religious, cultural, charitable, and political purposes. But do men and women show such a degree of unified dedication in common pursuits for profits? It is doubtful if they could spontaneously generate shared zeal for such an endeavor. This is particularly true if they are expected to accept from sheer joy a common goal of profit from engineering, production, and marketing activities.

How then are people encouraged to throw their lot in with such uninspiring pursuits? How can a member of a firm be encouraged to join in organizational life requiring the forfeit of certain freedoms and beliefs of value? One gives up a portion of individuality since some degree of conformity is inherent in all institutionalized arrangements (marriage is by no means an exception). One also yields a share of freedom because mutual decisions are required to further the progress of the organization. And, one loses a bit of equality because an organization is, among other things, a status and authority hierarchy within which unequal rights and privileges are conveyed. Equity, or fair treatment, however, is one of the basic rights a person will not easily give up when joining an organization. This has major consequences for leadership and will therefore be the subject of further discussion in Chapter 9.

Why, then, would a person tradeoff a portion of such treasured rights to join an organization that has as its objective goals for which the person feels little identification, much less dedication? The answer is that a participant will receive adequate rewards for providing certain contributions to the overall goal. One is rewarded for one's contribution; the arrangement is, consequently, a matter of trade-offs. The participant trades off some self-determination to join an enterprise requiring mutual determination. In return, the newcomer will realize benefits, or paybacks, from the organization—paybacks in the form of financial, psychological, and social rewards.

People join organizations for varied reasons and in response to different inducements. Some join because they must. During time of war, draftees are conscripted into the army, in which control toward goals is usually coercive. Some persons come into organizations to gain financial rewards. Business concerns, among others, provide such rewards together with utilitarian control to ensure that the common purpose is supported. People also join organizations as volunteers for varied reasons. Charitable, service, church, and social organizations, among others, provide intrinsic rewards and informal social control to guide participants toward enterprise objectives.

Commonness of purpose, or goal acceptance, is fundamental to the ideal of unified effort. It is attained largely through an elaborate network of role expectations, norms, values, and rewards. Unfortunately, in complex organizations, where tasks must necessarily be highly specialized, participants often cannot see the contribution of their individual parts to overall goals. How, then, can they relate to the fact that their rewards are based upon their part in moving the organization toward its goals? The results of their participation should be clear to members. If it is not, leaders' demands for true involvement or dedication are unrealistic. Lacking devotion, subordinates perform their roles listlessly. Leaders sometimes fail to recognize that identification (which is a prerequisite to dedication) is impossible if members do not perceive their part as it relates to the total effort. Concerned over the lack of enthusiastic support for overall goals, leaders react with added controls, reinforced norms of behavior, and stronger penalties for nonconformity.

Patterns of high performance are unlikely to occur until participants see (1) their part in the overall effort, and (2) their specific accomplishments as means toward that end. Workers need to believe that their contributions and commitments to organizational goals will bring them symbols of personal achievement. These symbols normally include money, status, personal recognition, and social integration. Leaders' ignorance or lack of understanding of these basic human needs too frequently results in inadequate performance.

SUMMARY

Organizations are necessary in unifying human effort to achieve the complex and large tasks required by society. They also represent the means through which their members fulfill a number of their physical, psychological, and social needs. Organizational effectiveness is particularly crucial to the well-being of societies wherein decentralized sources of authority influence the major social activities—economic, religious, charitable, cultural, educational, and governmental. In large measure, the strength of our society depends upon the vitality of pluralistic institutions in which power has been vested. Their vigor begins with an understanding of the nature of organizations so that their benefits can be maximized and their weaknesses minimized.

There are certain traits that are common to all organizations. People join their efforts to achieve a goal beyond their individual capabilities. The system that emerges is a social invention, designed, organized, staffed, and managed by people. Thus, it is an imperfect arrangement. It develops in response to functional needs for certain structural arrangements. It also develops in response to forces of a nonfunctional nature such as overcorrections, traditions, and idiosyncrasies of leaders.

An organization has traits that distinguish it from a loosely knit assemblage of people, or group. Its purpose and need for unified effort give it a higher degree of structure. A simple formal organization is defined as a *contrived open system of coordinated activities by two or more participants to achieve a common goal or goals.* The implications in this definition make the study of social structures much more complex than studies of biological or physical structures. We observed further that an organization is a system of activities. As a consequence, each develops its distinct character, or personality. The nature of a specific organization can be understood only through studying the entity in total, as an integrated system.

DISCUSSION QUESTIONS

1. Why are organizations needed? (Consider both the needs of individuals and the needs of society.)

2. "Why should I study organizations? They are the way they are. I'll just try to fit into one and do the best I can. There's no way I could change one even if I believed there was a better method of doing things." Comment.

3. Why are organizations so heavily structured? Why not rely on more informal arrangements?

4. In what ways do systems called human organizations differ from a biological system such as man?

5. I just want some ideas on how to succeed and some tips on how to manage people. How will study of the nature of organizations make me a better participant (or leader)?

2

Types of Organizations

> Society is sustained through the rewards of its economic system, which provide powerful instrumental motivation toward socially-required behaviors; by the maintenance structures of education and religion, which inculcate the general norms and specific behavioral codes and; by the political structures which pass and enforce law.
>
> *Daniel Katz and Robert L. Kahn*

In Chapter 1, we considered the basic role of organizations—their importance, commonality, and development. We observed the formation of an organization to perform the simple but awkward task of moving a crate from a loading dock to a truck. By analyzing this event, we developed a definition of an organization. We can now turn our attention, in this chapter, to differentiating the two basic types of formal organizations—social institutions and economic institutions—and to analyzing the implications of that distinction.

BASIC TYPES OF ORGANIZATIONS

As explained previously, an organization is formed when a task, because of its magnitude or complexity, requires the efforts of more than one person. Today, most activities require planned, coordinated effort because they are both large and complex. Thus, organizations provide the means through which societal needs are fulfilled; they can also be the means for fulfilling that need efficiently, that is, by minimizing the use of resources relative to output. Additionally, organizations can be the vehicles for the efficient, productive use of human capabilities through specialization of skills and integration of diverse abilities.

The basic purpose of all organizations is to fill a social need. Society, or one of its segments, wants a given service or product or experience, and organizations form to supply it. Thus, all organizations justify themselves *first* socially. This can be seen clearly in the following list of societal wants and the complex organizations that have arisen to satisfy them.

Societal Want	*Type of Social Institution*	
Spiritual guidance	Religious	
Economic and social order, progress	Governmental	
International security	Military	
Domestic civil security	Law enforcement	Category I
Philanthropy	Charitable	
Informed public	Educational	
Aesthetic values	Cultural	
Competition, health	Amateur athletics	
Goods and services	Businesses	Category II

It should be clearly understood that with the exception of businesses, other social institutions are justified *only* by social needs. This is because as a people we believe that certain organizations are socially desirable even if they cannot justify themselves economically. By *economic justification* we mean that revenues from the *prices* of services or products pay for the resources used in their production. We support organizations engaged in socially desirable efforts with voluntary and nonvoluntary donations. For example, a church receives voluntary financial and nonfinancial contributions from its members based upon its intrinsic value to them. Or, the U.S. Army gains nonvoluntary support from taxes and voluntary support from enlistees.

Most people believe that organizations producing services in Category I are doing so in the public interest; therefore, they require only social justification. Economic considerations bow to social necessities here. It is futile to attempt to fix a price, for example, on the benefit rendered by a church to a particular community and to society in general, or to place a dollar value on the serenity brought to a community by law enforcement authorities. It would be vain to attempt to estimate such intangibles as the freedom from fear, the security for self and loved ones, and the peace of mind derived from police protection. Consequently, organizations in Category I above concentrate on rendering social services consistent with the needs of society at a cost the general public, its representatives, or a special interest group is willing to pay.

BUSINESS ORGANIZATIONS

Businesses are found in Category II. The business organization, first, justifies itself socially. That is, it must find a social want or need to fill. Second, a business also justifies its existence economically, *justifies it in the sense that revenues from the sales of its products or services return to the organization sufficient funds to pay those to whom it is obligated.* Among those who have claims upon its revenues are apt to be owners, bondholders, employees, leaders, suppliers, and leaseholders. Revenues generated by the sales of products or services offered must be high enough to reward the people who supply the factors of production, that is, the inputs required to generate the production of goods or services.

Economic Justification

In the final analysis business activities are directed to fulfill society's wants for goods and services—but are normally confined *only* to those areas that are economically justified. To do otherwise a business would shirk its responsibilities to its owners and creditors, who rightfully expect economic reward. Because of this, activities that are socially desirable, but clearly imprudent economically, are undertaken by other types of organizations, which are supported for their social value by both private citizens and businesses.

As an example, assume that an obscure disease is killing 500 people a year. Obviously, it is socially desirable or justifiable to invest in whatever research is required to discover an effective inoculation to prevent the deaths. Notwithstanding, it is unrealistic to expect a pharmaceutical firm (as a business) to invest in what might be a multimillion-dollar research effort which, even if successful, may generate only a token financial return. It is apparent that to impose such demands is damaging to any institution that must justify itself economically. As a consequence, a research endeavor of this type would commonly be diverted to government, university, military, religious, or foundation laboratories. These institutions are charged with burdensome social responsibilities, but they are not expected to generate sufficient revenues through sales of services or products to pay fully for the factors of production used, nor of course, to return profits from their operations.

Efficient Uses of Resources

Businesses have an acute need to use resources efficiently in the production and distribution of goods and services. A business organization is obliged to manage efficiently the factors of production used within the firm and the resources used to influence markets.

On the one hand, the leadership of a company attempts to introduce efficiencies that minimize the amounts of claims placed on the revenues of the firm. It attempts to establish the least wasteful routines and procedures; to mechanize or automate certain phases of production; to decrease duplication and increase coordination so that raw materials, space, machine costs, and man-hours can be saved. In this way, claims on revenues from suppliers, leasers, lenders, and employees are decreased; costs of the goods or services produced are thereby minimized.

On the other hand, leaders attempt to cultivate efficiently markets for the company's products or services. They do so through promotional strategies designed to attain maximum revenues for the dollars spent. Toward this end, they invest in research to delineate their markets, to understand patterns of consumer behavior, to identify those who influence and make buying decisions, and to find methods to influence those decisions. Based on their research findings, leaders design promotional strategies capitalizing on trends in the marketplace so that they maximize returns in sales revenues from each dollar spent on promotional efforts.

For instance, management may decide that the cost of personal selling is prohibitive and that effective appeals can be made through advertising and displays where the product is sold. As a consequence, the economic efficiency of the second promotional strategy would persuade managers to promote sales through nonpersonal sales techniques. Sales revenues, in turn, would be maintained but claims on them would be minimized by eliminating unnecessary marketing costs.

A business must operate efficiently in an economic sense, compared with its competitors, if it is to survive. Bear in mind that the resources it uses can be quantified and expressed as costs. More significantly, its output can also be quantified and summed to represent revenues. For the firm to be economically efficient, these revenues must be sufficiently large to pay the costs of all factors involved in production. In contrast to all other complex social institutions, a business *in competition with other firms* strives to perform efficiently both in its use of resources to produce goods or services and to justify themselves economically.

NONBUSINESS ORGANIZATIONS

The social institutions found in Category I—such as governmental, military, and religious organizations—are also concerned with internal efficiencies to reduce costs. However, since their products or services are not priced, their costs cannot be measured in relation to income from sales. Thus, one can only evaluate their use of resources as a cost for "something produced of social value." In the absence of the ability to measure its economic contribution (relating costs of producing to income generated), an organization must base its justification on societal needs as others perceive them. In turn, social organizations promote voluntary or nonvoluntary contributions from support groups to cover their costs of production. A preoccupation with the cost of "something produced of social value" might lead to an undue concern for efficiencies within, to the neglect of seizing opportunities to serve outside.

Adaptability

Businesses have a need to maintain a keen sensitivity to changes in their environment and must be able to react appropriately to them. A firm must stay attuned to the changing needs and expectations of society. If it does not, other competing enterprises will rise to fill the new demands. This need to keep attuned to change is difficult to achieve when one considers that the markets are often widely scattered, diverse, and stratified segments of society.

By contrast, most other social institutions, those with purely social justification, are able to gauge the necessity for change by analyzing the expectations of a more narrowly defined support group. For example, a charitable organization has an active constituency comprised of interested citizens, foundations, philanthropists, and recipients. The need for change is normally introduced by some segment of this identifiable and definable constituency. It is relatively easy for the charitable organization to remain sensitive to views from the members of these specific groups.

Some organizations—government agencies, the armed forces, utilities, unions, law enforcement agencies, and universities—are either monopolies or oligopolies. If an enterprise is a monopoly, it has no close substitutes for the service or produce it provides. If an enterprise is an oligopoly, it has only several competitors that produce substitute services or products. As monopolies or oligopolies, they face less threat of being replaced by another institution than do organizations in more highly competitive fields. In the absence of such threats to survival, these organizations can easily grow less sensitive and adaptable to changing expectations from their markets and the broader society. However, when acute market changes pose a threat to a monopoly, its leadership must adjust—sometimes dramatically—or see their edifice crumble.

For example, universities are often monopolies in certain geographical areas. No other organization provides a close substitute for university education, at least within a certain town or metropolitan area. In the 1960s, when students were plentiful and resources abundant, many universities languished in that security, fascinated with their own internal affairs and preservation of the status quo. Now those same universities are competing for scarce students through public relations campaigns, market research, advertising promotions, and product (curriculum) redesign. No organization, including the highest governmental agencies, can long forestall change if its external environment is changing.

When structures do not bend to the forces from the powerful social system calling for change, they break.

Often organizations exempt from competition to ensure their efficiency and adaptability are regulated by outside authorities. As examples, state utility commissions regulate power, telephone, and gas companies; the Interstate Commerce Commission governs railroads; and the Department of Labor controls unions.

A business organization in a competitive setting strives to be aware of, and responsive to, the expectations of a plethora of diverse, sometimes unidentifiable, constituencies. Individuals who make up its markets for products and services are scattered and dissimilar. Those on whom it relies to purchase shares of ownership and bonds to provide its capital are far-flung. Men and women representing its sources for employable talents are dispersed geographically, with varying occupational and professional backgrounds. A competitive business, therefore, develops keen awareness of the changing needs and expectations of the multiplicity of persons upon whom it relies for support.

Succinctly stated, all organizations compete for resources and users of services to greater or lesser degree. All must therefore strive actively to use their resources carefully and to adjust their output to society's changing needs to some extent. Hence, all organizations—whether business or not—must fulfill certain requirements for survival.

For instance, if churches fail to care for the poor, government steps in. If universities fail to provide needed programs, businesses step in (General Motors' masters' program and Northrop Aviation's Ph.D. program, as examples). If the Boys' Clubs fail to care for our youth, churches or municipal government agencies step in, and so on.

Hence, all forms of organizations attempt to be the most efficient producers of goods or services available to society. All must also be adaptable if their survival is to be ensured.

DISCUSSION QUESTIONS

1. Is the distinction between business and nonbusiness organizations based on a value orientation or a basic truth? Why?

2. Examine the implications for organizations, (1) in a highly competitive setting, and (2) in a monopolistic environment.

3. Every organization has constituents who must be served and won over. These constituents use diverse yardsticks to measure an enterprise's success. With business organizations, the stockholders' yardstick measures economic success. What does the yardstick of the public-at-large measure to evaluate the contribution of nonbusiness organizations?

4. Resolved: The Department of Agriculture is efficient. Defend the positive and negative positions of this statement.

5. Define "business" and "nonbusiness." Define "competitive" and "noncompetitive." Are they the same things? Are there parallels between them?

3

Needs of Organizations

The idea that an organization must maintain dynamic equilibrium is no mere pretense for knowledge, as some might conclude. To the contrary, the concept concisely discloses the fundamental needs for organizational survival.

Robert Desman

In Chapter 1, we identified the basic role and elements of human organization, while in Chapter 2, the major types of organizations were classified. We found that all forms of these systems strive to ensure their survival by efficiency in the use of resources for production and effectiveness in adjusting to changing environments. The degree of efficiency and change varies with the type of organization, but all must meet the challenge or perish. Let us now analyze the functional needs of organizations for survival and, by contrast, the major malfunctions that weaken organizations. We can then infer certain of the challenges facing leaders.

SURVIVAL OF ORGANIZATIONS

An organization has needs of a practical nature that must be fulfilled if it is to survive. These needs are of a higher order than simply its ability to attract the people and economic support with which to maintain itself and generate output of services or products. They are needs functionally related to the ability of the enterprise to attain efficiency and maintain its effectiveness. The word *efficiency,* as used here, refers to gaining maximum output from the inputs of resources used for a productive effort. In the employment of people, efficiency would mean a coordinated, or synchronized effort to achieve a high rate of output in comparison with similar or competing enterprises. Low performance, redundancy, voids, and unnecessary conflict or friction would be removed. Efficiency is normally measured in the short run by month, quarter, or year. Effectiveness, as discussed here, refers to adaptability to changes in the external environment. It requires that the people in the organization be able and willing to bend to meet changing expectations, new technology, revised procedures, and other conditions. Effectiveness is required for survival. Contrasted to efficiency, it is a longer run requirement.

Let us return momentarily to the definition of an organization presented in Chapter 1. An organization was defined there as a contrived open system of coordinated activities, with two or more participants, to achieve a common goal or goals. Now, we can simplify this statement through use of Figure 3-1. The term *social system* implies a dynamic structuring of relationships among people who may elect to participate with varying degrees of involvement, or who may choose not to participate at all. *Common purpose,* or *goals,* provides the object for which the social system is formed. In other words, the formation of an organization's structure is functionally related to its common purpose, or goals. Goals are oriented to the future. Goals suggest required functions that are then designed into the structure. An examination of the model presented above would lead us to conclude that an organization can sustain its operation as long as it has a purpose that is commonly endorsed and supported by the people who aspire to achieve it.

History, however, shows that most social arrangements are short-lived. The Catholic Church, the Swiss government and, perhaps, the Hudson's Bay Company are noteworthy exceptions. These exceptions notwithstanding, organizations that function around us—whether designed to fulfill religious, political, economic, or other needs—are largely young structures, young, that is, in the long view of history. Though organizations can outlive the lives of their participants, they can also break apart at the seams and dissolve before their founders intended. Those that are operating now are the survivors of hundreds of thousands, if not millions, that have failed in the past. Heirs to the few tangible remains of past endeavors, we are lulled into the false belief that organizational arrangements are generally durable. This is an understandable conclusion, because we see only those enterprises that have been successful, and so are continuing to function. It is difficult to comprehend the countless numbers that did not succeed, for, in truth,

Social System ←———————— Common Purpose
                                    (Goals)

FIGURE 3–1. Formal Organization

there are few lasting symbols of the remains of defunct enterprises—little left to remind us of the frequency of the demise of these efforts.

As a weak substitute, we tend to identify an organization by its trappings, that is, its buildings and equipment. Though it simplifies our thinking, it is misleading to study organizations by merely observing their physical artifacts when in reality they are systems of human activities. Physical items that remain after the original venture collapses are usually converted to the uses of other organizations. Our ability to recognize the failure rate of organizations is clouded. Our concern with physical objects misleads us.

The truth is that the life span of most organizations is often sharply curtailed—governments, businesses, churches, and marriages (if included as organizations). But, why are such undertakings normally short-lived? What elements lead to the early demise of social arrangements when all that is apparently required is a common purpose and a coordinated human effort to support it? To deal with these questions, we must first understand the implications of maintaining both a social system and a common purpose.

THE NEEDS OF ORGANIZATIONS

A system of people striving to attain a goal has special needs to be filled if it is to survive, just as a mechanical system requires fuel, lubricants, oxygen, and maintenance to perform. The needs of organizations transcend the needs of the people who comprise them, yet the participants are inseparably tied to enterprise success.

A Goal-Seeking Social System

All organizations have the same basic design. They must have people participating and interacting in a structured way for a common purpose, or goals. The logic of designing an organization takes the following sequence: First, a common purpose (stated as goals) is adopted for the organization. Second, the goals adopted demand execution of certain functions (such as innovation, manufacturing, and selling). Third, the functions (such as research and development, production, and marketing) are built into the organization's formal structure. And, fourth, the functional units are bonded together to form the overall organization into a social system. Conceptually, the basic configuration of an organization can be stated in the same shorthand form presented previously, as seen in Figure 3-2.

Let's analyze the real meaning of this statement. It is clear that encouraging a group of people to accept certain common purposes would be relatively simple in some organizations because of the general appeal

Figure 3–2. Formal Organization

of the mission. For instance, individuals in a group might unanimously agree to forming a charitable venture through which food and clothing are gathered and provided to less fortunate people; or private citizens might generally accept the goal of achieving victory for a certain political issue, party, or candidate; or a group of parishioners might unanimously support a certain program of a church. With such clear, compelling objectives, they would doubtless organize themselves into an interrelated structure of activities to reach the goals. But would such a mutuality of purpose automatically prevail among participants in other forms of endeavor? Would they rise as one to support the building of a "widget," even though an astonishingly good "widget" might be produced? Most economic ventures, or other less compelling pursuits, lack the emotional appeal to hold people together without supportive internal subsystems.

Common purpose is not often automatically achieved. It is encouraged through the design of incentives, roles, role relationships, authority, and control so that each participant is rewarded for contributing to the attainment of the overall goals. In return, a participant expects to receive such rewards as equitable wages, fair treatment, a sense of social involvement, a chance to achieve and to win recognition for it, and personal growth. As long as people believe the trade-offs are in their favor, they will accept a part in the pursuit of organizational objectives.

An organization is weakened when its participants are not made aware of their part in the several key relationships that act to integrate the social system. These are: first, their relationship to one another; second, the relationship of their contribution to the overall objectives; and third, the relationship of their contribution to the incentive subsystem. Without these insights, employees are unable to integrate their role behavior appropriately with others, to see how aspects of their work are crucial to the overall effort, or to feel that their rewards are equitable based on their contributions to the enterprise. The degree of integration of the social system is functionally related to, and dependent on, the ability of its members to discern these integrating elements clearly. When they are understood, efforts are coordinated, activities assume direction, and rewards support achievement. When the unifying relationships are not grasped, activities lack coordination, continuity, direction, and support. Communication among the individuals, the units, and within the total organization are essential for the coordinated integration of the social system. One major impediment to the efficiency and success of a complex organization can be the inability of its leaders to communicate the common purpose as it relates to individual members of the organization.

Internal Consistency

An organization must be economically efficient when compared with its competition if it is to survive. Efficiencies are introduced through the design of subsystems—such as communications, incentives, and control—which fit the overall social scheme and support efforts to attain the common goals. They must be designed and calibrated so that they do not introduce unwanted conflict into the organization, but instead reinforce each other as means to goal attainment.

As an example, assume that a company wins a contract to design and build a prototype of a sophisticated piece of space hardware; the agreement stipulates that there is an extremely small tolerance for malfunction. Coupling this condition with that of producing the first component, the contract is based on the actual cost of providing the part, plus a fixed rate of profit. With the goal clearly defined, the company's leaders design subsystems appropriate to reach it: A "zero defects" control program is instituted, incentives awarded for innovative engineering and quality production, and a communications program launched to build pride within the employees for having a part in the space program. The subsystems of activity support each other, the program, and the total company, and act as means to goal achievement. They are internally consistent.

An organization strives for internal consistencies because they are a crucial element of efficiency. The arrows in Figure 3-3 indicate the logical steps required to design an efficient organization. After the common purpose and functions are set, one can then design the formal structure and overall social system required to fulfill the functions and attain the common purpose. However, internal subsystems (such as authority flows, communications, and incentives) are generally needed to tie the common purpose of the enterprise back to the people, or social system, carrying it out. When each of the subsystems within compliments and strengthens the other subsystems *and* goal attainment, they are internally consistent. Conceptually the organization model develops a new dimension (Figure 3-3).

Now let us look at the opposite of internal consistency. To view internal inconsistency, consider that the example given above changes. Assume that this same company completed its original assignment satisfactorily and was subsequently awarded a contract to produce in

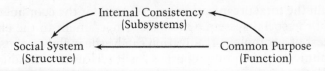

FIGURE 3–3. Efficient Formal Organization

large numbers a relatively unsophisticated device for missile weaponry, with a comparatively high tolerance for malfunction. In view of these new requirements, the contract was granted on a straight-bid basis as opposed to the earlier cost-plus profit arrangement.

In response, the firm restructures its social system and certain subsystems to pursue the new goal. But in so doing it neglects to redesign all relevant subsystems. The original "zero defects" program remains as an institutionalized way to control performance; and the related subsystems of authority, communications, and incentives are retained to encourage a high degree of innovation, premium quality, and pride of craftsmanship. Though such traits have merit when required for the task at hand, they cause economic inefficiency when they are not essential. Further, those subsystems that remain unchanged will doubtless conflict with other subsystems of activity for resource allocation, control, and production scheduling. The original functional units should probably be redesigned to accommodate the demands of the new contract. If they are not, a number of internal inconsistencies may exist, causing unnecessary friction and conflict, and leading initially to inefficiency and, ultimately, to increased costs.

The idea of internal consistency is in no way intended to remove healthy conflict and competition arising from interaction among the subunits of an enterprise, for these conditions usually stimulate desirable efficiencies and innovations.

As one example, leaders of subunits in an organization compete with other leaders for allocations of resources. Scarce resources such as employees, building space, and operating funds are distributed, in part, in response to the ability of a manager to justify a greater need for the items in his or her operating unit than in other units. Through this process, the allocation and use of organizational resources is justified. In another way, the competition (if not actual conflict) that exists between financial conservatism versus liberality within an organization provides a prime example of necessary confrontation. In all complex organizations there are individuals charged with diverse responsibilities and varied role behavior. Some look after the purse strings of the organization; others spend its funds to generate income. Treasurers, accountants, controllers, budget directors and auditors, among others, are accountable as stewards protecting the use of the organization's resources. In contrast, directors of such activities as public relations, research and development, and marketing are accountable for spending resources to generate revenues. Conflicts of drives will arise naturally from such arrangements but these checks and balances can also mitigate abuses of both overindulged and undernourished programs.

Finally, the design of subsystems of activity that support goal attainment in an internally consistent way should not attempt to rid an organization of the natural conflict between persons charged with continuity and those responsible for introducing changes. Both efforts are mandatory, the first to ensure efficiencies within, the second to maintain social and economic justification in a changing outside environment.

Internal consistency is the design and management of subsystems of activity that are supportive of each other and, in tandem, serve as the means to goal attainment. Although supportive, complementary subsystems remove pointless conflict and the accompanying fruitless frustrations, the establishment of constructive points of confrontation may be entirely consistent in reaching certain goals. It is a matter of "fitting" appropriate subsystems to each other to reach a predetermined objective.

Environmental Consonance

The conceptual model of an efficient organization can now be stated as a *goal-seeking, internally consistent, social system.* But is an organization with these traits alone sufficiently equipped to survive in the long run? Are internal efficiencies enough to ensure continued success? One can easily consider a situation in which an efficiently (that is, internally consistent) producing organization failed. Though a simple example, it seems reasonable to conjecture that there probably were certain efficient "hula hoop" producers a few years back who abruptly found themselves without a market and, as suddenly, left the plastics manufacturing industry. Others, however, may have sensed the short life span historically experienced by novelty products and diverted their activities to a newly demanded article such as Frisbee (a plastic disc which, when properly thrown, illustrates entertaining aerodynamics). This sensing of changing behavioral patterns and expectations external to the organization is required if appropriate reactions to new demands are to take place. And, appropriate reactions to its support groups' needs permit an organization to continue to fulfill its social or socioeconomic justification and thereby continue its life. *It is a primary and fundamental need of an organization to maintain a consonance between its oper-*

ation, its purposes (goals), and its external environment. Illustratively, the basic conceptual organizational model now assumes its final form (Figure 3-4).

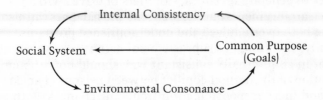

FIGURE 3–4. Efficient and Effective Formal Organization

An organization, particularly a competing unit, must attain the degree of internal consistency necessary for short-run efficiency, and it must maintain a consonance with its external environment to sustain long-run effectiveness. If these basic needs are to be filled, it must prepare itself to attain a degree of stability while at the same time striving to remain viable.

MAJOR ELEMENTS CAUSING ORGANIZATIONAL WEAKNESS

It is now possible for us to readdress our attention to the questions posed in the first part of this chapter. These, you will recall, dealt with the reasons for the short life span of many organizations and the conditions that contribute to their failure. Common purpose, carried out through a functionally related design and expressed in a managed social system, is all that is necessary for the perpetuation of an organization. Why then is its life often unintentionally curtailed? Why does it cease to function and, therefore, to exist?

By studying the final configuration of the conceptual model of an organization presented above, the reader can identify three major ways in which an organization is weakened. First, its participants can lose sight of the venture's major goals. When the common purpose of the enterprise becomes obscured, the people lose direction and the social system loses integration. Second, the subsystems of activities designed to serve as means to goals can lose synchronization with each other, or lack compatability with changing major goals. Internal inconsistencies leading to economic inefficiency result. When these appear, internal frictions erupt. The organization is drained of the physical, intellectual, and emotional energies it requires from its human resources, a condition that necessitates activities to offset structural imbalances. Third, the organization as a whole can grow impervious to changing demands and expectations from its support groups, or it can fail to adapt in a way appropriate to their new needs. When an enterprise loses consonance with the environment upon which it depends for resources, and to which it must prove itself socially and economically justified, it fails.

IMPLICATIONS FOR LEADERS

A properly designed and managed organization is enabled to continue existing through a state of *dynamic equilibrium,* a moving balance. On the one hand, it will bend with changing patterns of behavior. On the other, it will have stability and continuity. The end result in the first instance is to maintain a consonance with the forces from its external environment, and in the second, to achieve efficiency through internally consistent balance. Organizational needs hold clear implications for leaders. The realities of organizational life also thrust certain challenges on them.

Challenge of Internal Consistency

Are on-going organizations internally consistent and consonant with their environments? Generally, no. Bear in mind that assemblages of persons formalized into coordinated effort are social contrivances of human beings, and are therefore imperfect systems. Not only do they emerge in response to evolutionary forces but they also react to forces causing revolutionary changes both from within the enterprise (technology, patterns of leadership, goals) and outside it (changes in environment and needs or expectations of its support groups). Often, when leaders initiate reactions to internal pressures they modify certain systems of activities, *but* leave unaltered other subsystems that should be changed. Reactions to external forces are frequently effected only as a response to changes that have built up over an extended period of time. Thus, the intensity of the accumulated impact is great. As a consequence of such delay, a major change can cause an organization to be the victim of "shock treatments," and undercorrection or overcorrection. Change is best introduced in response to shifts in perceptions by leaders as to what constitutes appropriate organizational behavior. Thus, it can be a smooth, continual modifying, as are evolutionary processes.

For example, internal consistency is easily lost when a major change is introduced, but the redesign of a significant internal subsystem is overlooked. Consider the organization operating under the leadership of the person mentioned in Chapter 1, who views financial incentives as unprofessional.

This viewpoint is then adopted by other leaders throughout the organization. In response, rewards of an intrinsic nature become popular. Rewards honoring professional accomplishment are granted: coveted symbols of contribution and prestige among colleagues and superiors. To support the unique incentive system, its influence is incorporated into policies for orientation and training, personnel performance ratings, status, promotion and kindred incentives, the way in which leaders manage subordinates, and other incentive-related phases of the operation. In sum, the organization under the new leader is reprogrammed to retain people with similar values and to rid itself of those who are misfits because they hold other values. Thus far, internal consistency has been attained.

Notwithstanding the consistency of these arrangements, consider the consequences if one long-standing area of activity remained unchanged. Let us suppose that the subsystems for the recruitment and selection of personnel had historically attracted employees by appeals based on the wider industrial tradition. As such, these subsystems offered high wages, favorable working conditions, and opportunities for upward advancement. Persons attracted by these appeals, upon joining the enterprise, would be confused and demoralized to find that financial reward did not follow contribution. Further, they would find that advancement within a professional level was held in higher esteem than advancement up the authority hierarchy. As a consequence, frictions would doubtless develop and rates of personnel turnover might soar.

Most organizations have internal inconsistencies. Some are caused by oversights when new ways of operating or new objectives are adopted. Others emerge when leaders fail to share the same viewpoints on matters fundamental to the design of an efficient enterprise: First, confusion can arise among leaders on what business the organization is in; second, misunderstandings can evolve as to where the organization is headed; or third, agreement can be lost on the means used to take the business to its intended goals. This form of inconsistency, rooted in clashing viewpoints, can easily arise if one considers that an organization is divided along functional areas of activities (attraction of resources, use of resources to produce a service or goods, and the distribution of the production). The tendency to inconsistency is heightened by specialized staff groups who assist the leaders of the major functional activities, thereby creating multiple flows of authority.

Internal inconsistency, though widespread, does not prevent a social system from reaching its goals unless it causes gross inefficiencies. One can move an organization flawed by certain incongruities from its present position to some intended objective by merely offsetting subsystems not designed to complement the effort. As a simile, one can fly an airplane with a defective stabilizer to a distant point by offsetting, through overcorrection, the effect of the internal inconsistency. By so doing the goal may be reached—but only with considerable loss of fuel and power, and perhaps with damage to other systems. An organization, in a like way, can survive and achieve its objectives by offsetting sources of friction, redundancies, or voids. But, also in a like way, there will be considerable loss in the form of the wasted physical, intellectual, and emotional energies of the employees—the human resource. Internal inconsistencies often lead to misunderstandings, confusion, and friction to culminate ultimately in a loss of identification, dedication, and effectiveness by the people who comprise the organization.

Challenge of Viability

Most organizations are unable or unwilling to keep in touch with changing external factors or to react promptly to them; this causes a failure in their consonance with the environment upon which they are dependent for survival. Three major factors seem to cause organizational rigidities, the inability to change.

First, as an organization finds that it can fulfill a given social need, it settles down to do so in a competent manner. Introspection, a turning inward, is necessary so that the system of activity can be refined and coordinated to achieve internal efficiencies. With continued operation, growth, and strength, the organization becomes secure. Its existence is justified. Fairly certain of survival, it tends to grow impervious to the changing demands imposed by its environment.

Second, though an enterprise develops a repertory of responses to common environmental events, it is not normally attuned to unique happenings. Its sensory organs are designed to "hear" particular events. For instance, business people are attuned to economic data such as those related to labor markets, capital sources, and product changes; but they are less sensitive to alterations in the factors underlying economic change such as values, expectations, and social mores. Other types of organizations also "listen" to particular events, those affecting their constituency. Organizational responses, then, are preprogrammed to repetitive matters. Often, however, the use of a prearranged response does not permit the system to react appropriately because the reaction does not "fit" the situation. The solution is to predesign responses to repeating events, but not to the neglect of isolated or random events.

Third, it is apparent that as an organization functions over time, it develops set ways of behaving, a tradition, from which it is difficult to depart. Individuals as well as organized groups tend to proceed in a manner that has worked well in the past. Because it poses unknown consequences, or uncertainty, change is anxiety-producing. The status quo is comfortable though at times grotesquely inefficient. It is preserved merely because people know their part in it and their relationships to others. Though the need for adjustment may be sensed, traditions, rituals, social mores, and institutionalized ways can erect formidable barriers to change.

The challenge of viability can be illustrated by the case of a small, nonprofit children's day-care unit. Its director, initially, is not sure that a sufficiently high need for a pre-school nursery exists. Once assured that an adequate number of children are in attendance, the director's attention turns inward to developing educational and recreational programs. The director and teaching staff listen carefully to new innovations in child care, but seem immune to financial implications. Over time, costly programs for training and recreation become fully developed as *the* way to serve children best. They become rigified, when the external setting is changing. The director does not sense that the location of the child-care unit is becoming inconveniently located for working parents because of demographic changes. As attendance falls, the high costs of traditional programs become pronounced. Fees increase to cover them, only to further decrease the use of the day-care center. When the use of the center reaches the point where fees for the care of a child is excessively high, and if no other support is given, the day-care unit falters and fails.

SUMMARY

An organization can lose its consonance with its environment and as a result forfeit its socioeconomic justification by its inability or unwillingness either to sense the need for change, or to react to it in an appropriate way. Such an interprise deserves to die. It can lose internal consistency through failure (1) to generate acceptance of common purpose, (2) to agree to the means to achieve that purpose, or (3) to reconceive and redesign all subsystems of activities necessary to support the means to the goals. Certain behavioral impediments interfering with organizational needs are nicely summarized in the following statement from "An Executive's Viewpoint," by Thomas M. Ware:

> A corporation. . . . tends to develop within it pressure groups and empire builders. It develops taboos, prejudices, policies, and rules of thumb. It develops sacred cows and scapegoats. . . . it has an inclination toward introspection; it is overly concerned with its own internal problems. . . . The energies of the more talented, more aggressive, more ambitious employees often seem to be taken up with internal problems of power, prestige, and position. The corporation that is well established tends to become complacent and set in its ways.[2]

These barriers to organizational strength, which can block the attainment of internal consistency and consonance with the environment, were taken from a business setting. Nevertheless, the basic elements in the situation are at work in all social institutions, government, military, religious, educational, cultural, charitable, as well as business.

The general challenge for leadership is apparent: It is the ability to recognize that organizations need change amidst stability. It is the skill to estimate the degrees of stability and viability needed. It is the sensitivity to internal and external forces that require reactions. It is the art of implementing change in an otherwise immobile social institution. A more detailed analysis of these implications for leaders will be made in Chapter 10.

DISCUSSION QUESTIONS

1. Consider the major differences between organization theory and leadership theory? What are the relationships between the two?

2. Give examples of *internal inconsistencies* that create inefficiency. (Remember, an internal inconsistency is caused when one subsystem fails to mesh with another subsystem, or with the organization's goals.)

3. Why are internal subsystems required in most organizations? What are certain exceptions in which formalized subsystems are not needed? (Give examples.)

4. Why is environmental consonance difficult to maintain? (Give examples.)

5. How do the needs for sound organizational arrangements relate to the responsibilities of leadership?

4

Life Cycle of an Organization

The whole that counts in building a system or in measuring its perfor-
mance is an increasingly larger whole, one that does not stop even at its
own boundaries but extends into the environment to which it relates.

John A. Beckett [1]

It is apparent that when one's endeavors exceed one's individual capacity in either size or complexity, it is wise to merge efforts with those of other persons. When joint activities of the individuals are structured and coordinated toward common goals, an organization forms. As indicated earlier, an organization changes as a result of changing goals, means to goals, environmental demands, and roles or role relationships of its participants. Pressures for change are perpetual. Though certain enterprises have managed to maintain a dynamic equilibrium—moving balances over time—most have been unable to do so. Some have failed to survive because they would not or could not change; others, because they could not maintain the degree of efficiency expected so that more efficient organizations filled the void.

In Chapter 3, we saw that organizations have functional needs required for survival, and that these needs stem from goals based on conditions in their environment. We found that organizations are born out of social necessity. Further, we learned earlier that although they are initially justified by social and economic needs, organizations are expected to use efficiently scarce resources—people, money, land, equipment, and/or raw materials—and to effectively adapt to the changing needs and expectations of support groups. To do so, the conceptual model of sound organization behavior shown in Figure 4-1 was introduced and discussed. Filling the conditions of this model, though important for all

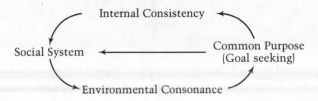

FIGURE 4–1. Conceptual Model of a Sound Organization

types of organizations, becomes critical for those that compete with other enterprises for survival.

We can now advance, in this chapter, to observe the behavior of a "living" organization and analyze that behavior as it relates to the conceptual model. From this account, the reader can gain an insight into the reasons organizations are strong or weak, efficient or inefficient, viable or rigid. A fictional case will be used to illustrate the forming, maturing, aging, and declining phases in an organization's life cycle.

Introduction to the Islander Case

Consider now an organization born out of functional necessity. It was designed to serve its purpose efficiently and effectively. Then the enterprise lost its ability to perform under newly imposed demands and finally dissolved. To take an organization through the complete life cycle, in a suitably brief discussion, it is necessary to assume a bizarre event. The situation was selected so that the demands on the entity could be changed abruptly and rapidly. The simplified fictional account that follows was chosen not for its eccentricities, but rather because its striking contrasts illustrate what can happen to an organization over its life cycle.

THE ISLANDERS: AN ILLUSTRATION

Picture a group of thirty to forty people enjoying a cruise on a pleasure yacht in the Caribbean Sea. Imagine further that the voyagers are taking part in certain popular shipboard activities such as fishing, swimming, shuffleboard, and card-playing. At this point, they enjoy casual, quickly changing social relationships arising from informal arrangements and a mutual desire for pleasure. Since pleasure can be achieved individually, in pairs, or in larger informal groups, no organization is needed.

Genesis of an Organization

Far out to sea, an unpredicted storm suddenly closes in on the yacht restricting visibility and making it impossible to navigate. As the boat pitches and yaws out of control, the hull strikes a floating object that severs the bow and makes evacuation mandatory. Passengers and crew man the lifeboats, setting their course for a land mass seen mistily on the distant horizon. In time, the castaways beach their boats and take stock of their situation. Though the lifeboats are sadly damaged, the people are at the moment safe from harm. But immediately two critical questions arise: First, is there enough food and water to support them? And second, are they invading a territory defended by hostile inhabitants?

Confronted with these threatening specters, mature people feel strongly the urge for self-preservation. They recognize the limitations of any single person in trying to conquer such obstacles. A reasoning adult (unlike the children who retrogressed to a primitive existence in *The Lord of the Flies*) becomes acutely aware of individual limitations on strength, endurance, and the diversity of skills required for survival. The people band together. Each sees strength in numbers and actively supports organized effort. Under the circumstances, it would be senseless for any person or group of people to try to dissociate themselves from the larger band and fend for themselves. It would be more reasonable to expect that the overall group would block attempts to fragment it, attempts that would sap the enterprise of its strength.

But can even a cohesive group fulfill the basic needs of its members? Probably not, at least not at a level of efficiency required by this situation. Efficient human effort comes when a group is structured so that its activities are patterned in such a way that they lead directly to goals. Stated differently, counterproductive effort that impedes goal attainment is minimized.

Leadership

First, the *group* needs a central authority to give it overall guidance, to allocate resources, and to keep its members headed toward the same goals. In a word, leadership is needed. It is required by functional necessity. Assume now that the members of the shipwrecked party assemble to choose a leader. Would it necessarily be one who acted as an informal leader in arranging social events aboard ship? Would it automatically be a ship's officer who had demonstrated ability as a seafaring leader? Or would it be a member of the group who was reputed to be an effective manager of a commercial enterprise at home? Perhaps any one of these persons would be candidates for the position of authority. However, none may have the background and attributes essential for leadership *in this particular situation:* a situation in which survival is possible, but only by using extreme measures.

Consider the appropriate traits of a candidate for a position of authority and responsibility here. It might be valuable to the group if the person had experience in leading others safely through trials brought on by a similar threatening situation. Under the dangers that seem to prevail, a candidate should probably possess the technical skills required to provide the group with food, shelter, and security. Stamina, strength, and authoritative bearing to command may be necessary to a group under stress. Further, the person may need to be decisive, mentally alert, an incisive communicator, and able to marshall group efforts. In sum, the characteristics of the situation suggest certain requirements of leadership:

Leadership Traits

Experience as a specialist in field (military or other)
Technical skills
Strength and stamina
Authoritative manner
Decisiveness
Mental adroitness
Ability to communicate incisively
Ability to organize

If leadership is to get results from people, it must be situationally appropriate—or contingent on operating requirements.

Authority

Second, the leader must gain and use authority to accomplish the required tasks. What is the source of this authority or influence? Authority generally comes from a formal source. These are usually private property (entrepreneurial), public property (governmental), spiritual needs (religious), or public decree (legal). Yet no institution now exists; there is only a group of people. Authority must originate with the group members. Each must agree to give up certain aspects of free will to the leader so that the total group may benefit. Such awarding of authority is akin to public decree, or consent, but without the institutional arrangements. In the place of an institution dispensing authority, it is generated by the people based upon their needs. It is often called the "authority of the situation." Rather than coming down from the top, it is acquired from each subordinate member and delegated upward.

Each member has effectively relinquished part of his or her self-determination to make possible group determination through an organization set up to reach goals. Each member also expects to reap the rewards of the affiliation: physical well-being, security, order, perhaps even social and psychological gratification. But is subjection to power worth it? Though authority is power over others, the idea of power is not at issue. Power has been legitimized, or at least rationalized to be perceived as "accepted authority." The negative feeling associated with power over free men has been transformed to "rightful power," that is, authority granted by the group because of the unusual situation. Often, rather elaborate symbols and complex rituals are projected upon those in power by those governed in order to provide an aura of legitimacy. In these ways power is converted to acceptable authority.

In any event, persons join the common effort because to them the rewards outweigh the sacrifices. Authority is accepted because leadership is required to fulfill the needs of the group.

Formal Structure

Third, the leader (with the followers' support) identifies the *major goal* of the group. The common purpose is survival. The *subgoals* required to reach the overall goal are providing food, shelter, and protection against attack. Subgoals are needed to further delineate what lesser objectives must be achieved to reach the overriding mission, or common purpose.

With the goal and subgoals defined, the leader can now move to the fourth step, that of providing for the fulfillment of *functions* required by *organizing* the people within the group so that the subgoals and in turn, the overall goal, are met quickly. With subgoals of providing food, shelter, and protection from portent attack, the functions would logically include securing food (gathering, hunting, seining, or whatever else is feasible), building (providing materials, trimming, framing, siding, thatching, and so on), and providing security (lookouts, listening posts, patrols, or other). When functions have been determined, they must be reflected in the organization, if they are to be accomplished. Functions are activities required to attain goals. They are the logical bases for organizing people.

Organizing deals with assigning members to one of the three major areas of activities so that each one can make the greatest contribution to the overall effort. This is a *division of labor* to bring about *specialization*. The organizing technique is based on the idea that individuals have unique backgrounds of experience, skills, and physical traits that make them better suited for one task than another. Further, the repeated performance of that task in cooperation with those doing related jobs will result in efficiencies beyond those that could be reasonably expected from a generalist—a "jack of all trades" working with first one work group and later another.

The leader would doubtless allocate the tasks to the individuals best suited to pursue each activity. For example, those with backgrounds and skills in hunting, fishing, or scouting might be assigned to gather food, those experienced in carpentry, to build shelters; and those with military or police training, to provide security from attack. *Departments of functional activities* would thus be formed. Since the activities would take place in different technical areas and places, the leader of the group would doubtless appoint leaders for each subgroup. At this stage in the life cycle of the organization, superior technical abilities would probably be the determining factor in the selection of each of the three intermediate leaders, that is, those functioning between the workers and the top leader.

In turn, the intermediate leaders would sort out the activities required within each major department. They would then assign subtasks to members within their respective work units. For instance, in the unit constructing shelter, several members would be assigned to gather raw materials for building, others to prepare the materials for use, others to build framing, while others would specialize in applying siding and thatching roofs. These finer degrees of specialization can bring about further efficiencies as long as the common purpose, and each member's part in its attainment, is clearly understood.

The basic framework that shows the way an organization should function has been formed. It is called the *formal organization*. It limits, and sets guidelines for, the relationships of those within the social system. It delimits areas of activities. It defines authority and communication flows and identifies points of responsibility. It suggests role behavior and appropriate role relationships with those within and outside each functional work unit. Such a framework quite simply acts as an outside governor on human behavior, defining the boundaries between activities and providing structure. The structure, based upon functions, serves as the primary means by which the enterprise can begin to pursue its goals. A formal organization chart can simplify (unfortunately, also oversimplify) human interaction by providing a graphic illustration of the basic framework. The charting of the newly formed or genetic, formal arrangements by the castaways would be as shown in Figure 4-2.

A plan for the organization of the group now exists. An unbroken line links the individual at the top of the structure to the subordinate lowest in the hierarchy. This provides the means for authority and communications to flow in a patterned way. Each of the three levels, or

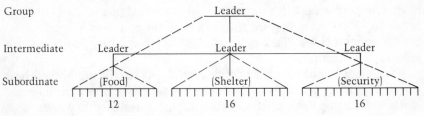

FIGURE 4–2. Genetic Organization

scales, in the hierarchy indicates an authority level that is the same horizontally across the chart. And each leader has clearly defined areas of accountability and authority. These are termed *spans of management*, or in the military, *spans of command*. They are identified by the broken lines on the chart. One can see that the span of management for the group leader in charge of food is twelve subordinates, while the group leaders accountable for shelter and security each supervises sixteen.

Delegation

At this point in the life cycle of the organization, a structure has been provided. The static framework of what will become an organization exists, and a group has been mechanically divided and arranged. But no organization exists because an organization is characterized by orderly activities, events, and movement among people—in other words, a dynamic social system.

The catalyst that brings about action is the delegation of authority. In the example used, the group leader delegates authority to the intermediate leaders to perform the duties or tasks assigned to them. The overall leader then holds them accountable to him for results. In turn, the intermediate leaders delegate authority to their subordinates to perform their respective tasks. They must then hold their subordinates accountable for the successful completion of these tasks.

With the formal organization serving as a structure to provide order to human endeavor, the delegation of authority triggers a chain reaction of decisions, actions, and obligations; a dynamic patterning of events or happenings commences to convert the original rigidly structured group into a social system. An organization is born.

Sources of Inefficiency

In the beginning, the command to produce food, shelter, and protection brings on a flurry of activities in the various departments accountable for these major tasks. Each member tries to perform the duties as he or she understands them. Some members in the section constructing shelter, for example, locate, secure, and prepare raw materials for construction, while others among them attempt to build frames or coverings. The varied activities, however, lack coordination. Raw materials of one sort or another pile up too high while others are unavailable; framing lags behind necessary covering; and the preparation of one material for use in construction is of poor quality, whereas another of an unnecessarily high quality is produced.

Coincidentally, confusion may arise as to the interrelationships among the intermediate leaders. They may in good faith vie against one another for the use of certain resources to fulfill the responsibilities of their respective areas of activity as they understand them. For instance, the security leader may be using building materials for, say, a vital lookout tower—materials that are then not available to the shelter leader, who also needs them. So, tradeoffs become necessary.

And finally, at the outset, the top leader may be uncertain about his role or role relationship to subordinate leaders. Confusion may exist over the best means to achieve the overall purpose of the organization. The leader may be unsure about the proper allocation of human resources to serve as means to reach the goals. This person may be taking tentative action and making interim decisions with a high degree of uncertainty.

The Emerging Organization

The organization has now been launched. Beset by pressures of unknown food sources and the possible presence of hostile inhabitants, this social structure would be formed and activated quickly after the party's landing on shore. It has a common purpose (goals) clearly understood by its participants. It is highly sensitive to external conditions and able to react quickly to changes. The organization is basically internally consistent in its use of authority, communications, and rewards. The social system, however, is somewhat inefficient because it lacks coordination of efforts at all levels. This is caused by no chronic ailment; it occurs because the participants have not been interacting long enough to develop common sets of roles, norms, and values. These are needed so that acceptable individual and interpersonal behavior can be molded. Each member needs to know what others expect and what, in turn, can be expected of others. In an organization, in contrast to more casual social groups, there is heavier reliance upon formally prescribed rules defining acceptable behavior.

MATURING OF AN ORGANIZATION

When an organization is first formed, its basic framework comes from structural-functional dependencies. For instance, in our shipwreck example, it was found that to achieve the ultimate objective (survival), certain basic needs (food, shelter, and security) had to be filled. In turn, the design of the structure of the organization was dependent upon how these tasks could best be accomplished. The ultimate objective (common purpose) required subgoals, which effectively identified functional areas of specialization needed within the social system. Expressed graphically, the sequential reasoning process for organizing looks like Figure 4-3. Once structurally organized, the delegation of authority from the leaders brought about human interaction to generate cooperative

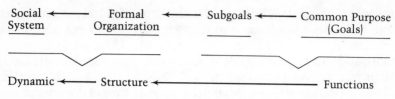

FIGURE 4–3. Reasoning Process for Organizing

effort. The simple production structure formed was sufficient to meet task demands. A primitive organization had emerged.

Coordination

Though goal-directed activities soon began, we found that the level of output by individual participants was unpredictable and uncoordinated. As a result, the organization was relatively inefficient when seen in light of its productive potential. A leader, uninitiated in organizational behavior, might assume too quickly that a redistribution of tasks is immediately needed to bring on desired performance. Probably reformation will be required, since the organization was originally designed with only a rough idea of the amount of work needed from each of the varied units. Reshaping of formal arrangements—a reorganization—should not be done, however, until the members have had a chance to perform acceptably and to merge their achievements with others.

Design of Formal Patterns

Acceptable behavior in organizations relies heavily on formal rules. The development of acceptable (as opposed to unacceptable) behavior is influenced by values commonly shared by the participants and gained from prior experiences within and outside the organization. More germane to the success of the total organization, however, is the need for the leaders to orient members to the norms necessary for the endeavor's survival. Formal patterns of conduct *that are largely predictable* flow from the participants' understanding of a system's norms, roles, and values.

Leaders in any enterprise establish formal patterns to guide behavior because they are the bases for the integration of organized social endeavors. *Norms* are the expectations shared by members in the organizing of performance. They are demands for the minimum results sought from by all system members, though the term *norm* may seem to imply average performance. To achieve the norms, *roles* are used to define expected forms of behavior appropriate to completing tasks assigned. Regardless of personal whims, roles are required of all members so that each plays a part based upon his or her functional relationships to others in the pursuit of goals. The interrelatedness of roles and interdependent sets of activities add cohesion to an organization. One member's goals act as another's means to reach different goals. Thus, well-defined and broadly understood roles enable all members to see their specific contributions in functional relationship with those of their fellow members. And finally, *values* are views shared by the members of the organization concerning the acceptance or rejection of system goals, subgoals, norms, and roles. Shared values, as they apply to individual participation, cause the individual to adopt organizational goals with varying degrees of commitment. They influence the degree of acceptance, support, and dedication propelling an organized effort.

Norms set minimum levels of acceptable performance; values act as appeals for performance superior or inferior to minimal expectations. As an example, norms establish standards of output expected from one of our castaways assigned to gather food. They also set the limits beyond which there will be penalties for not attaining the goals. But if the idea of securing food is viewed by the gatherer as a contribution to the security and survival of the organization, it would be the consequence of an appeal to values above the norms. Stated another way, acceptance of the task based on values would come from an understanding of the importance of superior performance by the individual to the welfare of all the people in the organization.

In sum, norms, roles, and values can bring on specialization of task efforts, provide the means for integration and continuity, give rise to the standards for individual conduct and performance. When participants understand clearly the demands imposed by these influences, they serve as means of control, that is, they reduce inappropriate behavior. Thus, acceptable behavior is ensured because it supports the functional requirements needed to reach organizational goals.

Rules

Now let's return to the hypothetical example of the organization formed to serve the shipwrecked castaways. Assume that the leadership at this time recognizes the need for standards to establish acceptable behavior patterns. At the second, or maturing, stage of the organization, leaders formulate and begin to enforce rules to govern behavior.

For example, you may recall that one problem appeared in the unit formed to build shelters. Coordination was lost because unusually high stocks of one type of raw material tended to be built up while other types of supplies were depleted. Therefore, construction lacked continuity and lost efficiency. This imbalance was the result of unacceptable behavior on the part of members. They did not understand what constituted acceptable behavior. Assume that the leader and workers in this activity soon find the best flows of materials for a balanced supply and develop shared expectations of performance to meet the requirement. The leader then can coordinate the activities to maintain a daily flow of a certain mix of materials, and to disperse it to given areas so that it can be processed for use in building. Each member is assigned a part in the overall task. Once the assignments are accepted, the members are provided with role requirements. Further, the leader encourages the gatherers to perceive the goal as their own. Once a mutuality of goals exist, norms are established. And finally, if the material gatherers sense the urgent need for shelter and throw themselves into dedicated effort that creates a stock far beyond that required for a single day, their behavior would be in response to values.

During the maturing stage, leaders and followers attempt to eliminate inconsistencies caused by confused role behavior and role relationships. This is done by formulating and enforcing rules, which then generate a higher intensity of authority. And this becomes the basis of the continuing use of authority for the self-maintenance and productivity of an organization.

Transformation

Following the establishment of rules, we can expect changes in role behavior. The effects of these changes in behavioral patterns as they influence production will then be felt and a reanalysis of formal organizational arrangements can take place. This is required to ensure the proper use of resources, the desired degree of specialization, the coordination of tasks within and among work units, and the desirable span of management. Once done, internal inconsistencies will have been removed or minimized. The organization has been moved into a stage of maturity in it life cycle.

Consider now the capabilities of this healthy, mature organization. The reader will recall that two major external forces impinge on the stranded voyagers' organization: (1) uncertainty as to adequate amounts of food, and (2) uncertainty as to the presence of hostile inhabitants. To analyze the status of this organization, it would be helpful to reintroduce the conceptual model of an efficient, effective formal organization originally presented in Chapter 3 (see Figure 4-4).

Now, let us evaluate this organization as to its ability to achieve both productivity and self-maintenance. To make the analysis, we need answers to such questions as: Is the common purpose of the organization, including the relation of subgoals to the overall undertaking, clear to its participants? Is it sensitive to environmental forces and adaptable to them? Is it internally consistent, that is, do the internal systems of activity support each other and provide the means to goal attainment? Is

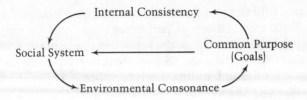

FIGURE4–4. Conceptual Model of an Efficient and Effective Organization

the social system cohesive, or is the system's self-maintenance threatened by potential fragmentation of members? Does it produce, thereby fulfilling its social function? Each of these questions will be examined in the following subsections.

Common purpose. The anchor to which any social system is tied is common purpose. In this instance, the threatening aspects of the environment (hunger, thirst, attack, even inclement weather) rivet the attention of members of the organization to the basic object (survival) of their mutual endeavors. Further, with such an uncommon, fundamental goal, it is also clear to members that the subgoals are part and parcel of the ultimate goal. Hence, they clearly understand and unanimously endorse both the ends and the means of their venture. Should a member do otherwise, informal groups would probably nudge the dissident back into line.

In addition, the participants can, at this point in the development of the organization, see progress being made through their joint efforts. Activities are set up and executed to provide the basic necessities for life. The payoff is clearly demonstrated to the individuals supporting the organized effort to achieve these goals, or common purposes.

Consonance with external environment. A social system must maintain a consonance, or compatability, with its environment to survive. To sustain this harmony between the organization and its particular setting, it must be both sensitive to external changes and able to adjust to new demands as they occur. Thus, an analysis of an organization's capabilities to maintain congruence between its activities and the demands from external forces should be conducted in two parts.

First, we must estimate the degree of its sensitivity to environmental forces. This does not include all environmental forces, of course, but only those to which the system must react. In the organization we have been following, such forces would include changes in food supply, weather, or signs of other threats. Again, fear of physical harm is a potent force in ensuring a perceptive organization. Among the castaways there are not only specially formed units to provide security, food, and shelter, but each person has also appointed him or herself to be a lookout for threats to survival or opportunities to increase security. This means that the objectives of the formal organization are also the goals of the informal groups. This condition, where formal and informal arrangements support each other, prrovides considerable organizational strength.

Second, if an organization is to be consonant with its external environment, it is necessary to estimate its ability to change. Though mature in one sense, the organization at hand is young in another. It has no rich culture or rituals, no tradition. Its members have not as yet acquired deeply set ways of acting and reacting. Nor is its leadership so confident of its methods of proceeding that it will not change. At this time and under these circumstances, it is easy to introduce modifications.

The seeds for inflexible relationships, however, have been sown. The mere acts of giving unequal shares of authority, of placing members into specific units of activities, and of insisting upon certain role behavior and role relationships will foster resistance to change. Structuring is mandatory for order, but order begets lethargy.

Internal consistency. Now we come to the subsystems of the organization. We must analyze these aspects to see if they support each other and the overall purpose. We must also find out if they are perceived as serving a rational purpose by the participants subjected to them. For this part of the evaluation, it is well to analyze the array of subsystems undergirding the island organization. Table 4-1 shows certain classes of internal subsystems, the reasons for their design, and, in addition, their impact upon the members as they might view it.

Internal consistency is attained when the subsystems of activities can be justified as means leading directly to an organization's goals. This condition of inner balance, or homogeneity, is strengthened when the participants accept as justifiable arrangements related to organizational needs and goals. Once they accept the rationale for the design of institutional subsystems, members can shoulder the demands placed upon them by such arrangements and direct their attention to their respective tasks. In the absence of a high degree of acceptance, paticipants spend much of their time and energies trying to change arrangements to meet expectations or to undermine areas that they see as inappropriate.

The mature organization of the islanders is internally consistent. The subsystems are justified as means to goals, both from an organizational and a participant standpoint. Now let us see if the internal systems support each other. Note that all arrangements are designed to facilitate quick, unified reaction to threat. The social system is command-oriented, in response to the demands of the situation. Regimented control is crucial to the venture's success, so leadership is militantly autocratic, delegation and communications unilaterally aimed downward. Authority relationships are clearly drawn to avoid confusion; functionally based formal groupings are charted on simple lines; and appropriate incentives produce contributions to the con-

TABLE 4–1. Designing internally consistent subsystems

Design of Internal Systems	Organizational Rationale	Participants' Perception of Rationale
Common purpose of survival	Threat	Threat
Subgoals of shelter, food, and security	Basic biological needs and protection of members; fulfill common purpose	Basic individual needs
Autocratic leadership	Fast reaction of total forces	Fast marshalling of members for individual protection
Formal groupings by major tasks	Functionally related to needs of organization	Logical means to provide basic needs of individuals
Direct delegative processes downward	Speed and simplicity	Efficient use of authority
Downward communications	Fast total reaction; little need for upward flow	Fast mobilization to quell attack; little need for upward flow because "experts" are in sensitive positions
Command and control basic to leadership	Cohesion, unity of direction urgently needed	Protection and self-support enhanced by safety in numbers with common cause
Rigorous control of participants' roles	Organizational well-being dependent on individual efforts	Must "pull together" to survive; self-control and informal control appropriate values
Clearly communicated incentives	Individuals share in protection and well-being brought on by organized efforts	Increased chances for survival if broader organization survives. "For my contribution, it provides protection."

tinuity, cohesiveness, and manageability of the total system. No internal inconsistency can be found here. The orientation of the organization continues to be toward emergency action.

Consider, finally, the effect of the introduction of an inconsistently designed subsystem. Assume that all internal systems are designed for command and control, with the exception, say, of incentives. Consider the effect on behavior of an incentive system geared to reward participants on the basis of their nonconformity and self-determination. The results would be ludicrous.—even fatal. Such a basis for rewards would weaken cohesiveness, control, and the ability of the total system to react rapidly and uniformly. Indeed, this internal inconsistency could weaken, if not abort, actions to achieve the common purpose of the organization.

In a relatively simple organization with a clear-cut mission, such as the organization of islanders, there is little chance for major discontinuities to impede progress. It is in more complex social systems with less clearly definable objectives, that inconsistencies of major consequence can arise.

We see, then, that the maturing organization is coordinated both internally and externally to reach its goals. It is thus efficient in the use of its resources and, by maintaining a consonance with its environment, is enabled to achieve long-run effectiveness.

An organization, however, is often subjected to a metamorphosis—that is, a change in form, structure, or substance—after reaching full maturity. The transformation usually is caused by changes or perceived changes in the external environment. In response, the structure is re-formed. Assuming it has developed a sound method of operation during its maturing process, there is little justification for its leader or other participants to change their behavior in any substantive way. Perhaps this is the reason leaders of mature organizations often react to issues rather than acting to anticipate change.

CHANGING ENVIRONMENT

Let us now imagine a major change in the situation of the islanders. Assume that the threat of physical danger is removed. Then the purpose, functions, structure, types of activities, and composition of the total system must in turn be changed.

After organizing, the leaders doubtless would initiate efforts to find out more about the threats imposed by shortages of food or possible attacks by hostile inhabitants. To do so, the top leader would direct an intermediate leader, the head of security, to reconnoiter the unknown areas of the island and report any information obtained. In response, patrols would advance around the island in a pincers movement and return through the midlands. On completing the mission, they arrive back at the base camp and report that no other persons or threatening animals inhabit the island. Further, on the other side of a nearby hill lies a valley holding a meadow rich with abundant game and edible plants and drained by a natural spring providing an apparently inexhaustible source of water. At that instant, threat has been lifted from the group—threat that had provided a common purpose. What happens?

The organization's mission now changes. Its functions are transformed. Its structure must be re-formed to serve as a means to new goals, and its systems reëvaluated to achieve the new objectives. The way in which its activities are performed will now change. Its patterns of leadership must be adjusted. In fact, the very nature of the total system will change. Let us look closely at the extent of these changes and their influence on organizational health, that is, efficiency and effectiveness.

Goals

The purpose of the organization changes. It was originally formed for its participants' survival. Now, it must provide the necessities of a small social order, and improved standard of living, and the means for rescue or escape. Though worthy objectives, they are not the sharply defined goal of survival, nor will these new goals inspire total agreement on the best way to reach them.

Functions

The functions of the organization must change since they are directly connected to its new goals. In general, there are two classes of functions to fulfill. The first, for which the organization was originally formed, is closely tied to the physical needs of the people. Yet these needs no longer have their initial urgency. The second function is to provide the institutional means to maintain the organization as a social system and, by doing so, to prevent forces of individual self-interest from destroying it. The organization must provide food, shelter, and protection. But, in addition, it must institutionalize levels of accepted behavior to harness the individual to community action. All of these functions must be fulfilled through means acceptable to the organization's participants under the now-less-urgent situation. In a word, a society must be created.

Structure

The structure of the organization must be re-formed to provide the means to achieve the new functional requirements. Under the newly relaxed environment (the only uncertainties being the time of rescue or the feasibility of escape), the members will need institutionalized means to develop fairly complete societal arrangements. Beyond providing for biological wants, the organization must now act to satisfy needs for such things as law and order, cultural events, spiritual guidance, and governance. In response, the organization necessarily would be dramatically reshaped from its initial form to fill a number of expected, though more nebulous, functions—in contrast to those that it filled originally. It undergoes a change in form called a metamorphosis. A transformation occurs, not unlike a major change in a physical organism, where it would be referred to as metamorphic. It would change from the simple genetic organization to the complex metamorphic organization depicted in Figure 4-5.

The organization chart, though only a crude estimate of the real changes, illustrates the intricacy of the evolving system required to meet complex functional needs. Note that though the same people are involved, when the organization is fragmented to accommodate new activities, an additional level of leadership is needed. Further, observe that with increasing complexity and the need to provide government, specialized staff advisors are needed. These staff units counsel the leader of the organization and, through this individual, assist the leaders of various functional activities. This is commonly required because line leaders are generalists who often need specialized assistance in a certain area. In sum, increasing functional needs lead to more specialized activities. Then, the activities bring on more organizational arrangements, multiple authority levels, line and staff units, and multiple authority flows.

Subsystems

As structural arrangements become more complex, the systems for such elements as authority, delegation, communications, incentives, and control become more difficult to design and manage. This is particularly true if common purpose is lost due to differing interpretations by various members of the group. In the beginning, for instance, authoritative power was used and accepted to make sure that at least enough food was obtained daily to sustain life. Now new expectations have doubtless developed concerning not only the quantity but also the quality and palatability of foods. What combinations of subsystems promise meeting such minimum standards for eating? Can they be merely ordered in the same way minimum quantities of food were? No, the use of authority alone fails to produce high performance when the primary requisite is quality. Perhaps through the use of minimized authority and control, along with maximized incentives and participation by the culinary staff, a high level of cuisine can be produced—assuming, of course, that general agreement can be reached as to what constitutes a "high level of cuisine."

Tempo

With a marked change in environment, the pace at which members perform the activities required by the organization shifts down from intense to relaxed. This adjustment is understandable since the new organizational setting now permits security, if not comfort. Not only is

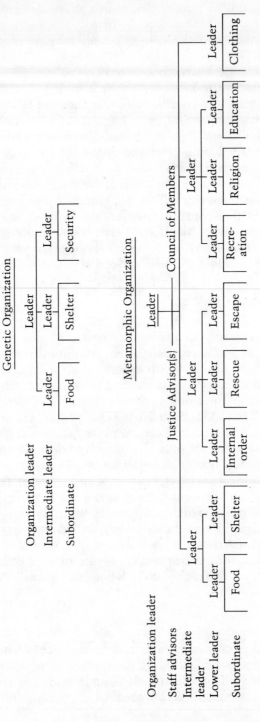

FIGURE 4–5. Genetic Organization and Metamorphic Organization

the rate of interaction slowed, but there is also an accompanying relaxing in the degree of integration. That is, as the demands on the organization grow less intense and its activities more diffuse, the tempo of interaction among members slackens. Thus, the integrating bonds are weakened.

Leadership

The role behavior of leadership changes both in intent and in content when the setting of an organization is altered. The *intent of leadership* here means its determination to act in a certain way toward subordinate members. The *content of leadership* refers to the composition of the leaders' responsibilities to the organization.

Reflect back to the behavioral traits and skills of the leader needed during the beginning of the survivors' organization. Recall that a person was chosen to act as an authoritative, strong commander who could decisively direct, organize, and control people under conditions of stress. This was the *intent of leadership.* Recall further that the situation required that the head be technically competent to provide bodily protection and security for the members. As a result, one with demonstrated abilities to command under adverse conditions, such as a former military leader, might have been selected. This technical ability was required for the *content of leadership.*

Now the organization has moved to a point where the people or the organization no longer need such a vibrant figure to lead, either in intent or content. Consider once again the leadership behavior and skills desired; then evaluate the attributes to be sought in the person who should now lead. The type of leader needed in the new situation must be able to cultivate the individual talents of the members to develop societal arrangements through which standards of living can be improved, commonly held values maintained, and escape or rescue made possible. The behavior and skills required to accomplish these would be quite different from those necessary to lead the organization under its original charter. To fill the leadership role posed by the respective situations, one would normally be expected to possess the following attributes:

Attributes of Leadership in Original Situation	*Attributes of Leadership in Current Situation*
Experience as a specialist in field (military or other)	Experience as a generalist (perhaps in government)
Projecting image of strength	Projecting image of stability
Authoritative in manner	Judicial in manner
Decisive	Deliberative
Mentally adroit	Mentally thoughtful; an arbitrator
An incisive communicator	An emphatic communicator
An organizer	A planner

Though these are merely an estimate, the differences seem necessary under the new situation. They seem more realistic for the leader who must assume the new role—a role shaped by the intent of leadership and the general membership to establish a small society.

The content of leadership must also change with the major organizational change. Leaders are expected to have competency in three major areas: technical, human, and conceptual. Technical skills are essential in mechanical or technological matters; human skills are used in interpersonal relationships; and conceptual skills are needed to solve problems requiring broadened perspective.

The original organization needed someone with specific skills and experience to guide it. Now the situation calls for a person with greater competence in the areas of human and conceptual skills to cope with the broadened fields of activity. Now members expect a less autocratic posture from their leader.

Leadership is effective when it is appropriate to the situation. And situations do change. Some leaders are psychologically prepared to vary their approaches with changing circumstances and are open to learning new skills. If organizations are to be adaptive and flexible systems, leaders must display adaptive and flexible behavioral patterns.

Some leaders, however, (as well as other people) become structured and rigid. They assume a certain approach to people and close out alternative approaches, even as the world changes around them. When unbending, structured individual behavior is confronted by forceful system changes, the system's structure cracks—or structured people are removed.

Assume for our purposes that the leader of the islanders is unable or unwilling to change behavior. So, replacement is required. A change in leaders presupposes that the members of the organization can remove the autocrat and install a new leader with capabilities suitable to the new needs of the organization. Often, however, dictatorial rule persists beyond the time when the organizational situation requires it, as do obsolete subsystems and procedures. It is not uncommon for a dictator to rise to power when an organization (or country) is in trouble and, by insulating the administration against reform, continue to rule beyond the critical stage of the endeavor's development, thereby preserving political power. Though examples of this sort of political self-perpetuation are widespread, it is more useful here to assume that a change in leadership will be made. It is also more realistic when one considers the speed with which the organization of marooned voyagers has been formed and re-formed. It seems doubtful that in such a short time span, leaders could have shielded their positions of authority from a pronounced need for change.

Total System

The final major change will make itself felt on the organization as a whole. And its impact can neither be clearly seen nor accurately understood by simply summing up the changes that have transpired to this point. A social system is greater that the sum of its parts. The impact of change races through it in such a way that the new organization typically develops a quality that is very different from that of the original structure. It is somewhat like a sweeping change of personality in a person.

If the original organization were described, one might hear the following description:

> In the beginning, the organization was designed simply to achieve basic and clearly defined goals. Its subsystems of authority, communications, incentives, and patterns of leadership were widely adopted as reasonable means to its goals. Its participants understood and accepted the roles, norms, and values as guides for acceptable individual behavior in merging individual efforts for the good of the organization. It was efficient and, under threat, sensitive to environmentally provoked needs for change.

Contrast this with a description of the new organization:

> Now the organizational arrangements are complex. Goals are diffuse and abstract. The organization must adopt and manage subsystems for such necessities as authority, communications, and incentives, which are uniquely designed to provide guidance for people working in groups with diverse activities and goals. Its participants accept their roles as they understand them. However, they may now be confused as to what manner of activity and level of productivity constitute acceptable behavioral patterns, particularly in merging individual contributions for the welfare of the entire organization. With nebulous goals, complex structure, complicated design of support subsystems, more highly specialized divisions of labor, and blurred definitions of acceptable roles, it is clear the organization will tend to be less efficient. And with situational security, it will also become less sensitive to needs for change.

THE AGING ORGANIZATION

During this final metamorphic stage of development, the organization of island castaways is not unlike many on-going, mature establishments. Over time, in a relatively placid environment, a social system will instigate rules, rituals, and other influences on participant behavior. As these social amenities are repeated, they become institutionalized. Such institutionalized patterns of behavior make up the cultural fabric, the social heritage of an organization. And people are hesitant to break with traditional ways of behaving. Even when behavior is grossly ineffectual and blatantly difficult, a person will commonly protect the status quo because at least there is comfort in knowing the task and security in understanding one's role relationship to others.

Rigidity

Thus, institutionalized arrangements tend to become fixed. As new goals and the means to achieving them become appropriate, they are imposed on the organization, but often without replacing long-standing behavioral patterns now grown obsolete. When abrupt, rather than evolutionary, changes are imposed on institutionalized behavior, internal inconsistencies tend to develop because certain systems of activity are not redesigned to support newly adopted goals.

Loss of Sensitivity

Further, as an organization becomes secure in its environment, it also becomes less sensitive to forces calling for change. It seems to become insulated from external forces and impervious to catalysts for change from within. Often, even after recognizing the need for a certain adjustment, it is lethargic in responding. This is understandable. In the absence of a threat to its security, there is little incentive to change.

The secure organization becomes more than only complacent. It inclines toward introspection, that is, it develops an overconcern with internal activities. Though natural, this can lead to further neglect of new developments in the external environment and divert energies from the pursuit of organizational goals. Organizational introspection is at work when large amounts of time and effort are used on activities having nothing to do with output, for example, political involvement; empire building; establishing "comfort zones" and taboos; harboring jealousy; and expressing pride, power, prestige, or position. Though it appears that it is natural for men and women to be so occupied, such activities can weaken organizational efficiency and effectiveness by (1) introducing internal inconsistencies (2) impeding alertness to the external environment and (3) diverting attention from the real competitor.

The organization now has lost the traits found in the original social system. Initially, a threatening situation gave rise to (1) explicit goals; (2) emergency of a cohesive, integrated social system; (3) internally consistent subsystems as means to goals; and (4) sensitiveness as well as adaptiveness to environmental forces. Weigh now the traits of the current organization by examining the conceptual model in Figure 4-6. The organization, though less cohesive than earlier, will continue to function, however, because it continues to fulfill the needs of its participants. It will, therefore, be supported until it demands more from its members than they believe they are getting from it.

Most organizations develop internal ambiguities and lose syn-

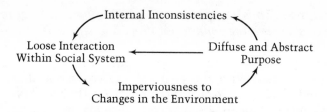

FIGURE 4–6. Conceptual Model of Aging Organization

chronization with their external situation, but they continue to function because they represent the best alternative available Though cumbersome, they are our best or only means to goal achievement. We know how to manage an organization so that, through corrections, it can reach its goals in spite of its imbalances.

DEMISE OF AN ORGANIZATION

Consider, finally, conditions that further weaken the bonds of integrated human effort, those that can lead to the ultimate demise of an organization so that the social system as it was formed ceases to function. You may recall that, unlike physical and physiological systems, when interaction stops the organization vanishes, leaving no remains other than the physical objects used during its existence. Physical and physiological systems, by contrast, leave structures that can be studied; these often provide explanations of the dynamics of the functioning organism and the reason for its failure. Unfortunately for students of organizations, no evidence remains of an organization's existence other than artifacts and historical records. These trappings usually are evidence of events, but often they do not reveal the causes of the disintegration of social arrangements. Thus, the study of organizational pathology is impeded.

The organization of our mythical marooned seafarers can be irreparably impaired in a number of ways. Among the more apparent reasons for collapse, the organization can lose sight of its goals; internal friction may become excessive and intolerable; the organization may fail to respond to new demands from either internal or external forces; or participants may feel that rewards are less than their contribution to the organized effort.

Pathology of an Organization

Let us now examine each of these causes of organizational illness in closer detail. Bear in mind that leaders of organizations must minimize these types of maladies if they are to preserve the continuing success of their enterprises. *Thus, recognition of these common hazards to organizational health lays the foundation for understanding the roles and goals of management.*

First, as agreement on common purpose wanes, the organization loses cohesiveness. With the goals of the enterprise more diffuse, abstract, and subject to personal interpretations, the social system loses structural sinew. Leaders are unable to develop and manage support subsystems when goals are not clearly defined. Participants are unable to see what behavior is acceptable. Leaders become indecisive in the absence of clearly stated aims against which alternatives must be weighed. Directives to subordinates lose effectiveness when they lack the "authority of the situation." Participants are unable to identify with organized efforts when the purpose of their efforts is clouded. In turn, involvement and dedication ebb. Then control is lost because goals are not there to set norms of performance against which actual contribution can be measured. All of these qualities lost are essential to organizational health.

Consider now how the individual voyagers will feel if the castaways' organization cannot be changed to meet new demands. Apprehensive members will seek a voice in the major decisions affecting their organization. Should its leaders continue to impose autocratic rule, subordinates will chafe because the situation no longer warrants such uncompromising behavior. Suppose the organization also grows impervious to demands from the external environment. Then, as a result, resources are wasted through overindulgence and contamination, shelters are inadequate to withstand tropical storms, and living areas become unhealthful through neglect. Confusion prevails as to appropriate roles, norms, and values. Coordination and integration are lost. The organization fades away and the group reappears—a loose assemblage of people engaged in casual interaction. As the trade-offs between inducements and demands widen in the eyes of participants, even casual arrangements weaken. Subgroups break away to seek self-maintenance through other arrangements. Finally, though the functional necessities of living are met in the fragmented groups, the original organization dies.

SUMMARY

Though an unusual example, the islanders illustrate the unfolding life cycle of an organization. At its formation, or genesis, both the members and their organization are insecure; hence, they are sensitive to the need for change and responsive to these demands. The system is inefficient until coordination and refinement of its subgroups and processes are attained. During an organization's maturation, it tends to refine internal operations while continuing to be responsive to environmental forces. As it ages, organizational ills are caused by malfunction in one of three major areas: First, and most important, an organization cannot be managed without clear goals; second, an organization cannot be efficient when fraught with internal inconsistencies; and third, an organization cannot survive over time if it grows immune or unresponsive to changing environmental demands. The organization of the castaways was viewed as a dependent structure, part of an environmental system, where external forces had an impact upon the design and functioning of organizational arrangements. The approach has certain strengths. It encourages an examination of cause-effect reactions and the influence of sudden environmental changes on an organization. However, the major weakness in viewing an organization from this angle is its overemphasis on the passive, or reactive, aspects of organizational life. That is, some would point out that it unduly emphasizes adaptation while neglecting leaders' strategies to defy certain unfavorable external conditions. Others might claim that leaders can use their organizations' strengths as instruments to make external conditions compatible with their organizations. The approach used in the example of the shipwrecked party, some may say, neglects consideration of the leader's capacity to change environmental factors.

Most professional leaders, however, have little latitude to change basic environmental influences. They are nearly as confined in this respect as the head of the organization of shipwrecked survivors. The commander could do little to eliminate a shortage of food or threats from hostile inhabitants. Likewise, leaders in other enterprises can do little to change values, attitudes, philosophies, life styles, family sizes, or concentrations of populations. And these are the basic causal factors that influence organizational behavior. So most leaders—political, business, clerical, charitable, military, or whatever—react, rather than anticipate horizontal necessities for changes. They are concerned with appropriate, timely reactions to maintain their organizations' internal efficiency and external consonance.

DISCUSSION QUESTIONS

1. In the first phase of the life cycle of the islanders' organization, what factors would tend to keep the people from becoming so formally organized as the text suggests?

2. What conditions impede organizations from maintaining a state of *dynamic equilibrium?*

3. Is the weakening and demise of an organization unusual, typical, inevitable, or merely one of several courses? Why?

4. Which phase in the life cycle of the islanders is most like conditions in most of the established, complex organizations around us? Why?

5. After the disintegration of the islanders' organization, how were necessary functions fulfilled that had been previously taken care of through its integrated structures? What are the implications here?

6. From the fictional account of the islanders' adventure, what do you see as the major implications for leadership?

5

Structure of Organizations

> *Organization tends to minimize conflict, and to lessen the significance of individual behavior which deviates from values that the organization has established as worthwhile. Further, organization increases stability in human relationships by reducing uncertainty regarding the nature of the system's structure and the human roles which are inherent to it.*
>
> William G. Scott[1]

To this point in our discussions, we have devoted attention to the overall nature of organizations—their basic elements, types, needs, and life cycle. This was done to provide a feeling for the gestalt, or an organization in total, and to point up certain features common to all organizations. Now we can narrow the focus of our study to the internal arrangements of these systems, to certain important details, but with an awareness of how the details fit into the overall scheme of sound organizational arrangements.

To do so, let us review the conceptual model of a strong organization, concentrating now on the structure of the social system—its goals, functions, and anatomy. (See Figure 5-1.) The reader will observe that the logic of the structural design flows from goals, and functions required to attain those goals, to the structure needed to fulfill those functions. As a reminder, the anchor for cohesive organized efforts lies in the understanding and accepting of goals by participants *at all levels.*

These fundamentals to organizational life, among others, were studied by the pioneers in the field.[2] Their early teachings provide the foundations from which more advanced analyses were made.

An examination of the goals, functions, and structures of organizations can help us understand their basic formation. Such an evaluation

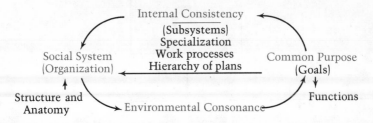

FIGURE 5–1. Conceptual Model of an Organization

can also make us aware in practical terms of the appropriateness or inappropriateness of structural arrangements. It will not, by itself, enable us to understand the intricacies of the behavior of a specific organization; nor will it permit us to develop solutions acceptable to a particular organization and its people. Goals, functions, and structures are common to all organizations. They are universals. Understanding common features cannot explain unique cultural differences. The type of analysis that is necessary to design prescriptions that fit a specific situation will be presented in Chapter 10. For now, let us consider the historical development of thinking about the structure of organizations.

EARLY STUDY TO UNDERSTAND ORGANIZATIONS

We usually attribute the classical, or traditional, school of organizational thought to that group of reformers who practiced, consulted, wrote, and taught during the late nineteenth and early twentieth centuries. The line of thinking, of course, was rooted in the centuries of humanity's experiences in dealing with the problems of organizing and directing people in unified pursuits. The various ventures were religious, military, political, utilitarian, and cultural. Valuable lessons on organizations sprang from such sources as biblical writings, the Roman republic, the Catholic Church, and Napoleon's armies. Contributions from early historical settings dealt with the fundamentals required to structure human interactions. Obviously the teachings could not deal with the complications of advanced technology, intricate economical considerations, or sophisticated human behavior.

For example, in a pre-industrial commercial enterprise, only relatively crude organizational forms were required. Craftsmen with varying degrees of skill often manufactured the entire product of a business under the general direction of an owner-manager, or master craftsman. The finished good was then taken to a central marketplace, usually in a nearby village, or was sold to buyers who came to the shop. Thus, the entire function was simple, as was the organization through which it took place. Size and complexity grow along with the size and complexity of the mission.

Historical Development

It was not until after the Industrial Revolution, in the early 1900s, that the intricate problems of merging workers and machines arose. The problems were further complicated, because the cottage manufacturers of the premachine age were unsuited to new goals requiring complex technological and economic structures. Problems of major proportions arose, problems without precedence. Mechanization was ostensibly intended to be an extension of man's physical capabilities to perform work. In reality, following the Industrial Revolution, workers often came to be viewed as merely appendages to the new machinery, necessary additions for its operation. In either event, the immediate task at hand was to merge people with machines; usually the variable element was the worker, the constant element the machine. (This condition often continues today in new applications of technology—mechanization, automation, and computerization.)

Conditions in organizations were dreadful by today's standards. Both human and economic inefficiency were widespread and appalling. Though a factory was usually selected to depict working conditions, similar organizational incompetence was common in institutions of government, religion, education, labor, and the military. However, such crude conditions should be viewed in the context of their historical setting, a period philosophically and technologically primed for progress and growth.

Public dissatisfaction swelled and the die for social reform was cast. During the period between 1880 and World War I, the *Age of Reform* as some term it, erupted. Others think it more accurate to call it the *Age of Revolt*.[3]

Leaders in industry heralded the work of pioneering students, largely made up of varied types of engineers, for their studies of leadership and organization. They were the forerunners of a reformation dedicated to bringing about improvements and efficiencies within organizations. They became known as the Classical School of organizational thought.

Object of Classical Teachings

Classical study was aimed at solving problems of a general, chronic, and universal nature. Understandably, early students concentrated on those widespread causes of inefficiencies that prevailed in nearly all types of organizations. They were compelled by the wasteful conditions they observed to offer broadly applicable solutions to the most common organizational ills. To alleviate the problems, they developed prescriptive models, that is, guidelines on how organizations should be designed rather than studies of how organizations were actually formed. These pioneer students developed ways to remedy chronic ills. Their models were based upon principles that were generally accepted as sound during that early period of study. Since these idealized guidelines were to be prescribed for use in many diverse institutions, their originators generally confined their inquiries to the structures common to all organizations. As a result, classical study provides templates, or patterns, for the design of arrangements integral to organizations in general; and these principles, or guidelines, are intended to be used to improve efficiency.

For example, virtually all organizations suffered inefficiencies because of poor planning. With little advance training, workers did not know what was expected of them other than to "keep busy." They were assigned awkward tasks. Often necessary supplies and tools were not available to them. And they found it difficult to coordinate their efforts with others. Leaders, on the other hand, were accountable for high output from the workers but were uncertain of their subordinates' potential. Their demands for increases in productivity were arbitrary and at times, in the workers' eyes, capricious. Frustration and inefficiency followed. The early "efficiency experts" observed that all organizations needed improved planning techniques. In turn, these experts developed theories for studies in such areas as work design, time and motion, methods engineering, and production scheduling to increase efficiency in all organizations.

So it followed that the object of classical interest was to solve the most pressing problems found in most enterprises. The concern focused on idealized arrangements for any organization. That is, students searched for the "one best way to organize." The prescriptions that they uncovered were based upon an ideal way of structuring an enterprise, constrained only by contemporary views of what constituted the "ideal way." As with other universal prescriptions, their application was limited by the unique conditions that prevailed in specific organizations.

Focus of Early Teachings

Classical thinkers viewed an organization as a means to production, much as one might think of a machine. Complex organization emerges when the demands imposed by its mission require a concentration of authority over a large number of employees. This makes it necessary for authority, incentives, and control to be continuously disseminated by communications through authority centers at intermediary levels. Early emphasis understandably fell on formal structure, with particular attention to downward flows of authority and communications, and to incentives for stimulating high output.

Classical theory led to the design of organizations that appeared to be stable, durable, pyramidal, and production-oriented, with high priority assigned to conformity and control. Classical thinking dealt largely with structural-functional relationships. The proposition that structured arrangements control the functioning of an organization was heavily emphasized. Though this view narrowly restricts the scope of organizational analysis, it led to valuable insights for improving organizational efficiency.

The focus of the reform narrowed to scientific studies of particular problem areas. Among these were the composition of work, workers' expectations, divisions of labor, and incentives; the interface between workers and management; the structural relationship of workers to each other and to management; authority and delegation; and line and staff relationships. The thrust of early study was aimed at resolving the common chronic problems of goal attainment, internal adaptation, integration, and patterned self-maintenance.

HIERARCHIES OF STRUCTURE

Let us now direct our attention to certain hierarchies of structure common to organizations and, thus, of major concern to the first contributors to organization theory. These structures are goals, plans, hierarchical arrangements, specialization, work processes and grouping work processes. Structures are required to provide order, to permit coordination, and to promote efficiency. The structures could be thought of as successive layers of frameworks. Each layer is related to all other structures. The process begins with goals.

Goals

As was illustrated previously, establishing the goals of an enterprise is prerequisite to designing an organization for their attainment. Setting goals is a part of planning, the fundamental managerial process required to fulfill the other adminstrative processes of organizing, directing, and controlling.

To Henri Fayol, a pioneer in the movement to improve management and organization, planning included establishing objectives, the action required to reach the objectives, scheduling of the various stages, and the means to be used. Fayol was the highly successful general manager of a large French mining and metallurgical firm. In that position, he initiated and used a series of forecasts, the forerunners of today's budgets. He used forecasts fifty years before he wrote on the subject, *Administration Industrielle et Generale*, which was published in 1908.[4]

Goals are the basic requirement of a stable social structure for group endeavor, according to the early classical school of thought, in which the logic of structural-functional design prevailed. From this base, other bonds of organized effort unfold—structure, job specifications, and grouping of jobs.

To some authorities, notably E. Wight Bakke, identification with the purpose of an enterprise must be broadened to encompass the *concept of organizational charter*. Organizational charter, an idea parallel to the notion of *collective representations*, refers to the image that its members have of the enterprise as a whole. This broader view is the mental picture that comes to a member's mind when considering the purposes, achievements, traditions, and symbols of the organization. It is the image that members have who say, "I work for Pepsi-Cola" or, "I'm a member of the Communication Workers of America" or "I'm a teacher at Cornell."

Organizational charter can provide the means through which members identify with an organization. Lack of identification with the purpose of the organization creates variations in participants' beliefs about its purpose, function, differentiating features, and often, what their appropriate contribution to the overall effort should be. When this occurs, internal inconsistencies usually result, followed by confusion, friction, tension, and, ultimately, weakened employee morale.

There is little disagreement among classical authorities that clearly defined goals are essential if united effort is to be nurtured. For that reason, management consultants continue today to ask such questions as "What is the purpose of this enterprise?" and "Where is the enterprise headed?" Responses are often fundamental to their recommendations. In the complex organization of today, confusion is frequently widespread as to its major goals and the individual's part in their attainment. As a consequence, strains and unwanted conflicts are common.

Disagreement over the need for common purpose does not arise because purpose is believed to be unnecessary. Rather, agreement wanes when leaders give a high priority to communicating the details of *what* must be done to the neglect of relating *why*. Disagreement over goals becomes even more pronounced with the high degree of specialization and high sophistication of technology found in most modern enterprises. Nonetheless, it often begins with a conceptual narrowness or disregard of the human element on the parts of leaders.

Hierarchies within Organizations[5]

For illustrative purposes, consider the relationships among the hierarchies of goals, plans, and authority. With this illustration, one major source of misunderstood objectives—with its accompanying damage to role identity, role relationships, and individual purpose—can be made clear.

All enterprises have functions to be fulfilled by people in pursuit of overall organizational goals. Goals ostensibly complement each other and are interrelated, from the top executive down to the lowest position in the enterprise. From the broad array of rewards received by the top leader to the earnings and fringe benefits of the employee working for a daily wage, incentives are granted to encourage individual support of institutionalized goals. In addition, a hierarchy of plans is devised to serve as a guideline for decision making and action throughout the organization. The plans range in degrees of definiteness from broad statements of philosophy and policy at the top to specific operating procedures at the bottom.

These hierarchies—goals, plans, and authority structure—serve as means to communicate common purpose and the role expectations required to reach overall goals. Most importantly, they are communicated activities that become relevant and meaningful at each level from top executive down to daily wage earner. The hierarchies of plans and goals required to give participants unified direction are in inverse relationship to the structure of the formal (or organizational) hierarchy. Figure 5-2 depicts these relationships.

You will notice that broad plans—policies, strategies, and programs—give guidance and direction to top management for decision making and action. However, it is also apparent that these plans are not detailed enough to provide direction to lower-level managers and workers. For this reason, the hierarchy of plans is reinterpreted in more precise terms to provide a finer degree of direction at these lower levels.

Hierarchies of goals and plans ideally should communicate common purpose throughout the enterprise in such a way that participants can gain a feel for their part, their reward, the parts of others, and their contribution to the overall effort. Haplessly, such close identification with overall goals is often lacking. One major cause, suggested previously, is that leaders in many institutional settings are quick to direct subordinates on the "what," "when," "where," and "how" of tasks, but less prone to explain the relationship of a subordinate's task to the overall effort. *Understanding the "why" of their activities, enables workers to see their role behavior and contributions in the context of the broader organization.* Failure of leaders to place subordinates into the overall picture may arise from a number of causes: They may not recognize the need for such broad comprehension by a subordinate; their own limited conceptual ability may prevent them from integrating a worker's part; or they may simply feel that they cannot take the time to give anything beyond the basic instructions required to get the job done.

Specialization (Division of Labor)

Organization is viewed traditionally as a necessary vehicle through which goals are accomplished, goals that lie beyond the capability of any individual, generally because of their size and complexity. It is axiom-

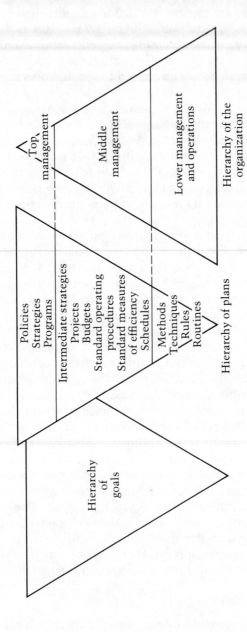

Source: Adapted from Robert Grandford Wright, "The Myth Inherent in Responsibility Center Management, *MSU Business Topics,* Spring 1972, Vol. 20, No. 2.) Used by permission of the publisher, Division of Research, Graduate School of Business Administration, Michigan State University.

FIGURE 5–2. The Relationship of the Organization to Hierarchies of Goals and Plans

atic that the magnitude and intricacies of organizational goals, and the functions to attain them, require divisions of tasks and the assignment of individuals best qualified to perform them. Herein lies one of the many paradoxes of organizational realities: People band together to pursue a common purpose, but their individual activities must be fragmented to permit specialization so that enterprise goals can be *efficiently* attained.

Divisions of labor permit specialization. Specialization, in a technical sense, permits high degrees of competence and expertise in varied, but narrowly defined, tasks. As a result, efficiency can be attained, assuming the diverse tasks are coordinated.

Consider, for example, a simple manufacturing process through which wooden chairs are constructed. Any one of us could learn the skills required to build the complete chair. We could prepare the raw materials; form the seat and doweling; assemble and glue the parts; and finish the chair with paint, varnish, or stain. But greater competence and speed would doubtless be gained if different ones performed more specialized tasks. This is particularly true if a high level of technical know-how is needed for using the equipment to make the chair. The use of electric sanders, bandsaws, lathes, and spray-paint equipment requires different knowledge and skills. Further, it is necessary to employ at a high rate of use such costly machinery to gain an acceptable rate of return on the investment. The necessity for greater efficiency causes us to specialize—that is, to divide the work into parts based upon the interests, capacity, and skills of individuals; the nature of machine capabilities and limitations; the physical layout; and the flow and timing of the production process. Assume the division of labor is made and that its final form takes on the features sketched in Figure 5-3.

Consider now the advantages gained from the specialization brought about as a consequence of divisions of labor. These benefits were of considerable concern to traditional organizational theorists

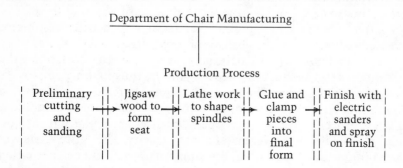

FIGURE 5–3. Process of Chair Production

such as Gulick and Urwick. They cite the reasons for the division of work as follows:

> Because people differ in nature, capacity, and skill—and gain greatly in dexterity by specialization;
> Because the same person cannot be in two places at the same time;
> Because one person cannot do two things at the same time;
> Because the range of knowledge and skill is so great that a person cannot within one life span know more than a small fraction of it.[6]

In essence, to traditional thinkers divisions of labor are a rational response to the limitations imposed by the nature of persons, time, space, and technology. Particularizing activities is required as a reasonable response to environmental constraints imposed upon people, work, and equipment.

Work Processes

A major thrust of early studies centered on the proper design of work. As indicated previously, neither the most experienced top executive nor the newly initiated production worker knew *objectively* what constituted a "fair day's work." Frederick W. Taylor, a preeminent pioneer of organization and management thinking, saw this dilemma as the major impediment to organizational unity:

> The greatest obstacle to harmonious cooperation between the workmen and the management lay in the ignorance of management as to what really constitutes a proper day's work for a workman.[7]

As a consequence of ignorance—ignorance of realistic individual contribution, ignorance as to the timing of various kinds of work, and ignorance of the proper role of management—no guidelines were available to determine what constitutes a "fair day's work."

Think about the implications of this situation, one found in all types of institutions during the early 1900s. What a source of confusion and frustration it must have been for leaders and workers alike. Leaders were accountable for production, but unaware of any way to achieve high output other than by "speedup" tactics. In response to pressures for increased output and in the absence of more effective techniques, they resorted to such measures as increasing machine speed, accelerating the work process flow, extending working hours, thus making employees work longer and harder. The workers frequently resisted in kind with individual or collective slowdowns (known as "soldiering"), equipment "failures," "accidents," or even open defiance, particularly if they already believed that they were working at capacity. The entire scene was a spawning ground for conflict, breeding frustration and consternation for a sincere leader. For the sincere subordinate it produced irritation, confusion, and despondency. The final consequence: human and economic waste.

This type of work setting was chaotic and, thus, ripe for yet another dimension of reform. A movement evolved to convince leaders that the remedy for inefficiency lay not in coercion but rather in a scientific approach to organizing and directing work.

The teachings of the movement began in the early twentieth century and grew in momentum, finally to be adopted throughout the then industrialized world. Its creator, Frederick W. Taylor, called it *scientific management*, and its precepts often carry that label today. Briefly stated, the principles of scientific management influence divisions of labor in the following ways:

1. Basing tasks on the scientific, accurate study of work as it relates to "unit times," that is, the time required for a divisible unit of work;
2. A division and a motion study of the elements of work on each position;
3. Rearranging the elements of work to facilitate maximum output;
4. Setting standards of output assuming a superior worker under favorable conditions;
5. Insistence upon work's being done the "one best way" developed, that is, standardized;
6. Rewarding the worker with higher wages for higher productivity.[8]

The idea offered leaders an alternative infinitely superior to practices in effect at that time. Ideally, as envisioned by its supporters, scientific management would enable (a) management to design *the* most appropriate division of labor, and to set *the* exact output to be expected from a "fair day's work"; and (b) workers to know precisely what was expected of them, and so produce to gain the high wages associated with high output. Ignorance of expectations and coercive tactics would give way to an enlightened design of work, work flows, realistic expectations, and wage incentives.

Scientific management after a time moved from the arena of work studies and divisions of labor to related problems. Its boundaries were broadened to encompass bonus systems to encourage cooperation (Henry L. Gantt, "Work, Wages, and Profits"),[9] scheduling and control to improve coordination of specialized units (Wallace Clark, *The Gantt Chart*),[10] industrial training and production planning (Gilbreth, *Bricklaying System*, 1909),[11] organizational efficiency (Harrington Emerson, *The Twelve Principles of Efficiency*,[12] and Morris L. Cooke, *Our Cities Awake*),[13] and the processes of management (Henri Fayol, *Administration Industrielle et Generale*).[14] Principles of scientific management were first published for the most part during that narrow span of time between 1909 and 1916. Demands upon productive capacity during World War I added impetus to the movement, stimulating applications of the new concepts in various organizations throughout the nation.[15] Today the basic tenets of these early teachings are used, implicitly or explicitly, to deal with the complex problems of efficiently merging people and technology. Often, the techniques currently in use are merely extensions of the fundamentals first enunciated by members of the early scientific school of thought. Methods engineering, operations research, work simplification, periodic evaluation and review technique (PERT), and preventive equipment maintenance are examples.

Early concern with the division of labor did not, however, encompass a number of issues that are pertinent to us now. The first studies failed to anticipate the dilemmas associated with overspecialization. They did not investigate human relations aspects, but focused primarily on the mechanistic elements of work. The analyses stressed the quantitative elements of output, but paid little attention to the qualitative aspects of work. And they ignored the impact of nonfinancial incentives. These matters, though important, were not the concern of the early contributors. They were concerned with widespread chronic issues, which could be solved through an understanding of work, the worker as an economic being, and the appropriate role of leadership.

Grouping Work Processes

After specialization has been instituted, tasks, processes, and activities must be regrouped to permit a unified pursuit of the enterprises's goals. Unification implies control of subgroup goals in the interest of the organization's goals, as well as a sharing of the endeavor's limited resources. This kind of balanced effort requires a hierarchy of leaders in ascending authority levels to pull the formerly fragmented activities (at times, these may be competing factions) into an integrated total.

Tasks may be grouped according to a number of bases, each with its own rationale. Initial clusters may reflect *product or services, function, activity, process, spatial proximity, territory,* or *constituency served.* Any groupings, or some form of combination, may be chosen as the most workable arrangement for a particular situation or institution.

Let us look at each of the bases for grouping activities in closer detail. To do so, it seems useful to reappraise the enterprise, presented previously, that was organized to produce wooden chairs. In this evaluation, however, rather than considering divisions of activities, we will examine the major ways through which they might be classified and drawn together. Reconsider the organization chart shown in Figure 5-4.

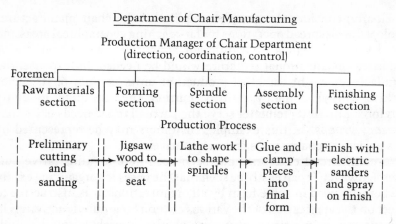

FIGURE 5–4. Organization of Chair Production

You will note that at the department level, the manufacturing phase of the enterprise has been grouped on the basis of *product*—in this instance, the Department of Chair Manufacturing. This method of assembling tasks could have been done on any level of authority. For instance, in the firm's early development, it could have had only one worker in each specialized activity—raw materials, seats, and so forth. Thus, the activities would have been grouped at the foreman level, the first level of authority. The growth of each activity required additional workers who then were formed into *functional* units, that is, areas of similar activities. Since each functional unit in this example requires a foreman to lead it, the groupings by product were made at the second level of authority—the production manager. You will observe further that activities have been clustered to enable production to flow over a course that begins with the gathering and preparation of raw materials, proceed through necessary intermediate steps, to end finally with the finishing of a completed product. This method of grouping, through which a product is aggregatively formed, is referred to as *process* grouping.

Now, let's turn to the remaining criteria for grouping. They are referred to above as spatial proximity and territory. Assume that the production department has need for a tool crib, a centralized facility from which small tools, hardware, templates, and other manufacturing essentials can be drawn. Assume further that only one worker is required to perform this activity and that the tool crib is adjacent to the finishing section. Though the tool crib may be used more by, say the forming section, it may be located and assigned on the basis of *spatial proximity* to the finishing unit because it is the centrally-located place, most convenient to the sections in total—raw materials, forming, spindle, assembly, and finishing—which require tool crib service.

Finally, consider the grouping required if the chair manufacturer developed widespread operations for far-reaching geographical areas and served varied demands from different constituencies, or markets. A broadened organizational structure would be needed. In response, the manufacturer might establish production units in each of its major markets, thus grouping by *territory*. Further, the firm might group its sales force into units to better serve the particularized needs of its *constituency groups*. In this example, customers may be represented by such outlets as chain stores and cooperatives.

A commercial enterprise has been used here for illustrative purposes. However, it can easily be seen that the bases for organizing exhibited here are used in some form by all organizations. It is instructive to reflect on the application of the various criteria for grouping activities in such enterprises as a city government, charity, church, hospital, or university.

SUMMARY

First teachings on organizations concentrated on providing ways to design efficient production systems. They contributed greatly to our understanding of the need for hierarchies of purpose, functions, and plans for the structure of work in organizations. The early theorists' primary concern was devoted to study work objectively, including its processes, specialization, and groupings. Their thinking provided a logic for designing the basic structure of organizations. They developed rational models, or templates, to be applied to improving the general conditions of work in all types of organizations. Because these were universal principles, or guidelines, limitations accompanied their application in specific organizations. Yet, they provided the underpinnings for later studies of particular organizations, that led to solutions of their problems.

DISCUSSION QUESTIONS

1. Why are heirarchies necessary in organizations?

2. Do specialization and hierarchical arrangements reduce or increase the personal identification of people within organizations? Why?

3. Why is the application of the general principles of organizations limited? Consider several major restrictions.

4. Why did classical thinkers seemingly neglect the so-called human side of enterprise? Or did they really neglect it?

5. Discuss the integrated relationships among the varied hierarchies of an organization. What are the implications when a change is made, for instance, in a goal?

6

Anatomy of Organizations

The most fruitful approach for those who want to learn about the nature of organization is to start with the understanding that if any collection of individuals is formed into a group . . . the function of the formal aspects is like that of a skeleton in the body. What you are mostly concerned with is the physiology of the relationships involved; but first of all you have to know anatomy well enough to know that there is a skeleton and that it keeps in place. . . . the organs which are mostly going to function autonomously.

Chester I. Barnard[1]

The anatomy of an organization is its structural form. It is a valuable key to studying arrangements of the system's basic parts, their identities, functions, positions, and relationships to each other. The anatomy of a formal organization is the skeletal arrangement illustrated by its formal chart.

The formal organization chart indicates only parameters. It depicts the way things are supposed to work. Though immensely useful to graphically illustrate relationships among people it can only loosely approximate superficial, albeit necessary, dimensions of social interaction.[2]

This view reduces an otherwise complicated system of activities down to its ultimate level of simplification. Yet taking this vantage point is valuable because the structure that is fundamental to all organizations can be clearly discerned and readily examined.

We must exercise care, however, by remembering that we have arbitrarily removed most of the intricate elements from real human interaction. In previous chapters we temporarily cut through layers of complex activities to gain insights into certain basic organizational arrangements. This approach is appropriate since it enables us to avoid tangling prematurely with complications. Later on we can consider certain intricacies required to understand organizations in real-world terms as total, dynamic, complex systems.

In Chapter 5, certain aspects of the structural nature of organizations were introduced: ideas about goals, functions, structure, specialization, work processes, and the hierarchy of plans. In this chapter, we will evaluate the ways in which the basic structures are tied together to form the overall anatomy of the formal organization. It is a static arrangement of people and groups of people. Then when authority is delegated, the members receive formal sanctions to use the resources of the organization, to contribute to the common effort, and to relate with other people in pursing enterprise goals. In this way, the static anatomy of an organization is converted into a dynamic social system. Viewed conceptually, we are now analyzing those traits of organizations indicated in bolder type in Figure 6-1. In analyzing these traits we will consider spans of management, unity of management, line/staff relationships, and the scalar principle.

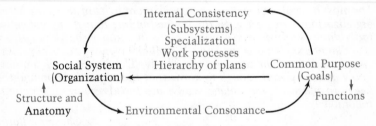

FIGURE 6–1. Conceptual Model of an Organization

SPANS OF MANAGEMENT

After activities have been assigned to people and grouped, organizers must give consideration to the number of subordinates a superior can effectively lead. The ratio of subordinates to a superior was originally called "span of command," a term derived from military usage. It was later termed "span of control" to emphasize what was considered to be the primary task of leadership at that time. Now the term "span of management" has gained popular acceptance because it conveys the relationship of subordinates to a superior authority in a more comprehensive way. A leader must "command"—that is, direct or lead. A leader must also be sure that activities are under "control"—that is, coordinated, continuous, and conforming to minimal demands. But even by combining these requirements into one definition, we are left with an incomplete definition of a leader. One who heads an operation must also *facilitate* the planning and organizing of group activities. Management has been viewed traditionally as a process through which planning, organizing, directing, and controlling take place in organizations. If indeed this is an accurate statement of its scope, then the newer phrase—span of management—is preferable to the forms used earlier.

Students of organization should be aware that the span of management goes beyond the accountability of leaders for the people only under their direction. The span also includes accountability for the equipment and funds used within their spheres of direct influence. For example, a leader must ensure that work area, machines, equipment, raw materials, and funds are efficiently employed and sufficiently protected. And this holds true, of course, whether the leader is in charge of a machine shop, a group of charity workers, a platoon of military recruits, or the Mayo Clinic.

Historical View

Concepts dealing with the span of management have been the object of as much controversy as any of the classical organizational principles. It is assumed that there is some upward limit to the number of subordinates who can be effectively managed by a single superior. Finding an appropriate degree of breadth, however, is difficult because concepts that should provide guidance are vague and, in some ways, misleading.

Yet finding appropriately broad spans of management is critically important for the efficiency of an organization. If spans are too narrow, management will become too costly; and employees may be overmanaged, lowering their morale. The resultant long chain of command can impede effective communications and result in less responsive organization units. Conversely, if spans are too broad, fragmentation into cliques can endanger group cohesiveness and autocratic leadership will be likely to increase. Subordinate concern for task success may lessen, member satisfaction dissipate, individual productivity fall, coordination be negatively affected, and, probably underlying most of the symptoms just cited, supervisors simply will not have time to lead.

Thus, finding realistic spans of management is fundamental to the effectiveness of organizational subunits and, in turn, to the success of the overall enterprise. The foundation of a sound organization is the appropriate structuring of its spans of management, particularly at the operating level.

Though the strength of lower units is critical to organizational success, the question continues to arise: What is an appropriate number of employees to be assigned to a supervisor? History provides little guidance in answering the question. Biblical writings such as those recorded in the Book of Exodus, suggest that ten subordinates for each leader is proper. This ratio was used in building early religious, military, and educational organizations. For instance, the term *dean* is derived from the word *decanus,* chief of ten, and the word decurion is formed from the word *decurionis,* head or representative of ten men.

The popularity of the long-lived idea of ten subordinates for each leader ebbed with widespread industrialization. A range of four to eight subordinates to a supervisor became a tradition. During that time, specifying rather precise limits on the span of management grew popular. This was an offshoot of a sweeping movement by management, searching for the "one best way" to proceed, to analyze work and the ways work is accomplished, scientifically. Two early thinkers serve as examples of this line of thinking. Sir Ian Hamilton, a British military leader, felt that the average supervisor could be most effective by directing from three to six subordinates. The typical human mentality, in his view, could only cope with a maximum of six other minds.[3] V. A. Graicunas, a French management consultant, applied a mathematical approach to seeking the maximum size of the span of management. His effort served to emphasize the complexity of a work group—that is, the relationships among individuals and also those between individuals and the group. After finding that the number of interrelationships can rise geometrically from forty-four with four subordinates to 1,080 with eight, Graicunas recommended a maximum span of four to five subordinates for each supervisory position.[4]

Present View

Today, we know that in practice the span of management is both broader and more flexible than traditional thought believed feasible. A well-known study of American corporations indicates that spans of management range from one to seventeen.[5] Though the number most frequently reported is six, giving credence to traditional theories, exceptions are widespread. For example, note the variances in the following well-known enterprises: During World War II, Dwight D. Eisenhower, serving as Supreme Commander of the Allied Expeditionary Forces, had three operating commanders reporting to him. Compare that with the president of a nationwide hotel chain having six executives reporting to him. Contrast both of these with the head of an academic department who directly oversees thirty-nine faculty members. Why the widespread disparity? What are the guidelines for finding appropriate spans of management?

The art of understanding organizations provides few pro forma solutions to problems under all conditions. Most matters are resolved in the context of each situation. Notwithstanding the cloudiness obscuring answers to the above questions, however, a logical approach to the answers exists.

Because determining the proper span of management is fundamental to studies of organization, it has been the subject of extensive discussions by authorities on the principles of organization.[6]

The majority of experts agree that the following conditions impose limits on a span of management:

Variety and nonrepetitiveness of work
Importance of work
Need for subordinate training
Inability to delegate
Absence of detailed plans
Absence of clear standards
Rate of change

A minority of the authorities also include the following inhibitors to a broad span of management:

Interrationships of subordinates' activities
Complexity or difficulty of work
Faulty communications
Operational duties and administrative responsibilities

Analysis of Critical Variables

Armed with these ideas, one is expected to attack the problem of establishing realistic ratios between superiors and subordinates in an informed way. Unfortunately, not only is the number of critical variables burdensome, but certain of the variables advanced are subject to serious misunderstanding. Consider the relationships between spans of management on the one hand and the nature, variety, and importance of work on the other.

The nature of work. Commonly, when persons are asked to identify aspects bearing on the scope of the span of management, they cite the complexity of work. Their idea is that if work is complex, the span of management should be narrow; if simple, the span of management should be broad. There is little doubt that the premise has certain support from authorities. For example, Longnecker states:

> The inherent difficulty of work is another significant consideration (in ascertaining the span of management). Some work is basically very simple. Few questions are presented by the work itself, in contrast to projects that are complex and that provide baffling problems. As an extreme example, consider the differences in managing a group of research scientists in contrast to the management of a group of file clerks.[7]

Let us consider, as the author suggests, the activities of scientific research and clerical duties as they relate to the assignment of a leader to a number of subordinates. The implication is that the research activities require a narrow span of management, the clerical duties a broad one. Nevertheless, one could imagine a situation in which a laboratory director might be responsible for a broad span of management, based not on the complexity of the work, but on the competence of the personnel.

Competence can give subordinates a high degree of autonomy or independence. By contrast, it is reasonable to conceive of a situation in
which a clerical supervisor might have a narrow span of management
due to the low level of training and experience of the clerical staff. The
simplicity of the work notwithstanding, a narrow span would be necessary because of the subordinates' dependence.

Professor Longnecker touches the issue when he states that certain
projects "provide baffling problems" because of their complexity.[8]
Nevertheless, it is the independence or dependence of personnel that in
part determines a realistic ratio of superior to subordinates; the complexity of their work merely indicates the degree of supervisory help
needed when their individual efforts are insufficient to cope with a
certain task.

The variety of work. The majority of authorities feel that a variety
of tasks and nonrepetitive work narrow the span of management. As an
example, William T. Greenwood explains the impact of the similarity of
work on superior-subordinate ratios as follows:

> At the lowest level in the organization, it is expected that the activities
> performed by the individuals will be highly similar if not identical, and
> therefore the problems to be resolved by supervisors at that level will tend
> to be similar if not identical, particularly if the jobs are not interrelated.[9]

Selecting the variety or similarity of work as a measure of supervisory
attention can lead to confusion. Serious errors in assigning subordinates
to a supervisor can occur if the span of management is viewed as a
function of the variety of work done. To illustrate the point, let us return
to the example of the head of an academic department; in that instance,
thirty-nine professors report to the chairperson. Is this broad span of
management feasible because the nature of the faculty's professional
activities is routine and repetitive? To the contrary, their activities
exemplify diversity in nearly every way: differing subject fields, teaching techniques, research areas, and professional activities. The underlying cause for the appropriateness of extreme breadth of management is
that the professors fulfill their responsibilities, in large measure, independent of superior direction. More importantly here, they perform
their work autonomously—there is little interdependence of employees' activities.

In contrast, consider a section of well-trained and experienced clerical personnel. Other things being equal, one would expect the supervisor to direct the efforts of a relatively large number of clerks because
they are independent of close supervision. If, however, the tasks of the
members of the unit are dependent upon the completion of work by
other members in the group, then the supervisor needs to coordinate the
individual activities of the subordinates one to the other, and with the
overall goals of the section. Coordination is one of the many elements of

leadership that cannot be ordered—it must be nurtured. To do so, a narrowed span of management is essential so that the supervisor will be able to sustain the unit's coordinated effort because of the great interdependence of employees' activities.

The importance of work. In assigning the number of subordinates to a superior, the importance of work does not in itself determine the range of the span of management. Rather, it is the degree of involvement by the supervisor in subordinates' activities that is relevant. Involvement, in turn, is determined by the extent of the staff's dependence on their leader. Hence, to consider the importance of work as a casual criterion is misleading.

In sum, the nature of work per se is a faulty basis for finding realistic spans of management. Whether light or heavy, its burden on a superior merely mirrors underlying conditions caused by the characteristics of certain relationships between subordinates and superior, among subordinates, and between the operating unit and the overall organization. It is to these key relationships that we can now direct our attention.

Defining Categories of Relationships

With certain major areas of confusion removed, it is now possible to place the remaining variables into three major categories. In this way, the classifications of variables most significant in determining a span of management can be identified and more easily analyzed.

Dependence of subordinates. The following conditions limit the size of the span of mangement: inability of the supervisor to delegate, lack of detailed plans and clear standards, a high rate of change in activities and procedures, poor communications, and the need for subordinate training. All of these conditions, together with the variety, complexity, and importance of the work done, cause subordinates to be dependent on the superior. If they are dependent, the span of management must narrow; if independent, the span may broaden if other conditions are held constant. Most variables commonly cited as constraints upon the number of subordinates reporting to a supervisor deal with the degree of subordinate dependence on direction from higher authority.

Two additional determinants, however, require analysis. They concern the interdependence of subordinates' activities and the interdependence of the various work units.

Interdependence of subordinates' activities. Professor Greenwood, among others, points up the importance of analyzing the interdependence of subordinates' work.[10] Where mutually dependent effort is required, the need for coordination increases demands upon the superior to cultivate the continuity and balance of effort. Assuming that a supervisor's time and effort are required to dovetail efforts, it then follows that interdependence of subordinates' activities is related to the assignment of a span of management.

Interdependence of Work Units

The interrelationship of a leader's unit with other units of the organization influences the span of management because such interaction requires supervisory attention. There are two types of interaction that should be considered: the involvement of the work unit with other units on the same level of authority, called *peer interdependence;* the degree of involvement of the work unit with the overall organization, termed *administrative interdependence.*

Peer. Consider the first type of interdependence. A section or department that must interact closely with other units on the same level requires the supervisor to maintain continuity and coordination, whereas a section or department that functions more autonomously needs relatively little of this type of direction. For example, the work of one section along a process production line must be integrated with that of related sections; however, the work from a unit of salesmen may require substantially less integration with other units because of the semiautonomous nature of their activities. In the first example the span of management would tend to narrow; in the second it would reasonably broaden, if other conditions are equal.

Administrative. The second type of interdependence is an extremely important consideration. Unfortunately, it is frequently overlooked or ignored when an organization is designed. There are two major aspects to a supervisor's responsibilities. The first entails the fulfillment of work within the section or department. It might be termed *operative.* The second requires attention to matters affecting the broader organization such as safety programs, community service, capital expenditures, and contributions to overall plans. This aspect could be called *administrative.* Though it imposes demands on the supervisor, in the short run its relationship is only incidental to the unit's operation. Nonetheless administrative work acts to drain time and intellectual energy from the line supervisor, and so influences the span of management.

As an illustration, consider what occurs when a span of management comprising six subordinates has been established based upon the idea that *operative* matters require six hours daily while *administrative* matters need two. Assume that administrative work expands to fill three hours of supervisory attention every day for a combined total of nine hours. If the leader puts in a normal eight-hour day, an hour must be taken from one of the two areas of activities. Since the supervisor's administrative duties are delegated directly from a higher authority, the time will probably be drawn from operative matters. The consequence is that operative inefficiencies occur because not enough time is being devoted to subordinates, their tasks, and the coordination of their efforts. It seems clear, therefore, that the interdependence of a supervisors unit with the overall organization causes administrative work and hence must be considered as a constraint on the span of management.

Summary of Categories

Three classifications—dependence of subordinates, interdependence of subordinates' activities, and interdependence of the work unit with other units—act as a keystone for all determinants critical to establishing appropriate spans of management. With only three situational determinants in mind, a relatively simple analysis can help us to develop optimum spans of management.

A Contingency Approach

First, we must set an upper limit on the capacity of the supervisor. For practical reasons, a span of time will be used to represent this maximum.

Second, we should consider the variations of conditions functionally related to establishing a specific span of management. Available time (A_t) is viewed as the limiting constraint on the span of management. Conditions that absorb the available time have been divided into the average dependency of subordinates in the unit supervised (a_t), the interdependency of subordinates' activities (b_t), and interrelationships of the work unit with other organizational units (c_t). Thus, stated symbolically:

$$\text{Span of management} = f(A_t, a_t, b_t, c_t)$$

The determinants can now be arranged to specify realistic spans of management by the formula stated below:

$$\text{Span of management} = \frac{A_t - (b_t + c_t)}{a_t}$$

where A_t = available time, a_t = average dependency of each subordinate; b_t = interdependency of subordinates' activities, and c_t = interrelationships of the work unit to other organizational units. In establishing a span of management, estimates should be made of the segments of time spent daily on work generated by:
  1. Interdependency of subordinates' activities (coordination)
  2. Interrelationships of the work unit with other organization units

(coordination and administrative duties: reporting, planning, organizing)

3. Average dependency of each subordinate (directing, controlling, training)

It should be noted that these estimates act as summations of expectations of performance from the supervisor in these important aspects of the work. Such qualitative supervisory traits as energy, stamina, competence, and charisma should be considered when the three estimates are made.

As one example of how to determine a span of management, consider the following situational estimates: Assume that in a certain area of activity, it appears that each subordinate requires an average of sixty minutes of supervisory attention daily. Further, the interrelationship of subordinates' work indicates that the supervisor should devote thirty minutes a day to coordinating their efforts. Suppose also that it takes thirty minutes to coordinate the section's operation with other subunits. And finally, the section head must invest sixty minutes in originating reports, pursuing special projects, and carrying out other administrative duties. By converting the supervisor's eight-hour day to 480 minutes, a realistic maximum span of management can be estimated.

$$\text{Span of management} = \frac{(480 - (30 + 90))}{60}$$

$$= \frac{360}{60}$$

$$= 6$$

We should be careful to make sure that estimates of time allocations are based upon enough observations of supervisory activities, and that the period of time during which the analyses are made closely approximates typical operating periods.

To illustrate a contrasting situation, consider the impact on the size of a span of management where there is no call for coordinated effort within the unit. In addition, only thirty minutes a day are needed for coordinating the unit's effort with other units and for administrative matters, while subordinates require only minimal direction, say an average of fifteen minutes daily. The supervisor's span of management could expand greatly.

$$\text{Span of management} = \frac{480 - 30}{15}$$

$$= \frac{450}{15}$$

$$= 30$$

It is clear that when supervisors prepare subordinates to be self-sufficient and when higher echelon managers can relieve lower level supervisors of burdensome administrative detail, substantial economies of organization are possible. Further, the flatter organizational structure that results from broader spans of management may enhance communications, efficiency, and morale.[11] Notwithstanding the strengths of broad spans, however, certain operating situations preclude them. Leaders in each organization should make such decisions to fit the particular needs of their enterprise, and then only after a thorough analysis in the context of the specific situation. Once the anatomy of an organization is fixed, however, it is difficult to adjust spans of management in response to changes in the determinants—dependence of subordinates, interdependence of subordinates' activities, or interdependence of the work unit with other units—of appropriate spans.

FUNCTIONAL MANAGEMENT

Early arrangements of organizations were based largely on line functions. Line functions are those positions that have direct and total accountability for the major sets of activities necessary for an enterprise to reach its goals. For example, in some manufacturing organizations, the primary activities are grouped as engineering, production/operations, and marketing. Though crucial to goal attainment, employees engaged in activities such as research and development, personnel, and purchasing may be positioned in the organization as staff specialists. These specialists assist line managers in their areas of expertise so that together—line and staff—they can attain enterprise goals efficiently.

Following industrialization and the accompanying increase in the complexity of work, a movement ensued to increase the degree of specialization of line managers. Frederick W. Taylor observed at the shop level the inability of foremen to achieve efficiency in the now-more-complex production areas of quantity, quality, raw material use, and equipment maintenance. So many supervisory qualities were necessary to oversee such varied facets of production, Taylor reasoned, that no one person could be expected to perform effectively all the duties delegated.[12] He proposed that the traditional line organization, with its unity of management, should give way to a finer division of tasks for management. Taylor termed the idea "functional management"; and because it was applied at the shop level, it became popularly known as "functional foremanship."

According to the idea of functional foremanship, each production employee would have four superiors; a "speed boss" (quantity), inspector (quality), repair boss (machine maintenance), and "gang boss" (accessories such as raw materials, jigs, and templates). An employee would be subjected to directives from one or all of these superiors, depending upon the sphere of activity involved. Depicting the arrangement graphically, draws the sources of conflict into clearer focus, as shown in Figure 6-2. Or, as seen by any particular worker, the functional foremanship model might have looked like the graphic in Figure 6-3.

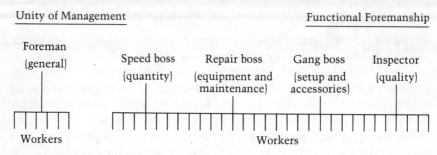

FIGURE 6–2. Basic Shop Organization (Overview)

There were many sources of conflict about the work expected of the subordinate employee. Not only were there misunderstandings concerning what activities were most important, but the various functional areas of activity also conflicted with one another. As an example, if the "speed boss" insisted upon maximum unit production, the employee would divert effort from quality of production, machine maintenance, and efficient use of raw material to achieve high output. And by so doing, probably provoked outcries from his other "bosses."

Why was such an inefficient arrangement prescribed even though it often led to imbalances of effort and demoralization of employees? The reasons are at least threefold: First, in that era the major preoccupation of managers was productivity and the "one best way" to achieve it. Second, the mechanistic dimensions of production overshadowed concern with humanistic matters. Third, and of particular significance to current problems, people with the general abilities necessary for line managers under unity of managment simply were not available. At that time a firm was unlikely to have an employee capable of planning, organizing, directing, and controlling the efforts of subordinates who was also competent in the broad areas of quantity, quality, equipment

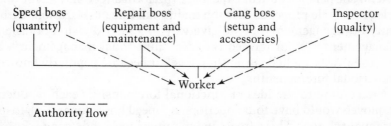

FIGURE 6–3. Basic Shop Organization (View by Worker)

maintenance, and production activities. In a word, generalists were not normally available.

With the exception of "functional management," line managers must be generalists, whereas staff people are specialists. Both types of skills are required in a modern organization because of the complexity and diversity of operations. One constructive result of functional foremanship is the present popularity of line staff relationships. In the absence of people skilled in fulfilling both functional needs of organizations, however, management must apply stop gap measures. As an example, Russia's heavy losses during World War II caused a chronic shortage of generalists for lower management positions there at a time of intense effort to expand and integrate the nation's productivity. Confronted with this shortage of managerial talent and also with the need for generalists or some workable substitute, many Russian enterprises resorted to the application of Taylor's "functional foremanship" until general managers could be developed. Though some subordinate comrades doubtlessly developed ulcers as a consequence, the arrangement did provide the talent required to improve efficiency and, in sum, to heighten productivity.

Current View

Today, the need for the generalist and the specialist is fulfilled by a combined form of organization. The hybrid anatomical structure places the former in line positions and the latter in staff positions. We recognize that organizations need general leadership to unify effort and direction. We also know that persons with specialized skills are wanted to deal with specific and complex problems in such areas as law, labor relations, public relations, and operations research. In response, staff people with highly specialized interests, educations, backgrounds, and skills are appointed and positioned to cope with such matters.

All authorities known to the author now support the idea of unity of management. Leaders in most institutional settings endorse the notion that no subordinate should be formally accountable to more than one superior authority. The strengths of this arrangement apparently outweigh its weaknesses. More correctly, the strengths of unity of management can be gained and its weaknesses overcome by the addition of organizational appendages—the specialized staff functions.

It is the role of many staff persons to attend to some particular set of activities lying within generalists' areas of responsibility. Often the basis for evaluating the effectiveness of staff specialists is their ability to gain support for their area of special interest, for example, control, planning, or some functional activities. It is apparent that this can bring on conflicts and discontinuities that throw organizations into imbalance.

In the next section, the varied nature of staff activities will be investigated. Then we will pursue the idea that in an operational, "real-world" sense, disunity of management is the rule and unity of management the exception to it.

The Nature of Staff Activities

There are various types of staff activities. The nature of the staff activity determines the extent of staff authority over line operations. This leads ultimately to the cause of disunity of management in organizations today.

It is generally accepted that there are four major types of specialized activities: personal, advisory, process, and functional. Commonly, all types of staff activites are grouped under the general heading of "staff authority." Thus, by failing to categorize differing kinds of activities, we also fail to recognize that each type has varying degrees of authority which act to withdraw or withhold line managers' prerogatives. As a consequence, misunderstandings arise concerning relationships within organizations.[13]

Personal staff refers to such specialists as clerks, secretaries, and "assistants to" a line authority. Some experts consider a general staff and key committees as subclassifications of personal staff because such groups carry out managerial work. *Advisory staff* is a type of specialized counsel to line managers. To some, this advisory relationship characterizes the nature of staff activity and defines its commensurate authority. This is an overly simplified conception. An advisory staff studies problems, prepares alternative courses of action, and offers suggestions that the line manager may accept, modify, or reject. *Process staff* serve as agents for a line manager and can exercise authority over line actions in the managerial processes of planning, organizing, and controlling. Though the common use of quality control staffs comes immediately to mind, this staff activity also extends to such diverse activities as limiting credit to customers, regulating various activities, managing physical distribution, budget planning, directing personnel recruitment and selection programs, or modifying procurement policies. *Functional staff* provides the organization with specialized service consisting of activities separated from line authority. As an example, early in a firm's history, requests for various undertakings in the area of public relations may be handled by people in the line departments. Examples would be a clerk leading plant tours, a salesman giving talks to civic groups, or a production worker drumming up support for the United Fund. When a public relations staff is established, all such activities fall under that staff group's authority.

The Nature of Staff Authority

As the reader may sense, each type of staff activity influences to varying degrees the extent to which authority must be granted restricting the scope of line authority. It is apparent that authority must be exercised initially to ensure, that the assignments are fulfilled and, later, to resist overlapping efforts or voids between line and staff responsibilities. Consider next the different degrees of authority over line activities. Personal staff members genreally do not restrict line authority.[14] Advisory staff and process staff restrict line authority in relatively increasing degrees. Functional staff usurps line authority to a large degree in those activities in which it is authorized to function. A summary of comparative authority relationships of various staffs to line management is graphically depicted in Figure 6-4.

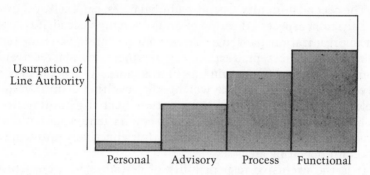

Source: George R. Terry, *Principles of Management,* 1964. Used by permission of Richard D. Irwin, Inc.

FIGURE 6–4. Types of Staff Authority

Though an approximation, the graph draws attention to the fact that varied types of staff persons or groups usurp, or draw away, increasing degrees of authority from line managers. It also suggests areas in which potential conflicts and imbalances may result because of disunity of management.

Potential Areas of Conflict

Two major areas of difficulty that may easily arise under disunity of management warrant our attention. The first is the problem of confused objectives and conflicting loyalties; the second is the possibility of imbalance if, in a given speciality, staff efforts are overemphasized in relation to the line manager's overall responsibility.

If conflict exists, it is difficult, if not impossible, for any subordinate to be responsible to more than one superior. Dissension can produce split loyalties, discontinuity of effort, confused objectives, and equivocal expectations in subordinates. Any one of these results of conflict can leave a subordinate perplexed, frustrated, and ultimately demoralized. For example, consider the plight of a secretary who reports to a middle-level manager, but is also expected to serve the personal secretarial staff of a higher authority at such times as the workload of the superior's staff is heavy. Assume further that the immediate superior and the secretary have agreed that it is essential to keep the main work current. After a commitment to this goal, consider the subordinate's dilemma when the boss's superior requests help causing the secretary's work to become backlogged. The secretary's frustration would be intensified if he believed that the tasks to which his attention was transferred were less important than his direct responsibilities and if, as a result, he became delinquent in his basic work. Even isolated experiences of this nature are irritating, particularly to a conscientious employee. If they happen frequently, the working conditions become intolerable.

The second difficulty, operating imbalances, can easily occur when any particular aspect of the total effort is overemphasized. It is apparent that an organization, particualrly a corporation, at a given time tends to run with its finances, production, engineering, sales, and receivables in reasonable balance. If a certain link in this mutually dependent chain of activities is given inordinate weight, the resulting distortion quickly ripples throughout the entire organization. Such disequilibrium is far-reaching in a system because frequently emphasizing a particular aspect of operations is apt to divert resources, thus effectively upstaging other important operating areas.

It is the exclusive responsibility of certain staff groups to focus concentrated effort from line forces onto a narrow, specialized area of activity. As a consequence, the staff unit's effectiveness is rated by the degree of success achieved by the line units in the specific segment of work for which the specialists are held accountable. For example, a section of the controller's office in a corporate headquarters may be expected to assist operating divisions in handling accounts receivable. The special unit is expected to facilitate a concentrated effort on collection activities, to provide procedural guidelines for managing accounts receivable, and to offer expertise to line authorities in all such matters. The unit's effectiveness is in turn measured by the line units' level of performance in this specific activity. Illustrated graphically, the line-staff authority relationships might be shown as in Figure 6-5.

Often the use of staff specialists is required to attain the degree of intensity needed for a desirable level of performance. If, however, it is not applied with judgment and discretion, it will foster unexpected inefficiencies in other areas. In the example presented, overemphasis on collections could easily detract from such important objectives as good customer service; current billing; and the maintenance of accurate, thorough records. Disunity of management can easily lead to operational imbalances. As one authority observes the problem:

> It is sometimes stated that staff assistance is impractical, unbalanced, and fails to take into account all the ramifications of the situation. What is offered stresses too much of the staff's particular speciality. The big picture is ignored.[15]

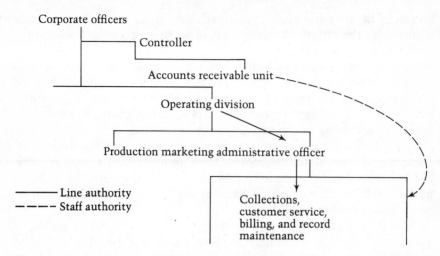

FIGURE 6–5. Line-Staff Authority Relationships

Unity of Purpose

Some disunity of management is unavoidable in line-staff organizations. Certain authority relationships blur the precision and clarity of unity of management, because many functional activities require the cooperative efforts of both line generalists and staff specialists. Though these kinds of authority relationships are functional necessities, management should be acutely aware of the weaknesses inherent in such schemes and actively strive to mitigate the problems they breed.

When multiple authority relationships exist, leaders must cultivate mutual understanding between line and staff groups on the overall goals, the groups' respective roles in goal attainment, the means through which achievements will be pursued, their role relationships, and their interrelationships with the overall enterprise. Only through increased and more effective communications can mutual understanding flourish; only through understanding can congruent relationships be cultivated; and only through congruency can the mutuality of goals be explicated by managers and then accepted and pursued by subordinates in both line and staff activities. The objective is unity of purpose. As the degree of disunity of management increases, efforts to promote unity of purpose become critical. We can effectively manage organizations with multiple authority relationships as long as the people in the organization are aware of where they are headed, what their relationships are to others, and what is expected of them.

THE SCALAR HIERARCHY

Now, let us review the state of the anatomy of organizations as we have delineated it so far. First human activities were structured by a hierarchy of goals and plans to achieve those goals. Then the activities required by the enterprise were divided so that specialized work processes could take place. Next, segments of related activities were grouped to form organized units: sections, departments, bureaus, divisions, or whatever the names. Leaders were then appointed to be accountable for the general conduct of activities within these units. Finally, specialized staff persons or units were designated to assist line leaders in attaining the objectives of the enterprise.

As the anatomy now appears, it is but an assortment of components—unrelated, uncoordinated, undirected as a total system. No provision has been made to this point to tie the units together, to provide the "backbone and central nervous system" so that the appendages hang together.

A unifying anatomic part is missing—the *scalar hierarcy*. Scalar, or graduated, hierarchy refers here to an unbroken line from the top to the bottom of organizations through which communications and authority can flow to ensure cohesive effort. It is a hierarchy of authority, as pointed out, that is in inverse relationship to hierarchies of goals and plans (see Figure 5-2). It is a scalar arrangement because it illustrates the authority levels of those persons in the line organization from the highest to the lowest. The scalar hierarchy provides the "backbone" linking units together and the "central nervous system" sending impulses from top to bottom to unify the enterprise.

An Early Example

The basic anatomy of an organization—spans of management, unity of management, line/staff relaponships, and the scalar hierarchy—is illustrated vividly for us in the Old Testament. In the Book of Exodus, we find a situation where organized effort was desperately needed. Yet groups fragmented, bickered, and worked at cross-purposes to the overall mission.

The story goes this way. Moses was selected to save the Israelites from Egyptian persecution by leading them from Egypt to the safety of Canaan. Apparently Moses was as much a man of the people as he was a man of God, because he elected to let his followers remain in fragmented clans and burdened himself with judging their individual problems and differences. By doing so, he prevented the development of organization and leadership. The wanderers' trek to safety stalled and danger threatened as the Egyptians pressed their pursuit. (You may note that in helping individuals to the neglect of organizing them, Moses was endangering those very people he was attempting to help. We point this up because in some areas the same type of neglect to the need for organizing hurts people today.)

Moses' father-in-law, Jethro, saw that Moses was burdened from morning until evening judging individual's problems, whether grave or petty. And he said to Moses,

> What is this thing that thou doest to the people?. . . The thing that thou doest is not good. Thou wilt surely wear away, both thou, and this people that is with thee: for this thing is too heavy for thee.[16]

Jethro knew that if Moses' time and energies were spent in counseling individuals, he would be unable to fulfill his major responsibility to the people of leading them to their goal.

So Jethro counseled Moses in three ways. First, he urged Moses to represent the people before God and to bring problems to Him for counsel. Second, he admonished his son-in-law to teach the people laws and ordinances, their duties, and their direction. And third, Jethro advised him to organize the people so that subordinate "rulers" could "judge the people at all seasons: and it shall be, that every great matter they shall bring unto thee, but every small matter they shall judge." By organizing, Moses was able to share his burden of leadership with subordinate leaders. More significantly, as a final consequence, Moses was freed to handle issues of major import to the organization. Jethro's recommendation for organization was as follows:

> Thou shalt provide out of all the people able men. . . . to be rulers of thousands, and rulers of hundreds, rulers of fifties, and rulers of tens. . . .[17]

And the organization shown in Figure 6-6 was formed.

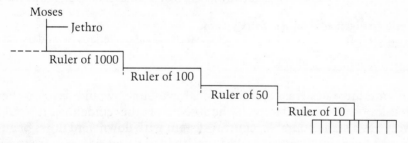

FIGURE 6–6. The Israelite Organization

Now, the fully formed organization of the Israelites took shape, with spans of management, unity of management, Jethro as advisory staff to Moses, and a complete scalar hierarchy. Unity of enterprise was established. The organization of the Israelites served them as an effective means to reach the safety of Canaan.

SUMMARY

The anatomy of an organization includes certain structures and components common to all organizations. These were some of the aspects of an enterprise that concerned those persons who comprised the classical, or early, school of thought scrutinizing organizational design. Their primary objective was to bring order, continuity, and efficiency into organized human endeavor. This was a noble contribution to the advancement of efficiency and to more humane treatment of people in complex organizations.

Nevertheless, understanding its anatomic form does not explain an organization's behavior. It throws no more light on the organization's actions than understanding the human skeleton illuminates human behavior. However, knowledge of the skeletal form is immensely helpful in creating an awareness of the anatomical arrangements of formal organization structure as a foundation for further study. The final object is to understand the behavior of a certain organization and the function of leadership.

In sum, early organization theory provides valuable insights into the basic nature of these social systems. Its value, however, is limited to understanding the formal anatomy of organizations, because thinkers of that era concentrated on dimensions of immediate and urgent concern. As a consequence, their contributions were largely confined to guidelines like the following:

Principles for application to organizations *in general*
Structures and subsystems common to all organizations
Prescriptive guidelines (a normative model), that is, what should be, rather than what is
Static arrangements rather than dynamic
Parameters to structural design to eliminate voids and overlaps (boundary disputes)
Structural/functionalism

An enterprise designed along classical guidelines would develop the-well-known pyramidal form. In the absence of other guidelines, it would evolve as a stable, durable, control system with downward flows of authority and communication. We know that all enterprises require these traits in some degree if they are to function. We know further that a specific enterprise has other requirements for functioning—it must accommodate the human resource *as a being*, and it must be *adaptable* to a changing environment.

DISCUSSION QUESTIONS

1. A philosopher once said, "Maybe there is a perfect number for order of all relationships in the universe." If this "perfect number" were discovered, would the art of organizing be transformed into a science? (Defend your answer.)

2. Why would the assignment of equal spans of management to a number of leaders probably be inequitable?

3. Why are overly narrow spans of management damaging to organizational efficiency? And why are unduly broad spans of management also harmful to efficiency? (Consider structural, economic, and behavioral factors here.)

4. Consider the hospital organization (functions of administration, with dietetics, pharmacy, nursing, physicians, x-ray, and so forth) where unity of management is often agreed to be impossible. From the standpoint of organization, what are the full implications of such a condition?

5. Why are both line and staff positions required in complex organizations?

6. What is the relationship of the scalar hierarchy of an organization to its other hierarchies? Now relate the scalar hierarchy of the anatomy of an organization to the anatomy of a person.

7

Subsystems of Organizations

Some excellent work has been done in describing and analyzing the super-ficial characteristics of organizations. It is important, but like descriptive geography with physics, chemistry, geology, and biology missing.

Chester I. Barnard[1]

In the last two chapters, we considered the design of structural components and the anatomy of an organization as they relate to its goals. Those discussions merely analyzed the formation of a static structure. In this chapter, we are concerned with certain organic subsystems that can bond the organization into a cohesive, enduring, and dynamic scheme of events. We will view the nature and development of common subsystems which, when related to goals and the overall social system, can produce an internally consistent organization. Figure 7-1 presents these subsystems, so crucial to an organization's success.

By *organic*, we are referring to those internal elements of the overall organization that influence the coordination of its parts. By *subsystem* we mean the type of internal element necessary to bond human interaction. And the term *bond* here means that which binds and combines individual and unit activities so that they adhere firmly to each other in pursuit of enterprise goals.

Consider the relationship of the life-supportive subsystems of a person to the organic subsystems of an organization. In complex systems, physical or social, a division of labor permits identifiable, special subsystems to perform essential life functions. In humans and other vertebrates, eleven organic subsystems are essential to survival: circulatory, digestive, endocrine, excretory, integumentary, muscular, nervous, reproductive, respiratory, sense, and skeletal subsystems.[2] It is clear that

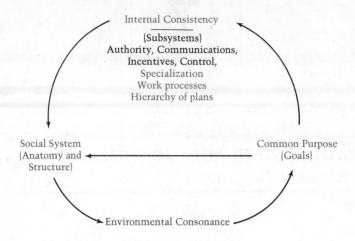

FIGURE 7–1. Conceptual Model of an Organization

each subsystem functions interdependently to support the others and the entire healthy human organism.

In complex social organizations, there are also integral organic subsystems: for example, authority centers, delegative processes, communications, incentives, control, and leadership. Here too, each subsystem functions to support the others and, ideally, the overall healthy social system.

This chapter introduces these organic subsystems, which individually and together can give cohesiveness to organized human effort. Particular attention is devoted to the nature of authority because of its traditional influence as a bonding agent between superior and subordinate units, that is, in ensuring vertical unification.

USE OF ORGANIC SUBSYSTEMS

All organizations, we have said, must develop certain common features if they are to function and survive. These aspects are demanded by functional necessities. They are essential if a large group of people is to contribute collectively to organizational goals in an orderly way. The arrangements do not come about arbitrarily nor by happenstance. Rather, they are consciously established to give the people the procedures they need to achieve enterprise goals.

Each organization *relates its goals back to a structured grouping of people* and, through the use of such subsystems as *authority, delegative processes, leadership, communications, incentives,* and *control* induces individual participants to support enterprise goals. Herein lies the reason for the need common to all organizations, to develop structures and systems.

But what does all this mean to one who is merely trying to understand an organization? It means that a person can cultivate a deeper understanding of an organization by simply analyzing goals, structure, and subsystems of activities that are required to reach those goals. One can then understand and satisfactorily explain certain elementary but important behavioral patterns in organizations.

For example, say that you are a new trainee in a department store. You find that it competes actively to attract a discriminating clientele in the middle and upper socioeconomic classes. To do so, it carries a wide selection of quality "soft goods" such as ready-to-wear clothing, housewares, fabrics, and notions. You know that the store must have the following subsystems to reach its goals through its employees:

Authority centers	Communications
Delegative processes	Incentives
Specialization	Controls
Groupings of people	Leadership roles
Hierarchy of plans	

You find that the enterprise has a *central authority* giving direction to the overall effort, and that the subordinate *authority centers* take care of operations activities (functions within the store), purchasing (procurement of high quality goods), and sales promotion (persuasive communication to prospective customers). Further, you find that the *delegative processes* for purchasing and promotion are the province of staff specialists in the upper hierarchy of the structure. Delegation in operations, however, flows downward to the salespeople so that customers can be given the personalized service they expect at the selling level. To encourage competence among the sales force, you observe that *specialization* by lines of products has been instituted. The selling force has been *grouped* into small boutique-like units to create an aura of specialty shops. This atmosphere seems to appeal to the customers. You also find that these boutiques carry complementary products and are dispersed within the store in a way that accommodates shopping patterns. To make the plan work, the structure shown in Figure 7-2 is necessary as a means to reach the enterprise's goals.

Further, the influence of common subsystems for authority, communications, incentives, control, and leadership patterns is evident. You find that these bonding elements of the firm take on the following configurations. *Communications* flow quickly and accurately throughout the organization with minimal distortion, repetitiveness, and omissions. You consider this condition crucial *in this setting* if high morale and support for overall efforts are to be attained. *Incentives* are designed to promote individual competition in areas where products require a high level of salesmanship. Rewards are tailored to generate cooperation in less competitive areas. Specialized staff units have been established to handle purchasing, sales promotion, and customer services. *Control*

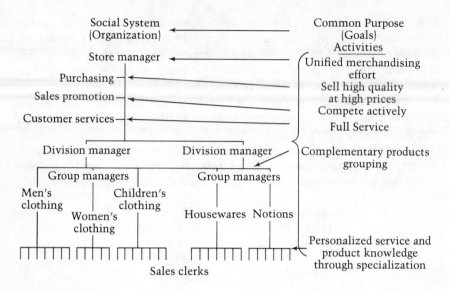

FIGURE 7–2. Analysis of a Department Store Organization

you observe to be effective yet not oppressive or stifling to the initiative required by the sales personnel in a highly competitive business.

Leadership patterns, you find, vary with differing situations but seem to meet the varied demands. The store manager is authoritative and autocratic, but she recognizes the necessity for participation by subordinates in solving complex problems beyond her competence. In most areas leaders foster a somewhat supportive attitude toward employees, though in the specific areas of furniture and major appliances, leaders tend to treat employees permissively because of their greater expertise. After considering the nature of each situation,

FIGURE 7–3. Internal Organization Analysis

you judge the structured subsystems of behavior to be appropriate, compatible, and effective as the means to organizational goals. In addition, your analysis of the formal organization leads you to accept the structural design as a logical, complete response to functional needs. A shorthand sketch of your initial findings might be shown as in Figure 7-3.

Through this sort of quick analysis, you cultivate an awareness of the *reasons* for the structural arrangements observed. Given the goals of the venture, certain organic substructures are inevitable. You will have satisfied yourself that a logical (structural/functional) congruity exists between anatomical components and enterprise goals. The explanation you gain is far superior to a simple description of an organization. In addition, you will not think of the firm as merely a self-explaining entity. On the contrary, you have recognized and identified the goals of the endeavor and its functions. Then, knowing the structural traits needed by all enterprises to reach their objectives, you search for the structured activities reflecting the traits. If your findings do not reveal that appropriate responses have been made to the organization's goals, you will have identified an apparent void, redundancy, or ambiguity—in a word, inconsistency.

Herein lies a compelling reason for appraising goals as they relate to the design of common components. You can critically evaluate ambiguities. When a structure or subsystem does not appear to fit because of a void, overlap, or inappropriate design, you recognize that constructive steps should be taken to correct the problem.

For instance, in the example of the department store, you find that one goal of the enterprise is to minimize losses from thefts. But the formal structure has no provision for people or incentives to combat stealing. Finding this omission in the structure and subsystems, you may recommend the establishment of a security unit and rewards to individuals for special efforts to strengthen security.

This is an instance of omissions in structure, incentives, and control. We may find in other analyses of this type problems with overlapping responsibilities (redundancies) or dysfunctional designs (frictions). These findings, together with voids, are all internal inconsistencies that sap organizations of efficiency.

Through this type of analysis, you also may learn *why* organic subsystems function as they do. And knowing the reasons for their being will spare you the irritation of believing them arbitrarily imposed, unfairly restrictive, inconsiderately capricious, and hence, crying for change. In the example of the department store, for instance, specialization by product line may seem confining, compliance with procedures tedious, and control to ensure personalized service oppressive. But one can more graciously accept one's organizational setting if the true reasons for its functioning as it does are clearly understood.

AUTHORITY SUBSYSTEMS

With this brief overview of the need for well-designed organic subsystems, let us explore in greater depth the nature of one major influence in organizations: authority. It would be desirable to discuss each subsystem in turn, because each set of influences—authority, communications, incentives, and control—is crucial to the internal strength of an enterprise. However, this book's general purpose and its limited length force us to confine the discussion to a single set of influences, authority and delegative processes. The authority subsystem was chosen for illustrative purposes because it seems to hold universal interest for students of organizational relationships. Though authority is the catalyst that activates social structure, each of the other subsystems plays a critical part in making organizations work. Excellent studies of organizational communications, incentives, and control are available to the interested reader.[3]

Nature of Authority

The nature of authority has been the object of considerable philosophic and pragmatic thought throughout recorded history. Though a consensus of opinion has yet to result, there is substantial agreement on certain of its traits. Authority is the ability to influence decisions and to initiate actions. This text is concerned with the human organization; thus, our discussion of authority will be limited only to its function as an influence exerted by some people over other people within an enterprise. The reader should recognize that authority also affects decisions and actions on other subsystems—capital, technology, structures, equipment, and flows of source materials—of an enterprise. Its force may also be felt by people and institutions outside the enterprise. If authority is viewed as an influence over people who would otherwise be "free," then authority is power, power to enforce conformity to the degree believed to be necessary by those in power to achieve collective goals. The term *power*, however, commonly connotes negative, even coercive, control: free persons flinch from power exerted over them. And indeed, by contrast with primitive cultures, this is not the type of influence that prevails in most organized settings today.

It is inappropriate to refer to authority as power because the terms are not synonymous, only related. To understand their relatedness, the concepts of authority and power must be seen in the context of a realistic setting. The similarity of the two terms is accurate up to a point; beyond that point it dissipates, as we shall find in the next section.

Legitimacy of Authority

Authority is influence, and influence *can be* power. Power can be made legitimate through its general acceptance by those people under it.

Even though power limits their free will, the limitation can be freely accepted where it is recognized as a functional necessity in organizing their activities efficiently. As with the island castaways, those who accept power under such circumstances recognize its legitimacy as a necessary adjunct of authority. Legitimate authority can, therefore, be accepted by free men and women, but illegitimate power is typically rejected as repugnant. Power becomes legitimate, first, by acceptance of the need for it by those exposed to it.

Second, power is given further sanction through rituals, cere-monies, and symbols to communicate and reinforce its legitimacy. It must be clearly understood that the legitimizing process is not only required for the benefit of those in power but is also necessary for those subjected to it. It is an essential part of the socialization process. Power, when viewed as necessary to organizational advancement, can gain sufficient legitimacy to become an acceptable influence over an indi-vidual's decisions and actions.

Illegitimate Use of Authority

Even with this narrowed view of authority, we must be careful to understand the limitations imposed on authority used in most institu-tions. Even legitimate authority is finely curtailed by the needs of the enterprise. As an example, say that you are appointed as a leader in a political action group. The scope of your authority is thus limited to the demands of the organized effort. This would be reasonable, for that was the source from which your authority emanated. You may direct your subordinates to perform such tasks as telephoning voters, passing out political pamphlets, and assisting shut-ins to get to the polls. But if you direct one of the workers to wash your private car, you are probably begging for an incredulous, "no." The worker will probably do a double-take to see if you are serious, and if you are, hand you a refusal and ask to serve elsewhere. You simply overstepped your authority by attempting to exercise it beyond the limits for which it was granted. Even in highly rigid authority systems such as certain military, police, fire, and medical organizations, the exercise of authority beyond the demands required by the mission is not accepted by subordinates.

Source of Authority

The nature of authority, to classical thinkers, was clear and abso-lute; the ultimate source of authority emanated from the institution of private property. An on-going enterprise acquired property, which commonly included land, buildings, machinery, raw materials, and funds. A professional manager or a daily-wage employee was hired to work with the properties, or resources, of the enterprise. Thus, its own-ers or representative leaders had a right to impose authority over the employee (whatever the level) to ensure the correct treatment of those properties. Classical theorists saw no conflict here. Organizational integration was achieved largely by downward flows of authority. Through procedures, rules, methods, and techniques, minimum levels for acceptable behavior and output were established. By the design of formal arrangements, individual participants and organizational components were directed to interact and relate to each other as required by the leaders. Popular ideologies of the classical era, such as Calvinism and Social Darwinism, gave broad discretionary latitude to leaders of the time in the use of their authority.

To more recent scholars the nature of authority is less distinct and more closely related to human needs. The sources of authority vary with the situation. To the modern theorist authority can be formal or informal. It in part is rooted in formal sources. But operationally it may stem informally from a situation in which a particular kind of knowledge or competency is required. A person possessing the intelligence or skill called for at a given time emerges to become the informal leader. Discussions by today's scholars in this area revolve around the real sources of authority, the relationships of formal and informal authority, the assumption of authority roles, the traits of the informal leader, and the nature of authority derived from varied sources. To some, authority over free people is simply a myth. Authority is a product of consent given by workers as well as of their need for representation.

Today, by contrast with historic views, it seems clear that authority is not understood as something exclusively vested in leaders for dissemination downward over subordinates. Neither is it viewed merely as a function of the situation nor as the emergence of informal leaders to fulfill a void. Rather, authority in a given enterprise is seen is a system of interacting influences partially designed and partially a product of human interaction. Some people seem to need to lead, others to follow. Whatever its nature, formal or informal, its influence on organizational members is profound and sweeping; it shapes their activities, behavior, relationships, aspirations, and nearly every other phase of their institutional involvement. By so doing, it also serves as a strong bond to maintain cohesiveness in a collective endeavor.

Subsystems of Authority

Authority is a subsystem of forces within all organizations. It includes multidirectional flows of influence—downward, upward, and lateral. It is a system because it is interacting: The imposition of authority from one source causes a reaction, or retraction, of authority over the matter from another source. Change takes place and social balance may follow, but at a different point of social interaction.

Authority is marshalled, it seems, as a consequence of a person, or a group of people, having access to certain scarce attributes or things that are needed by others. They may be physical (property), intellectual (expertise), contractual (the will of a group), or sociopsychological (fulfilling the needs of a group).

Authority was traditionally understood to stem from owning valued *property*. Today we also know it to be enjoyed by a person with a special area of *expertise* making him or her a valuable source of information and/or an assistant to decision makers, for example, a computer systems analyst or an executive secretary. Further, authority is bestowed on those persons who by *contractual* arrangement represent certain interests of a large constituency. Lawmakers, judges, clergymen, among others, are invested with authority over some specific segment of human affairs by large numbers of supporters who believe the particular activity to be needed. Such leaders often have an exclusive mandate, sometimes for a specific period of time, to influence the institutions through which these activities are conducted. And finally, authority is won by those who possess *sociopsychological* qualities that are needed by other people; an example is the commanding figure possessed of charismatic attributes. These traits may be appropriate to fulfill certain wants or needs as *perceived* by those requiring leadership *at a given time*. Given the need for leadership, people will give support (albeit at times grudgingly) to a person who they feel has the qualities to fulfill the needs of the enterprise and its members—not merely material, intellectual, or contractual needs, but also social and psychological ones.

So authority appears to arise when an individual possesses something that is needed by others. This might be termed the socioeconomics of authority. Authority, influence centers, emerge both formally and informally.

The scene is now set for us to generate an organization into motion, to change it from its static posture to one of dynamic interaction. It is the point at which the inert structure and anatomy of a formal organization are converted to a social system. The phenomenon is somewhat like watching a military formation from a raised reviewing stand. The formal groupings and leaders are gathered into a static, structured assembly, like an organization chart. Then the military leader barks a command, delegating authority downward for the order to be fulfilled. This act transforms the structure of soldiers into a dynamic social system of interrelated activities.

All systems—mechanical, chemical, biological, physical, or whatever—require a catalyst to start their activity. Delegation of authority is the catalyst that puts motion into a social system.

Delegation of Authority

Authority centers have now been established over each of the units of the organization considered to be critical to its goals, while the scalar hierarchy ties the units together. Let us return now to the simplified illustration in Figure 5-3 of the Department of Chair Production. But we will extend the example to include upper management. Figure 7-4 shows the various formal centers of authority from the president to the workers. The main stem of formal authority centers has been emphasized by bold lines. One can see that a single line of authority flows downward over an unbroken line from the head of the firm to the workers. That scalar authority arrangement in a classical sense provides the means for effective delegation of authority, communication, and control. By contrast, organizations with more complex forms—line, staff, and committees—as we discussed previously, diffuse accountability and bring on multiple authority flows.

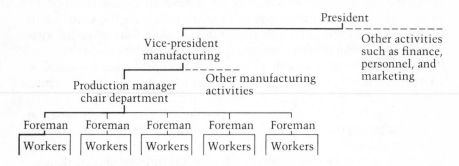

FIGURE 7–4. Broadened View of Chair Manufacturing Company (Partial Structure)

Authority and Responsibility[4]

A major misunderstanding prevails on the delegation of authority and responsibility. The error begins with the idea that authority and responsibility should be coequal. And the myth that grows from the error can make leaders frustrated and unhappy. It is reasonable to believe at first brush that if one is held responsible for certain activities, one should expect an equal share of authority to get the job done. Or stated in another way, if one lacks sufficient authority, one cannot be expected to assume the full burden of responsibility for results. The ideal of coequal authority and responsibility may appear reasonable to some, but it is unreasonable when viewed from the standpoint of the overall organization. Though the belief conveys the idea that coequal authority and responsibility are fair to individual leaders, it overlooks an even greater need by the overall enterprise for inequality in these factors. The belief that these elements are equal or should be equal is misleading because it gives a distorted impression of how organizations really work. The following illustrates this point:

A common complaint heard among first-level (or lowest) leaders is,

"Around this place, I have plenty of responsibility, but I don't have enough authority to do the job." Indeed, the situation seems that way to them because directives from higher authorities often sound something like this: "Now this is your unit, and as such, I hold you responsible for results on this new program. However, if it requires overtime work, I must get approval from 'upstairs.' And if it takes added supplies or equipment not budgeted, we'd better talk it over. And as a matter of procedure, you'd better give me a weekly report on the progress of the program. Let me know if you hit any snags, particularly in working it through with other units. Now go to it! It's your baby."

What has happened here? The superior holds the subordinate leader accountable for putting some program into effect but has also narrowly limited the subordinate's authority. Restrictions have been imposed in three areas, (1) the use of resources: work hours, supplies, and equipment; (2) feedback reports on performance; and (3) reports concerning other units helping to implement the program. In effect, broad responsibility has been given but the latitude to exercise authority has been narrowly limited. Is this fair? Or is it required to achieve organizational goals?

Authority/Responsibility Inequality

To answer these questions, it will help to analyze an alternate situation where authority and responsibility are coequal. Picture the unit used in Figure 7-5 in the context of the broader organization. Consider that the subordinate leader accountable for Unit A is responsible for implementing the program with the cooperation of Units B, C, and/or D. Assume now that the leader of Unit A is given full authority over the task. This supervisor would have full authority over the use of resources, control, and relationships with other units. As a consequence of having coequal authority and responsibility, the leader of Unit A is

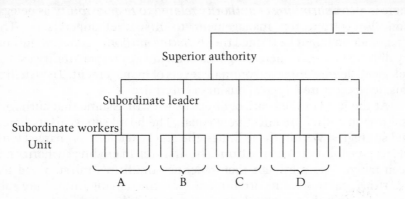

FIGURE 7–5. Formal Organization (Partial Structure)

enabled to function independently. Because of this freedom this unit can be withdrawn from the broader enterprise. The leader is independent— free to use resources he or she considers necessary but ignorant of other units' needs for scarce resources; free to control the performance of the unit when, in fact, the leader's superior is also accountable for its performance; and free to relate to other units and the broader organization in a way required for the attainment of Unit A's goals, but without the benefit of the broader comprehension required. In a word, the delegation of authority equal to accountability disintegrates an organization when integration is the real key to organizational success.

Withholding authority is one essential means to give cohesiveness and unified direction to collective human endeavor. It acts as an interlocking mechanism through which vertical integration, coordination, and balanced control are made feasible.

Now, let us return to the questions asked above. Is it fair to subordinate leaders for their authority and responsibility to be disproportionate? It is not fair if their superiors do not recognize that this natural disparity exists and, as a result, make unreasonable demands on subordinates. It can be handled equitably, however, if those in all positions of authority are aware of this "natural" limitation. Through awareness leaders can limit their expectations of subordinates to the same degree as their authority is limited.

Shrinking Authority Concept

The issue of authority/responsibility becomes clear if one considers a few facts about formal authority.

It is well known that institutional authority is delegated downward in diminishing amounts required to accomplish activities of narrowing scope and lessening importance to enterprise goals. The process creates the so-called tapering concept of authority. I propose, however, that there is also a *shrinking of authority related to responsibility* as delegation flows from top management to first-level supervisors. The phenomenon might be termed the *shrinking authority concept;* authority diminishes at an increasing rate compared to responsibility as it is delegated downward to subordinate levels of management. To visualize this, let us picture a typical business enterprise.

At the level of the board of directors we will assume that authority and responsibility are effectively equal. The board sets goals, policies, and strategies. Within those limits, the chief executive is charged with the responsibility to run the firm. The first step in eroding authority has been taken. The president then redefines the firm's mission and the activities required for its attainment, in turn charging immediate subordinates with their particular area of responsibility. But at this second step, additional authority is necessarily withheld to coordinate the now more specialized activities and fragmented subgoals, which are all vying for the company's resources. At the third step in the delegative process, specialization proliferates; more finely drawn guidelines are needed; budgets limit resources; procedures restrict discretionary action; schedules limit random timing; and controls grow more pronounced and stringent to ensure integration and coordination of major divisions of activities. Following the process to its ultimate end, the first-level supervisor's authority over his or her section is circumscribed by limits on resources, fixed production processes, preset technology, standards, procedures, and routines. These constraints on authority are imposed by superior authorities.

Figure 7-6 is reproduced here as it appeared in Chapter 5 because it presents the range of constraints that effectively usurp lower managers of the authority to make discretionary decisions and to act independently. It is clear that each level of authority from top to bottom is increasingly bound by predetermined sets of regulations. Withholding authority not only causes a chain reaction, but it also has a snowballing effect that produces the shrinking authority concept.

Figure 7-7 illustrates in another way the effect of increasing constraints on authority, this time as they relate to responsibility downward over a chain of management. Although the chart only estimates the relative impact of withheld authority, it depicts the basic concept of shrinking authority as it relates to responsibility. Scopes of responsibility are functionally related to groupings of interrelated activities. Scopes of authority, however, are not regulated by activities for which a line manager is responsible. Authority is withheld by present limits on resources, procedures for role behavior, and programs for control.

The actions of lower management are constrained by regulations imposed from above, and these constraints impinge even more stringently as they percolate downward from the top through the chain of management.[5] As a result, lower managers feel the pressures for performance but sense the futility of their efforts arising from the lack of means to control results. They are charged with full responsibility for the activities of their units, but because they do not have sufficient authority, they must gain support from their immediate superiors to fulfill their responsibilities.

It becomes evident that a person in a first- or second-level position without such support would join the chorus of lower management complaints, "Around here we have plenty of responsibility, but we don't have enough authority to do the job as it should be done." There exists a shrinking authority law, because authority is curtailed in higher degrees relative to accountability as it flows downward.

Return again to the questions dealing with the fairness and necessity of disproportionate delegation. Living with a burdensome degree of responsibility but with limited authority can be fair only when people in

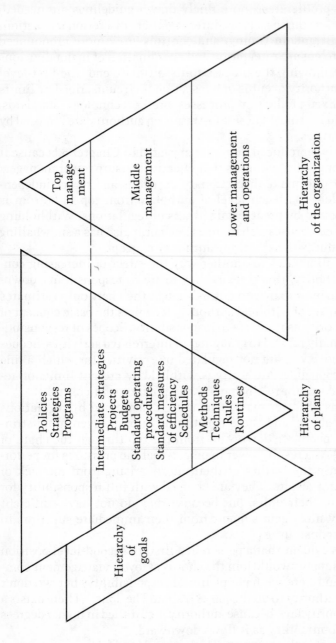

Policies
Strategies
Programs

Intermediate strategies
Projects
Budgets
Standard operating
procedures
Standard measures
of efficiency
Schedules

Methods
Techniques
Rules
Routines

Hierarchy
of plans

Hierarchy
of
goals

Top
manage-
ment

Middle
management

Lower management
and operations

Hierarchy
of the organization

Source: Adapted from Robert Grandford Wright, "The Myth Inherent in Responsibility Center Management," *MSU Business Topics,* Spring 1972, Vol. 20, No. 2. Used by permission of the publisher, Division of Research, Graduate School of Business Administration, Michigan State University.

FIGURE 7–6. Continuum of Constraints on Managerial Authority

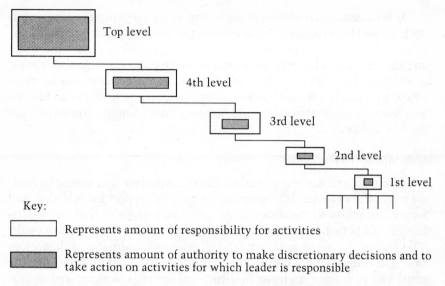

Key:

☐ Represents amount of responsibility for activities

▨ Represents amount of authority to make discretionary decisions and to take action on activities for which leader is responsible

Source: Adapted from Robert Grandford Wright, "The Myth Inherent in Responsibility Center Management," *MSU Business Topics,* Spring 1972, Vol. 20, No. 2. Used by permission of the publisher.

FIGURE 7–7. Estimated Relationships Between Authority and Responsibility

authority positions superior to the one so burdened recognize and understand this limitation. When the superior in our earlier example held the subordinate supervisor fully accountable for the implementation of the new program ("It's your 'baby'"), the superior failed to recognize the many prerogatives denied the subordinate. Accountability must be shared jointly, initially by the two leaders directly involved and in turn, by superiors up the chain of management. The interrelationships generated by jointly shared authority creates a major bonding agent to weld an organization together vertically, whereas functional mutual dependencies can bond organized effort horizontally.

When people who manage fail to recognize authority/responsibility inequalities and consequently make unreasonable demands on subordinates, it is disconcerting to the subordinates. If lower level leaders are allowed to cherish the fallacious idea that authority and responsibility should be equal, this is also cause for concern. Such myths lead to distortions of organizational realities; to internal inconsistencies, disappointments, confusion, frustration and, at times, demoralization. Failure to recognize the effects of the shrinking authority concept impedes the use of sound leadership techniques such as participative decision making, mutual dependency caused by this linking process, leads to further disregard for the mutual involvement among superiors and subordinates required to bring an organizational success.

It is necessary to withhold authority in relationship to responsibility because this process is basic to bringing about integration, coordination, control. It is also required to ensure the pursuit of common goals and the efficient allocation of resources to strive for those goals. Certain of the negative effects of the shrinking authority concept can be mitigated. By frankly acknowledging what is occurring, leaders can behave in a more congruent way. Sound superior-subordinate interaction can then be cultivated.

Limitations to Authority

According to early classical thinkers, authority was vested in leaders to greater or lesser degree throughout an enterprise. Each leader used formal authority to make decisions and take actions so that the contribution of his or her unit enhanced the attainment of enterprise goals. The leader also used authority to influence subordinates' behavior so that individual output contributed favorably to the productivity of the unit. The influence, in most institutional settings, was viewed as curtailed only by the precept of private property rights. Leaders, in the traditional view, were either owners of property or represented property owners. Thus, authority was given legitimacy and its use was clearly justified.

Early thinkers expressed little concern for the subtleties of authority and its use. Informal alignments and concentration of informal authority were not at issue. Restrictions placed on formal authority were of little import among classical theorists. They focused mainly on formal authority based upon a formal structure of positions. As with other facets of organization, traditional thinking about authority dealt with mechanistic necessities. Hence, it was impersonal and aimed largely at providing for conformity and control. The use of authority to create an organizational culture within which creativity and innovation might flourish was not envisioned. The basic problems of the era dealt with mechanical and economic efficiency.

Traditional thought conceived of the use of authority as a way to bring about efficiencies that could come from conformity, integration, control, and accountability. As a consequence, the traditional formal pyramidal organization symbolized strength, a vehicle of compliance and control. In the organizational environment that prevailed during the early 1900s, this approach was needed. After its initial impact, mechanization progressed in an evolutionary manner. In contrast with today's great demand for services and short product life cycles, a market for long-lived goods prevailed. Many enterprises were effectively monopolies or oligopolies in the labor market because employees' skills were not readily transferable and workers were relatively immobile.

Further, the comparatively narrow range of operations and simple technologies prevalent in enterprises at that time tolerated a closely held centralization of authority to make decisions.

Considering those conditions, traditional thinking about the use of authority was quite appropriate. Authority was not needed to spark employees' participation and contribution; nor was it needed to encourage employee development. Instead, authority had been viewed down through history as a device to ensure the compliance of individual will to the will of leadership. Influence was employed to gain the physical dexterity of workers. Today, authority often is also needed to produce an organizational climate within which members will want to contribute intellectually and emotionally to enterprise objectives; this use of authority is in response to current conditions and workers' expectations of greater job satisfaction.

SUMMARY

The first test of a soundly developed organization is that it brings about unified, or orchestrated, effort. To do so, the structure and integral subsystems must generate an interlocking, interrelating adjusting of individuals and various parts so that a single functional unit emerges. Authority, and the relationships of authority centers, were historically conceived as the critical bonding agent to achieve this.

The subsystems of formal communications, incentives, and control, together with authority and its delegation, are interwoven to bring on economic and technical efficiency. Though space permitted us only a discussion of authority, all of these other components are required by enterprises. They provide the impetus to collective human activity and thus move the organization from a static condition to dynamic interaction—from rigid anatomical arrangements to fluid social system.

The contributions of early thinking on organizations dealt largely with formalized, structural arrangements as the basic requirement for attaining goals. Viewed in one way, major concerns of the first organization theorists might be illustrated as in Figure 7-8. Early theories are useful and valuable as guidelines to form an economically efficient, production-oriented system. They provide insights into the design of structural/functional frameworks and of the internal subsystems serving as basic bonding agents in all complex organizations. One can view the structure of the organic subsystems by adding the dimensions of communications, incentives, and control to Figure 7-9. Here one can picture the structure of certain of the major subsystems common to all organizations. You should bear in mind that in practice the operating

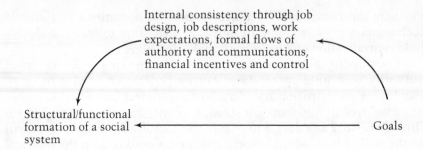

FIGURE 7–8. Logic of Early Organization Theorists

structures are dynamic interrelations of activities and events. The structures are needed to deal with the problem every organization faces:

> That problem is the maintaining, with respect to the organization as a whole, an evolving state of dynamic equilibrium consistent with its Organizational Charter [purpose, policies, and values shared] in the face of internal and external conditions and changes in those conditions.[6]

While early guidelines have application in forming organizations, they are limited to internal arrangements of a mechanical nature. Viewed alone, they obscure other elements of organizations. The inner workings—interrelationships of people in formal interaction and the emerging pulse of human activity—are excluded from the scope of early teachings. Recognition of these aspects can add new dimensions to an understanding of the nature of organizations. It is to these areas that we direct attention in Chapter 8.

DISCUSSION QUESTIONS

1. What major benefits can one derive from understanding the reasons for the emergence of certain internal subsystems in an organization?

2. What varied influences can these subsystems have on a person in an organization? In what ways do they modify behavior?

3. Discuss the relationships among internal subsystems—authority (emphasized here), communications, incentives, and control—which can ensure internal consistence. Use a specific enterprise as illustration.

4. Is the phrase "illegitimate authority" a contradiction in terms? Why?

5. It has been said that *power* often brings on negative connotations, while *authority* is a more acceptable term. Discuss the distinction between these words and the reasons for their acceptance or rejection by persons subject to their influence.

6. What are the consequences of coequal responsibility and authority?

7. Some would suggest that grasping more responsibility than one has the authority for is partly a ritual of initiation to gain higher rank. What are the full implications of such an act?

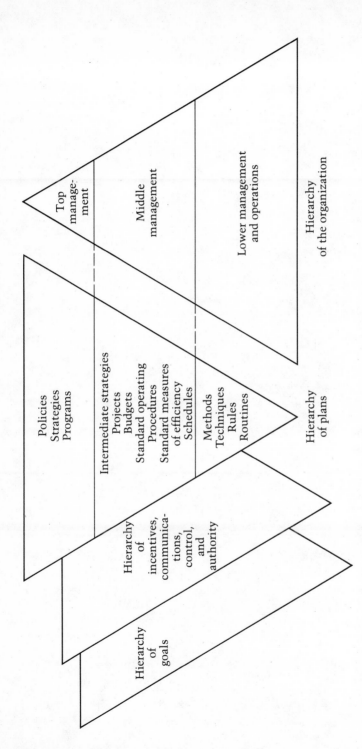

Source: Adapted from Robert Grandford Wright, "The Myth Inherent in Responsibility Center Management," *MSU Business Topics*, Spring 1972, Vol. 2, No. 2. Used by permission of the publisher.

FIGURE 7–9. Organic Subsystems of Organizations

8

Culture of Organizations

*In describing an organization, it is observed that there are a number of
features or facilities which support the activity process and which make
them more dependable and systemic. . . . Taken together these facilities
come very close to being what the anthropologists mean by "culture."*

E. Wight Bakke[1]

To this point in the book, we have studied features common to all
organizations—structure, anatomy, and sybsystems. Here we depart
from our explorations of how things *should* work to inquire into the way
things *do* work in organizations. We will consider those aspects that
make each organization unique, differential aspects, rather than those
factors that make them alike, common aspects. For it is as true with
organizations as with individuals that they are to an extent:

1. like all other organizations,
2. like some other organizations, and
3. like no other organizations.[2]

We have concentrated in previous chapters on the first two, that is,
aspects of commonality among organizations. Now we can turn to the
third aspect and explore the differentiations that make it impossible for
any two organizations to be the same.

To do so, we must study the culture of social systems. By culture, we
mean the knowledge, behavior patterns, language, beliefs, artifacts, and
habitat of an organization—the whole of its society. Walter
Goldschmidt put it this way:

Man lives in a time continuum; that is, present behavior is made up out of
past experiences and is projected into the future. It is impossible to understand any social system without taking this "cultural heritage"—as it is

119

generally called—into account . . . Every social system has a past and is directed toward a future.[3]

These elements promote cultural continuity in organizations. They are influences, or forces, from inside and out that shape an enterprise's behavior and make up the "field" within which any social system must operate. The field of cultural forces that partially form the behavior of an organization comes from three major sources:

1. People within the organization in sensitive positions (leaders)
2. Internal traditions
3. External forces[4]

Forces from each of these classifications will be presented. Then we will observe the way these forces are analyzed by authorities on organizational awareness. We will cite interviews with twenty-five authorities in management consulting, people seasoned in organizational planning. These consultants have examined the cultures of thousands of enterprises in settings as diverse as missile testing centers, synagogues, police departments, schools, businesses, penal institutions, governmental agencies at all levels, and the Vatican.[5] So they serve us well as experts. First, we will consider briefly the relationship of this cultural approach to understanding organizations to the conceptual model, and to its place in the so-called schools of organization theory.

Culture and the Conceptual Model

In earlier chapters we concerned ourselves with those aspects of organizations that make them "like all other organizations." These are the common attributes designed to achieve structure, integration, and internal balance (equilibrium). Such arrangements lead ostensibly to efficiency. These structural/functional requirements are presented again in Figure 8-1, bracketed and screened.

In this chapter we are concerned with aspects that make an organization "like no other organization." These are differences that emerge over a period of time as the unique culture of a social system, tempering and changing common aspects. The cultural factors are shown in bolder type in Figure 8-1.

Culture and Schools of Thought

As noted previously, early schools of thought to understand organizations centered on the logic of function and structure common to all organizations. Concern for the influence of culture on the behavior of an enterprise was in effect absent. Study of other dimensions of organizations was needed if their behavior was to be understood.

The later, neoclassical, school of thought developed in response to

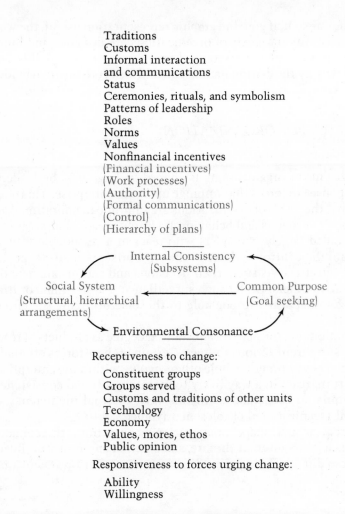

Traditions
Customs
Informal interaction
and communications
Status
Ceremonies, rituals, and symbolism
Patterns of leadership
Roles
Norms
Values
Nonfinancial incentives
(Financial incentives)
(Work processes)
(Authority)
(Formal communications)
(Control)
(Hierarchy of plans)

Internal Consistency
(Subsystems)

Social System
(Structural, hierarchical
arrangements)

Common Purpose
(Goal seeking)

Environmental Consonance

Receptiveness to change:

Constituent groups
Groups served
Customs and traditions of other units
Technology
Economy
Values, mores, ethos
Public opinion

Responsiveness to forces urging change:

Ability
Willingness

FIGURE 8–1. Conceptual Overview of an Organization

unanswered questions. Its contributors included people who studied such external environments (legal, economic, political) of organizations as social psychology, anthropology, organizational politics, informal communications, and systems theory. Their findings threw new light on the nature of organizational realities and, as William Scott views it, refined the pillars of earlier classical teachings on organizations.[6]

In a similar way, the cultural appurtenances studied in this chapter will help us to differentiate one organization from another. Differentiating cultural aspects refines our understanding of why structures are formed as they are. Or, if you find graphic representation useful, the way in which the common aspects of organizations are designed and function (shown in bracketed and screened print in Figure 8-1) will be influenced heavily by the distinguishing cultural aspects (shown in bolder print in the same figure).

MAJOR ASPECTS OF ORGANIZATION CULTURE

The behavior of organizations is shaped in large part by leaders' rational responses to forces that impinge upon the enterprise. This does not imply that the heads of organizations are immune to nonrational, or even irrational, decisions and behavior. It simply means that organizations are molded largely by leaders who react in a reasonable way to forces beyond the control of those in the enterprise. Leaders are at the forefront of activities. As such, their decisions and actions are usually clearly visible to others. Under such surveillance, a nonrational or irrational act would appear irresponsible to those scrutinizing the enterprise.

Organizations are formed to a substantial degree as products of reactions to pressures from various sources. Certain of these forces originate in the external environment, whole others evolve within the enterprise. Leaders, in turn, react in a way to try to maintain internal consistency and environmental consonance.[7] In this way, internal inefficiency is lessened and organizational obsolesence avoided.

The forces which shape organizations come from three major sources—leadership, internal climate, and external environment. Reactions to these differentiating stimuli give an organization its cultural pulsebeat.

LEADERSHIP

To understand the cultural dynamics of an organization, one must understand the characteristics of people in sensitive, namely, influential and powerful, positions. Leaders interpret goals and means as well as internal and external forces. These *interpretations are basic and fundamental to their reactions and the impact of their reactions on the behavior of the organization.* Thus, understanding its key leaders is crucial to understanding an organization.

Observe that a study of "people in sensitive, namely influential positions" is recommended. They may be found at the top of an enterprise or elsewhere within it, depending upon who dominates activities during different periods in the system's life cycle. For instance, in the

federal government the Secretary of Defense may assume a commanding role in times of international conflict but may be relegated to a
position of influence subordinate to the Secretary of Health, Education,
and Welfare when domestic problems are urgent. But, take note, the
formal organizational arrangement does not change. It neither indicates
distinctions in the degree of influence wielded by persons on the same
authority level nor reflects informal arrangements that place a subordinate in a role with greater influence than upper echelons display. Formal
organization charts are presently incapable of accurately recording such
realism.

You will observe further that when we study people in organizations, we confine our inquiry to those "in sensitive positions." This
restriction is made to narrow the study to include only relevant variables. Such focusing is also required because *differences in organizations are not understood by studying differences in people within them.*
Concentrating on personal traits is unsound for several important reasons. First, an organization is something more than the people who
make it up. In situations of collective interaction, the sum of the total
organization is greater than its parts. The whole system evolves as a
distinct entity with a tradition, culture, an identity of its own. And second, the technical and social demands of a work position may be more
decisive in determining the behavior of its incumbent than is the individual's personality. This means, among other things, that a thorough
analysis of all the people as they behave in an enterprise could result in a
distorted view of their individual personalities. Worse for our purposes,
at the least it would lead to a misleading view of organizational behavior, for it neglects other influences on it. Further, it would tend to un-
cover similarity of certain roles across organizations rather than the
points of difference that explain distinctiveness. The point can legiti-
mately be made that the role behavior in certain work positions common to a number of enterprises is more uniform than the behavior of the
individual enterprises. For instance, positions such as controller, public
relations representative, cost clerk, secretary, and production foreman
attract certain types of people with specific backgrounds of education
and experience. Further, the diverse natures of the positions impose
certain role behaviors to meet technical, social, and authority demands.
As a consequence, the individual filling the position develops set behavioral patterns, whatever the enterprise served. By contrast, however, the
behavior of the different organizations is distinguished by various functions, goals, and cultures. Indeed, all its participants help to shape the
culture of an enterprise, but our study will be restricted to those whose
shadow of influence falls over a significant segment of the organization.

Let's begin by observing the backgrounds of leaders. Then we can
consider their attitudes, values, and beliefs.

Backgrounds of Leaders

There are at least two major segments of one's background that influence behavior as a leader—education and professional experience. Exposure to certain types of knowlege and activities shapes a person's perceptual field while indicating areas of strength, weakness, and predisposition. For instance, it is well-known that one is more comfortable in areas of activity with which familiarity, competence, and identification have been cultivated. Hence, an authority asserts authority:

> If I find a leader of an enterprise with sound technical training, say in engineering, there's a good chance that he will over-manage activities in this area of speciality, perhaps to the neglect, imbalance or jeopardy of directing important related activities. It's simply a tendency among us.

Or, as another authority on organization behavior stated:

> When I find a person in a highly sensitive position who has a unique kind of professional education, say a legal officer promoted to head an enterprise, the organization may be caused to assume a bent toward conservatism, together with an inordinate concern for internal affairs, as opposed to a liberalizing innovation, with pioneering efforts in areas such as research, promotion, and diversification or decentralization, or other reform. There is simply a propensity toward more concrete efforts, rather than less tangible programs.

Carefully consider the impact of this single leadership trait on the design of the organization structure and common subsystems for authority, communications, and control. Analyze further the internal pulse of the operation, the ideas that will gravitate upward, and the type of people who will find the corresponding culture suitable to fulfill their particular needs.

The background of the person, or people, in sensitive positions can also make an indelible mark on the culture of an enterprise:

> Take an individual who owned and managed a firm where nepotism or paternalism is practiced. It can lead to unique behaviorisms. Incentives may be provided in the form of bonuses rather than high wages. Authority may be used to overly protect employees rather than build them into more capable people. And control may be erratic and personal because of the lack of procedures.

Compare this form of leadership with that of professional management in a large institution: leaders hired to manage for an absentee constituent group (for example, parishioners, citizens, contributors, shareholders, and the like):

> The professional man is conditioned to behave as did his predecessor. I'll call this the "ex quotient man" influence. He is entrapped by the behavior of the former leader who recognized the frailties connected with giving promotions to men based only upon their demonstrated ability at the next

lower positions. Thus, he has provided a number of "pigeon-holes" for incompetents rather than dismissal. In a way, the procedure is humane but it distorts the real organization and creates a corps of malcontents impervious to most commonly used incentives. Perhaps the new leader's hands are tied by a practice that has now become institutionalized.

Can you sense the impact of this leader's behavior on the pulse of the organization? If this practice was unknown, the organization would seem to suffer a nonrational, split personality. The logic of the paper organization (formal) would depart widely from the real organization (formal and informal). Consider one further example of a leader's background and its implications for workers' activities:

> Leaders are influenced by their industrial experience and its application to current practices. You see, if you understand the background of an industry, you can better understand the type of people who gravitate to it. And industrial atmospheres vary widely. As an example, consider the contrasting types of men attracted, say, to the oil industry versus the banking industry. On the one hand, a leader may wear his hat in the office, find expression difficult without employing four-letter words, and rule things with an iron hand. On the other hand, a leader may be ill-at-ease if not nattily attired, internalize his frustrations, and perhaps give wide discretionary freedom to employees, limited only by the most apparently needed restrictions. Each will impute a profound influence upon employee behavior and the corporate culture. Sure, some departures from character do occur, but cultural heritage is very persuasive.

There is little disagreement that the professional backgrounds of people in positions of leadership have an impact on the behavioral atmosphere of an enterprise. Further, their attitudes can bring on unique organizational patterns.

Attitudes of Leaders

The attitudes of leaders also have widespread influence which, in turn, affects the physiological fabric of an enterprise. A seasoned outside consultant cites the importance in this way:

> Consideration of leaders as critical elements is highly primary [to understanding an organization]. As in an indigenous culture, so you find it with each enterprise. It is made up of people with their special characteristics. The traits of leaders—their skills, attitudes, and resulting approaches—shape the life and dynamics of the organization.

Further, attitudes are instrumental in molding leadership patterns. By leadership patterns, we refer here to a leader's concept of his or her relationship to subordinates. Leadership patterns, or styles, range from autocratic to democratic, with varying shades in between. One way of sorting these patterns of behavior might be shown as in Table 8-1.

Leaders' attitudes, values, and perceptions cause them to adopt one

TABLE 8–1. Patterns of behavior.

Brief Description of Leader's Attitude	Resulting Leadership Pattern
It is my responsibility to make decisions and act autonomously concerning the enterprise.	Autocratic
It is my responsibility to make decisions and act alone in the best interests of all aspects of the enterprise and its workers, as I define their best interests both on the job and off.	Feudalistic
As a leader, it is my duty to make decisions and act autonomously in the best interests of the enterprise, as well as to protect its employees.	Paternalistic
It is my role to make the final decisions and implement them; however, for technical and/or humanistic reasons, those affected should be consulted.	Participative, consultative
I have obligations beyond decision making and operative matters to work actively to develop subordinates to their fullest potential.	Developmental
It is my role to set broad guidelines for decisions and action to be taken largely by subordinates, with minimal controls.	Permissive
My functions entail establishing an atmosphere in which the dominant responsibility for decisions and actions is assumed by subordinates.	Collegial
My role is as a steward to ensure that decisions and actions reflect the views of my subordinates based upon an expressed majority rule.	Democratic

pattern of supervision or another. It is easy to see how each of these patterns can infuse its influence into organizational culture. For instance, paternalism would introduce a whole set of cultural variations. Authority, bolstered by excessive controls, would be held tightly at the top of the enterprise; upward communications and ideas would be inhibited; and both financial and nonfinancial rewards would be bestowed benignly, often for conformity or loyalty. Though consistency prevails among subsystems, it is questionable if a paternalistic approach is compatible with the goals of the enterprise, the demands from its environment, or the needs of its participants.

Whatever the reasons behind a certain leadership pattern, it can modify the subsystems and the overall behavior of an organization. An experienced analyst shares the following observation with us:

> A good part of the soul of a company is the result of management attitudes, which in turn become a part of tradition. They create the atmosphere for receptivity, rigidity, and inflexibility. You may sense a pattern of dictatorial behavior; then you confirm or reject it by listening to the members of the enterprise to determine if management has been receptive to ideas from below. If confirmed, you watch for its impact on related activities and processes. In sum, you can then identify unique behavioral patterns of the firm.

Awareness of the type of leadership also helps us to understand distinctive behavior in organizations.

> Typically, professionally managed corporations with ownership separated from control are formed to maximize profits, while companies owned and managed by the same individual or family are organized for other purposes.
>
> For example, there is a tendency for entrepreneurs to develop a benevolently autocratic attitude toward their organization and establish supporting programs to fulfill this role that have little to do with profits.
>
> In addition, leaders of privately owned enterprises are usually more innovative, while firms run by professional managers tend to react rather than to act.

Imagine the variations in organization behavior brought about, let us say, by a benevolently autocratic leader who is relatively free-wheeling and adopts noneconomic goals. Organizational members who are aware of the leader's personal ideosyncracies and mutually competing goals could function well by understanding the causes of their treatment by the leader and ambiguity among objectives. Members who fail to discern causes could view the situation as merely frustrating and demoralizing. Can you imagine further the individual adjustments required to perform in the atmosphere of an individually owned private firm compared to a publicly owned, professionally managed corporation? One setting would be personal and intimate, rewarding effort and loyalty, while the second could be impersonal and aloof, and reward achievement and competency. And finally, can you imagine the degree to which ideas would have to be modified to work in one enterprise, after working in the other? Though the idea may be suitable to each setting, it would have to be redesigned to fit the new culture: a culture not only influenced by technology, economics, and structure, but also shaped by leadership attitudes.

Values of Leaders

Values, as you may recall, are views shared by individuals that underlie their acceptance and support of enterprise goals, subgoals, norms, and roles. Values engender varying degrees of individual support for institutionalized activities. Experts assess the values of leaders to determine the intensity of their commitment to institutional arrangements.

> One leader may be retiring within several years. He would like the *status quo* preserved. He has fought his battles, won a few and lost a few, and now he would like a "don't rock the boat policy." Another man is intensely involved building an "institutionalized dynasty" to assure his progress. Yet, another leader has become distractingly involved with supporting programs of the Catholic Church. And a final manager observed claims that "he just wants to make a decent living." Such differing values can be found on the parts of men in different organizations or in various sensitive positions in the same organization.

The values held by a leader of an enterprise can affect the degree of integration in the organization. Divergent values among heads in a single enterprise can give the organization the appearance of schizophrenia. Varying values can also lead to conflicting behavioral patterns in various units of an organization.

Analyzing values is one approach to a more thorough description of organization behavior. A "feeling" by a leader at the top can pervade the entire organization and make its mark on all aspects of human affairs within the enterprise. One senior consultant put the matter this way:

> The value of the chief executive dominantly influences the temperament of the organization. Values are manifested up to six or seven levels down into the enterprise. As an example, in an aerospace firm with over 40,000 employees, the top manager did not feel that financial rewards were fashionable or relevant to professional employees. Instead, intrinsic types of rewards such as those representing prestige and professional accomplishment became important because of top management's feeling. As a result, it now has influenced personnel selection, incentives, promotion policies, management processes, training, status, and other phases of the operation. This concept is reinforced by attracting people with similar values and shedding those who prove to be misfits.

Values are often omnipotent in shaping major subsystems. In the example given above, the "feeling" of a leader influenced the design of all of the subsystems of procedures concerning personnel policies. In fact, if all related procedures concerning personnel are not designed to support the leader's view, an internal inconsistency will surely result. Consider the ambiguity that would be caused if the attitude on incentives were not designed into the process of selecting personnel. Misunderstandings and confusion would become widespread concerning expectations, trade-offs, and rewards. It could lead finally to employee unrest and high rates of turnover.

Perceptions of Leaders

Perceptions, as used here, are one's beliefs about (1) who one is, (2) how one relates to others, and (3) what one believes the operating situation to be. In sum, a leader develops a stable, unified belief about him or herself, the leadership setting, and the makeup of the organization. These definitions are fundamental to decision making and actions as a means to cope with that world. They, in part, form images (cognitions) that influence attitudes, values, and other elements of individual behavior. Let us look at the importance of the leader's definition of the organization as it influences decisions and behavior.

To understand the behavior of an organization, we can ask people holding key positions several simple but often perplexing questions. The following inquiries are helpful in gaining an initial grasp of organizational realities: What business are you in? Where are you going with the enterprise (three to five goals)? What are the most important external factors that pose constraints to reaching those goals? And what internal activities are critical to attaining them? The views of leaders on these points can provide sharp insights into organizational behavior. Responses can also point up areas of serious, harmful disagreement.

Further, human relationships within an organization can be brought into finer focus through inquiries into more specific classes of perceptual interpretations. A veteran analyst has put it this way:

> Patterns of perceptions from people on where the enterprise is going and how they relate to the organization help to understand the *real* organization. There are the status relationships and the contractual relationships. When you find out how the boss "sees" relationships, often as contrasted to the way subordinates see relationships, you start to describe the *true* organization, as opposed to the formal organization chart.

Perceptual frameworks of leaders are important for they have marked influence on the behavioral patterns of the organization. They take an analyst far in describing what is *really* going on. As such, studies of leaders are important as one way to differentiate the culture and behavior of an organization.

ORGANIZATIONAL CLIMATE

The study of organization culture also includes the climate of an organization, the internal culture from which behavioral patterns emerge. Organizations develop traditional ways of thinking that become institutionalized. They are like social mores, a people's ethos, or the superstitions of a primitive tribe. These ways of thinking are important because they establish an institutional image with which participants may identify and communicate an image of what the institution stands for. Beyond that, the culture in part gives legitimacy to the activities of the entity. It also sets a consistent pattern of expected, and thus acceptable, behavior based upon historical precedence. Beliefs establish an ideological setting or operating condition. They include concepts, such as roles (status), occupational kinship relationships (acceptable social interaction), negative and positive sanctions (punishments and rewards), rites of passage (orientations, initial management training, retirement dinners), "religious" (beliefs unquestioned super directives, including myths), social strata, and related sodalities (unions, foremen's club, management association, and professional societies). Culture is not only ritualized behavior, it is also often symbolized by material objects, for example, offices, furnishings, telephones, and various types of equipment. Cultural arrangements in organizations are frequently designed and institutionalized. If they act to fulfill the needs of the people as well as to guide them towards organizational goals, they are internally consistent. They become traditionalized to create the social environment, or organizational climate.

Understanding the traditions of an organization is helpful both to describe its behavioral patterns and to evaluate its capability to assimilate change. An analyst gave this example:

> In the defense industry, you find "major religions" and "minor cults": Reliability may have become a cult, while R & D may develop into a major religion. They are above question, as edicts. Then they tend to become institutionalized, to become entrenched, even when the goals or needs of the organization change, making them obsolete. These are certain parts of culture. Culture *is* the internal environment. It's the culture of a small society.

Beyond simply cultivating a "feel" for the behavior of an enterprise, one can generate an awareness of those ideas that will fit an organization and can sense tolerances for various degrees of change. Truly, things do become ritualized; a subculture emerges with rituals and folklore from which people do not like to depart. Reluctance to alter established patterns of behavior is a commonly recognized tendency of human beings and is one of the elements of organized life that can be better appreciated by analyzing its cultural aspects. A senior management consultant put it this way:

> We look at things historically to get an idea of why things are the way they are today, how long they've been that way, and what would be a persuasive rationale where changes are required. People have a characteristic to develop "sets." We get conditioned by tradition, habit, and so on. They develop sets of ways to do things, and resistance is conditioned by these sets. From a practical standpoint, you can't just legislate against them. You have to persuade, coax, and motivate because if you do otherwise, the organization will recoil against abrupt changes.

> The condition is not only prevalent with people in the lower levels of organization. Most leaders tend to oppose change even when they're in trouble. Change should usually be gradual, unless the situation is so imminent that the "earthquake treatment" is the only solution. If abrupt, leaders will fight your ideas. So, it's a matter of finding out how they have acted in the past. Then, introducing change becomes a logical process and an intuitive process at the same time to break from the magnetism of culture.

The subtle nature of cultural aspects and their impact on a social organism make organization studies absorbing. An organization is a microsociety in which culturally steeped modes of behavior are at times central to its activities. As such, cultural nuances represent a major sphere of influence on organization behavior.

EXTERNAL ENVIRONMENT

Influences on the nature of an organization's behavior are also exerted by its external environment. To a high degree an enterprise is an adaptive organism—a dependent variable responsive to outside stimuli over which it has little control. Industrial customs and changes, economic trends, market composition and movements, product and service advances, and technological progress are some of the stimuli requiring adjustments if an enterprise is to survive. At least as important because they often precede economic changes are variations in human wants, values, life styles, philosophies, and the social norms of relevant segments of society. It is imperative that organization members pay close attention to these.

Some developments outside require changes of goals or of the means to goals. Changing goals may be in response to such variations as market shifts, business cycles, or public opinion, while changing the means of reaching the goals may be a reaction to new technology, advanced needs of participants, or different feelings about rewards. Therefore, by understanding external pressures one can anticipate reactions and better describe organization behavior. As an example, a senior organization analyst once stated:

> To really know a company, you have to know the external situation, so we start by evaluating the impact of its markets and competition. . . . And also, we try to understand the peculiarities of the industry and the historical performance of the client firm related to its competitors. By looking at external factors, in quite some depth, we can better understand why the company functions as it does.

Though a business enterprise is used here as an example, any organizational behavior can be better understood by evaluating the ecological forces impinging on it. A church, a military unit, a charitable enterprise, a governmental bureau, or a social action group—all are in part shaped and understood by their responses to outside forces.

We are not suggesting here that institutions do not have a countervailing impact upon their environments. Certainly it is apparent that they try to neutralize threats to their well-being and decrease uncertainty surrounding their operation. Such efforts, however, are only as effective as the organization's capacity to control environmental aspects.

In today's milieu of many diverse enterprises—large and small, strong and weak—only relatively few, with extraordinary power, can create and constitute their own environments. Even the behavior of these enterprises can be better explained through an awareness of their external pressures. Giants with huge capabilities for influencing their environmental fields—General Motors, The Tennessee Valley Authority, the Catholic Church—are not impervious to external agents requiring reaction. Though adaptation may indeed take the form of altering an environmental force rather than reacting to its pressure for change, the countervailing strategies nonetheless help one to describe and to cultivate a "feel" even for organizations of great power.

Understanding organization behavior is considerably simpler with middle and small-scaled enterprises. In these the ability to influence external forces is minimal when compared with their need to adjust operations to maintain environmental consonance. And these enterprises make up the great preponderance of organizations in a society. The demise of an organization is usually preceded by its failure to adjust to its environment. Put another way, an enterprise is approaching collapse when its leaders tend to view it as a closed system (classical thinking) rather than an open one (neoclassical and current thinking).

SUMMARY AND CONCLUDING REMARKS

In this chapter, the reader has been asked to consider the culture of an organzation. It is culture that summarizes the past of an organization *and* shapes its future dynamics, or interaction—the processes, activities, and phenomena characteristic of its life.

In addition, it was pointed out that the dynamics of organization are concerned with human relationships, informal arrangements, individual behavior, motivation, and organizations as open social systems. Particular attention has been devoted of late to the way in which these factors alter earlier, classical teachings on structure.

Indeed, a cultural perspective of the nature of organizations, coupled with the earlier viewpoint on their structure, should render a complete portrait of an organization's behavior. Unfortunately, it does not! The behavioral studies that could illuminate dimly seen features of organizational life have not followed an orderly, integrated plan. As a consequence, we largely find ourselves with bits and pieces of disjointed data. For instance, we know something of the social interaction of a bomber crew; the socio-psychological makeup of restaurant workers; the bureaucratizing elements of a state employment agency; and the effects of decentralization in a department store. But, as William Scott notes, observers "generally seemed content to engage in descriptive generalizations, or particularized empirical research studies which did not have much meaning outside their own context."[8] Though many findings emerged, they did not appear to be relevant to understanding the behavior of other specific organizations. Later studies were not related first to classical theory and then to a new theory to explain the total organization. And we would also agree with Scott when he observes:

> The neoclassical approach has provided valuable contributions to the lore of organization. But, like the classical theory, the neoclassical doctrine suffers from incompleteness, shortsighted perspective, and lack of integration among the many facets of human behavior studies by it.[9]

The teachings, mostly descriptive, deal with studies of the dynamics within specific organizations as contrasted with earlier analyses of the structure of organizations in general. These aspects are the chief elements that distinguish one organization from all others. To some degree, neoclassical thinking deals with variations among organizations, or differential aspects. Three classifications of these aspects were introduced—leaders in influential positions, internal climate and external forces—as major causes for the unique behavior of an organization.

We now have the advantage of a number of viewpoints: structural, anatomical, subsystemic, and cultural. In Chapter 9, we will integrate these viewpoints and place them within an analytical framework. With a means for classifying information observed and analyzing it systematically, we can acquire a new organizational perspective—an explanation of the character of organization.

DISCUSSION QUESTIONS

1. Compare and contrast the cultures of, say, Mother's Bakery, City Bank, and Acme Toy Company. What types of persons and behavioral patterns would be compatible with these varied cultures?

2. Why are social systems (1) like all other organizations, (2) like some other organizations, and (3) like no other organizations?

3. Give examples of cultural appurtenances, or factors, lingering on to cause internal inconsistencies with goals and other internal subsystems, such as authority, incentives, communications, work processes, and control.

4. Evaluate the influence of two chief executives with diverse backgrounds and behavior on the culture of a soft drink bottling enterprise.

Chief Executive 1	*Chief Executive 2*
Professional accountant	Liberal arts education
Seasoned manager in firm	Heir to business
Internal orientation to firm	Sensitive to external affairs
Believes in work ethic	Believes in achievement,
(loyalty, perserverance)	whatever the arena

5. Outside study: Discuss the influence of behavior modification, organization development, cultural diffusion, and other ways to change an outmoded organizational culture.

9

Character of an Organization

Even though its existence is seldom recognized . . . , personality has an important bearing on an organization's fate. In fact, one might say it is important because it is so rarely recognized.

Gellerman[1]

When one attempts to understand a specific organization, it becomes apparent that it is different from all others and that some analytical framework is needed. One cannot simply add up the parts, describe their arrangement, and conclude that the system is understood. Nor can one expect to gain overall comprehension merely by summing up structure and culture.

An organization, as a social system, develops a distinct, unique character. Though two organizations may be designed to pursue the same goals and have like functions, over time each will acquire distinctive traits peculiar to itself. For example, though two churches of the same faith are established to provide spiritual guidance and community services, each will ultimately come to have its own identifiable character.

Organization character is the result of complex influences on a social system out of which a unique personality develops. The idea has been widely accepted by authorities who have studied organizations from varied viewpoints—or disciplines. Some call the phenomenon "personality,"[2] some term it "institutional subculture,"[3] another will call it "character," while yet another will refer to it as a "peculiarly characterized bureaucratic situation."[4] Perhaps the sociologist Robert Presthus put the matter best when he said:

> Organizations are indeed miniatures of society. They have a hierarchy of status and of roles, a system of myths and values, and a catalogue of expected behaviors. They are probably more significant than most associations because of their concern with economic and status needs. . . Organizations, then, are defined here as miniature social systems.[5]

As a small society (not unlike that of the island castaways of Chapter 4), each organization develops a particular character.

IMPORTANCE OF UNDERSTANDING CHARACTER

Why attempt to study something as nebulous and abstract as organization character? Isn't a description sufficient? Or can't one merely analyze the inner workings of an enterprise based upon logical responses to its needs? Let us consider the answers to these questions by looking at the advantages in seeking to understand the character of an organization.

First, despite superficial similarities, each organization develops an atmosphere that differs from any other. Analysis of this personality, coupled with an awareness of the organization's functional needs, *explains* why an organization behaves as it does. And this is a more incisive, practical plane of knowing than mere description can provide. To the student of organizations, such insights can be invaluable. This is particularly true when one considers that the insider rarely has a real awareness of the organization. This is true because the analysis of an enterprise's personality requires a level of objectivity nearly as difficult to attain as a realistic self-appraisal. An outsider enjoys the aloofness of "stranger value"; an insider does not.

Second, analyzing the inner workings of an organization solely on grounds of logical responses to practical necessities is both insufficient and misleading. It is mistaking fiction for truth to believe that organizational arrangements are the result of critical analyses of hard facts followed by rational responses. It is giving credence to a myth to believe that mere flesh-and-blood managers are somehow immune to biases and thus can contrive human organizations as an engineer designs some physical system. To the contrary, there is a strong emotional tide in every company. It stems from the hopes, aspirations, anxieties, and attitudes of people in sensitive positions, and it guides their judgments to at least as great an extent as do knowledge and reason.

Third, the personality of an organization is the major influence on its acceptance or rejection of new goals, ideas, procedures, and other patterns of behavior. As a consequence, the naïve advisor may recommend a certain idea that appears practical, but is incompatible with the distinctive character of the enterprise. Leaders will reject the recommendation not on practical grounds, but rather on feelings that somehow "It doesn't seem to fit our situation."

There is an excellent old example of a well-intended, otherwise well-founded, recommendation that was totally ill-advised because of the character of the institution. It seems that a management consultant firm was engaged by the Catholic Church. The consultants apparently based their study on similar assignments from major business concerns such as General Motors. Uncovering comparable problems, but unable or unwilling to recognize institutional variations, the consulting firm recommended that the Church maintain depreciation reserves and delegate part of the Pope's authority to subordinates. The plan fell on deaf ears! Beyond its ludicrous element, the story serves to illustrate the fate of good ideas made ill-advised by their incompatibility with a particular organization.

The personality of a social system forms a pattern of unwritten laws for analyzing proposals—a program for their acceptance or rejection. Though technically sound, new ways of operating are often turned down on temperamentally justifiable grounds.

Fourth, understanding organization character is basic to understanding the types of people who will or will not fit a certain enterprise. To some authorities such as Saul Gellerman, a psychological consultant, *"compatibility with the company personality is as much a requisite for success for employees as aptitude, experiences and other qualifications."*[6] To illustrate the point, Gellerman describes a firm that he classified as having an "impersonal, aggressive" personality. It had adopted a hard-sell strategy. Salesmen were selected for their aggressive manner, impersonally pressured by their leaders, and handsomely rewarded for performance. Those who survived were a hard-boiled corps—independent to a fault. Other salesmen became demoralized and accepted jobs with other firms, often at a financial loss, to get personalized interest and attention from management. Frequently, highly competent, well-qualified employees will fail in a job because of their incompatibility with their organization's character.

And last, by studying organization character one can develop an awareness of a total, specific enterprise. This has more practical relevance for each of us than a partial estimate of the behavior of some generalized organization. To explain the character of a particular enterprise requires a comprehensive framework of the following nature:
1. A sufficiently broad viewpoint
2. A logical analytical framework
3. A situational, exploratory study
4. An integration of findings applied to the organization *as a system*

In sum, here is what one gains from an understanding of organization character: (1) perhaps most important here, a perception of why an organization behaves as it does rather than a description of how it behaves; (2) an awareness of both rational and (seemingly) nonrational decisions and behavior; (3) the kind of ideas that will be accepted by its members; (4) the kind of behavior that will fit; and (5), an understanding of the behavior of a specific organization rather than general impressions.

Difficulty of Analysis

Choosing among various approaches to studying organization behavior (or any other complex issue, for that matter) calls for difficult trade-offs. For instance, if one's study is too narrow, one misses total comprehension. If the study is too broad, detail is lost. An unstructured analysis leads to the weak conclusion that everything is somehow related to everything else, while one that is overly structured may exclude some critical element. If one waits for scientific proof for every finding, understanding organizations through analysis is delayed. Yet if one explores with tentative means, the specter of replication of findings rears its troubling head.

The study of organization character brings forth its share of research difficulties. But we know that to understand the behavior of an organization, one must use bold means of analysis. Further, we know that only through a comprehensive study can the nature of a total organization be understood. And, finally, we have found through researchers' experience that more satisfactory explanations of organizational behavior come from studies of its character than from other approaches. So we must use the best tools available to us and adopt the position of other students faced with the same type of dilemma:

> Those who aim to be social scientists are entitled to invent their own ways of mastering their materials, and to challenge the skeptic to doubt the reliability of their results.[7]

Relating Character to Other Theories

The analysis required to evaluate organization character ties together a number of ideas put forth in earlier chapters. It must do so if we are to be able to explain organization behavior. Early classical teachings did not do so. Later teachings by behaviorists did not do so. We must attempt to integrate past lessons in a way that explains behavior.

Chapters 5, 6, and 7 presented, in order, the structure, anatomy, and subsystems common to all organizations. As you will recall, these were the areas of major concern to early, classical students of organizations. Chapter 8 then described certain cultural influences that differentiate each organization from the others as a unique entity. These aspects dealt with human behavior and the environment of a social system. As we said earlier, these were dimensions of concern to later, neoclassical students. Classicists considered organizations largely as closed systems, while neoclassicists viewed them as open systems. Figure 9-1 below illustrates the relationships among these schools and the analysis of organization character. The arrow indicates differentiating influence and the dashed line, effect.

Chapter 8	Chapters 5, 6, 7	Chapter 9
Culture	Structure, anatomy, subsystems	Character
Behavioral/environ- mental aspects	Mechanistic aspects	Character
Open system	Closed system	Character
Differential aspects	Common aspects	Character
Neoclassical origin	Classical origin	Character

FIGURE 9–1. Analysis of Organization Character

One must be aware that if organizations were designed purely on the basis of the conceptual model—internally consistent and environmentally consonant—those with like goals and environments would resemble each other and be perfectly designed, logical responses to those demands. Yet their characters do differ, a result of different cultures and individuals. Shown graphically, the symmetry of common features (solid line) becomes assymetrical when one recognizes the influence of differential aspects (broken lines) (Figure 9-2). The influence is somewhat like the effects of genetics and culture as observed in a normal human being. By analyzing genetic influences, we find similarities among people as to structure, anatomy, and internal organs. A scrutiny of cultural influences uncovers the reasons for dissimilarities. In human beings nurture (differential forces) to a degree alters nature (common elements), as it does with organizations.

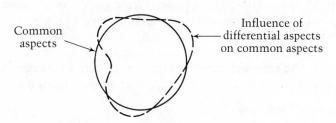

FIGURE 9–2. Impact of Differential Aspects on Common Features

So, to study the character of an organization, we evaluate the effect of differential influences on those structures and subsystems that are common to all organizations:

Authority centers	Formal communications
Contrived grouping of personnel	Spans of management
Divisions of labor	Control systems
Formal hierarchy	Incentive systems
Delegative processes	Functional roles of management

THE ANALYTICAL FRAMEWORK

Let's now consider how one analyzes organization character—how one finds his or her way around in a complex organization. To do so, we will present the analytical framework, the classifications of variables found to influence character, and a study of one kind of organization. First, certain assumptions about the analysis of organizational character must be made:

1. We accept the proposition that each organization is a unique functioning whole and, as such, requires individualized analysis.
2. We assume that an estimate, or first-approximation, of an organization's character can be gained by analyzing logical responses to forces from its external environment, internal culture, and influential leaders.
3. We assert that a tentative explanation of character can be rendered through a systematic analysis of the effect of these influences upon (a) each other, (b) the structure and subsystems of activities, and (c) the total organization.

If these premises appear reasonable, our approach to analyzing character is merely the application of accepted scientific methods to the study of a total object—in our case, an organization. First, we identify strategic variables that act as forces to which the organization must react. Second, we make tentative estimates (inferences) as to the influence of the variables on each other, on the design of subsystems of activities, and on the total organization. Third, we observe activities to see if our tentative inferences are supported. If the inferences are supported by observations, we can assume that they represent reality; if not, they are rejected. At the conclusion of the analysis, we should have an understanding of why the organization has adopted its particular mode of operation and, with a sufficiently broad perspective, we can also explain organization personality. The approach is well-suited to research into organizations, because it can combine causal analysis with system thinking.

Classifications of Strategic Variables

It is commonly felt that the strategic variables that shape the personality of an enterprise come from three major sources: (1) *external environment,* representing the ecology of the organization, (2) *internal climate* representing its heritage, and (3) *traits of leaders* representing the influence of individuals. Under each of these classifications of major sources of influence, we find such strategic variables as those illustrated in Figure 9-3. Though this is not an exhaustive set of strategic variables, it represents the basic forces considered to be critical by management consultants.[8]

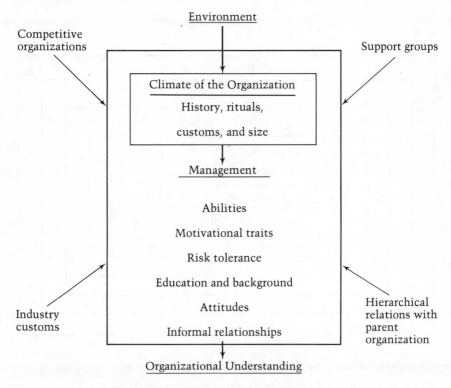

Source: Robert Grandford Wright, *Mosaics of Organization Character,* 1975. Used by permission of Dunellen Publishing Company, University Press of Cambridge Series.

FIGURE 9–3. Strategic Variables Commonly Cited as Crucial in Determining Organization Character

The Path of the Analysis.[9]

A study of the character of an organization begins with a broad view of strategic variables in the firm's extended external environment. It is the entire "field," "life space," "supersystem," or "ecology" to which the total entity must respond in order to exist. Next the study focuses on the organization's immediate external environment so that the influence of such factors as its location, competition, and markets can be analyzed. The investigation is then narrowed to the enterprise's internal climate, its traditions, history, customs, and rituals. Honed one step further, it examines the traits of the leaders, their professional backgrounds, attitudes, motivations, and tolerance for risk. Finally, the analysis relates the findings originally expected to actual operations through visual observations of the enterprise—its work place, processes, and subsystems. In this way, an estimate of its character emerges as patterns of reinforcing behavior are observed. Figure 9-4 depicts the path of the analysis.

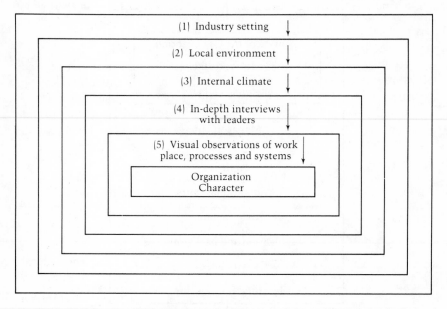

Source: Larry Senn, *Organization Character As a Methodological Tool in the Analysis of Business Organization* (Ph.D. dissertation, 1970).

FIGURE 9–4. Path of Analysis to Explain Organization Character

CHARACTER OF ONE KIND OF ORGANIZATION

To illustrate the use of the analysis, it is helpful to turn to an example. Though the case provided is a brief composite, it is sufficiently thorough to display the method of investigation.

Suppose that you are a management consultant retained to study a business organization that specializes in physical testing of products and parts. It is equipped to perform environmental, vibration, fluid flow, and leak detection testing. The firm—let's call it Allied Test Laboratories (ATL)—is purely a service business to manufacturers.[10] It does no manufacturing of any kind. Annual revenues are $800,000, 95 percent of which comes from government contractors such as producers of aerospace components and missiles, while the remaining 5 percent comes from commercial manufacturers of electronics and aircraft.

Allied Test Laboratories is modestly housed in a 30,000-square-foot structure that includes a test laboratory, administrative quarters, and sales offices. The firm is located in a metropolitan city near its customers and has easy access to all commonly used modes of transportation.

ATL's organization is staffed by forty employees. The people are formally arranged somewhat along functional lines of engineering, sales, and laboratory, as seen in the formal organization chart depicted in Figure 9-5.

As an analyst, you know before going further that the organization is a system of activities. You also realize that the firm must have aspects common to all organizations such as delegative processes, formal communications, systems of incentives and control, and functional roles of management. What you do not now know is how and why they are designed and maintained in their unique way. This is your object in analyzing ATL's character.

You need to consider first the nature of the firm's industry. Then you can proceed with the inquiry, converging from this wide view—local external environment; internal atmosphere; traits of the firm's leaders; and the work place, processes, and subsystems—to specific observations of the firm's mode of operation.

Industry Setting

You find the *industry* to be relatively new. It emerged in response to a need for independent testing of missile and aerospace hardware and, to a lesser degree, for outside testing of increasingly sophisticated commercial products. The industry is loosely structured with individual firms clustered around major companies requiring their testing services. These large firms subcontract testing jobs of varying types to small labs for several reasons: First, tests by independent sources are often required to ensure objectivity; and second, tests made by producers carry high overhead rates for fixed costs (as high as 280 percent over the cost of the testing job, which we find "kill cost comparisons" to the advantage of small laboratories). If testing equipment is purchased, its high cost makes it difficult to enter the industry. Leasing the equipment, or purchasing it only as required for specific testing jobs, makes it easy.

Now you analyze each aspect of the industry to learn what its probable role relationship is to other aspects and what its impact is on ATL.

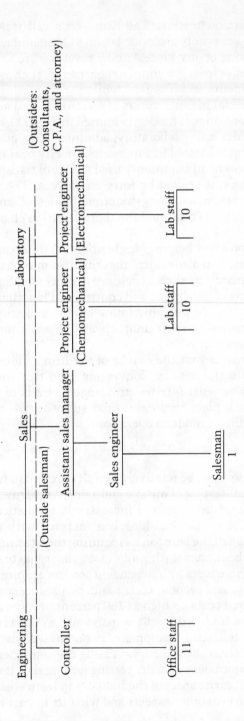

FIGURE 9–5. Formal Organization Chart—Allied Test Laboratories

One reason that few industrial customs have developed is the youth of the industry and its lack of concentration. As an analyst, you believe it to be keenly competitive because of ease of entry into the business; therefore, you think ATL would need aggressive sales efforts with an accompanying flexibility to compete for various kinds of testing jobs. And further, you infer that ATL leases its equipment and space to keep fixed costs low. If the volume of testing business is as "hot-and-cold" as the competitive concentration and customer needs suggest (coupled with the need to keep fixed costs down), you might also tentatively reason that ATL probably hires certain employees when business is active and dismisses them when it slackens. Remember, all of these inferences are temporary. They will be reinforced, or rejected, based upon your subsequent findings.

Local Environment

You then identify and evaluate certain aspects of ATL's *local environment.* You find that the market for testing services, while sufficient to support the local industry, is erratic. At a given time the demand for these services can be great or small. Further, eight small laboratories and one major laboratory all compete for the available testing business. Customers expect reliable, prompt, and convenient testing service of a highly technical nature. They are represented by some 700 purchasing managers and engineers who heavily influence buying decisions. Contracts are generally awarded on the basis of competitive bids.

Further inferences can now be drawn and prior assumptions given support or questioned. It seems reasonable that ATL would minimize capitalization, maintain a high degree of flexibility, and offer employees incentives for technical innovation and ingenuity. Further, the company probably would provide high monetary or nonmonetary incentives for the sales force, but the technical personnel would enjoy higher status due to the innovative nature of their work. And, finally, since the testing jobs frequently require crash programs at full speed, one would expect to see a sort of freeform organizational arrangement. By freeform, we mean an organization in which members' roles and relationships vary depending upon the different demands of changing situations. In such a fluid system, formal arrangements are temporarily changed, communications and delegation are direct, authority centers vary in relationship to each other, and controls and incentives are adjusted rapidly to respond to the demands from the work engagement. As an example, though one manager may carry the title of engineer, on a certain major testing job this person may be assigned to the "graveyard shift" to fill the need for a mechanic or technician or both.

Cultural Aspects

Now you narrow the analysis inward to ATL's *internal traditions.* You study aspects of its history, customs, and rituals that may give it distinctiveness. You find that ATL was formed three years ago by an engineer gifted in the field of physical testing. Needed: business knowledge, capital, and contacts in the markets! The founder aligned himself and his aspirations with a cousin, well educated in business, and a friend, well respected in the testing field. Capital was needed; however, the partners did not want to lose control of the enterprise. They assigned high priority to the technical phases of the venture instead of marketing and administrative activities, because 75 percent of the revenues came from so-called "house accounts"—those developed by management. Because of their inexperience, the managerial trio was filled with anxiety, if not trepidation, about the general welfare of the business in a fast-moving environment.

ATL, though a small organization, envelops a number of different groups specialized by skills, interests, and authority levels. They include top management, middle-level technical personnel, sales force, and administrative office staff.

Although coordination of the enterprise is mandatory, at ATL's formation it was agreed that each of the three partners would hold equal authority for the top-level decisions. The partners hold evening meetings for policy decisions, because the demands during the business day preclude their getting together then to make decisions.

One can now reason that a status hierarchy has emerged within ATL whereby technicians have more prestige than nontechnicians. In turn, formal arrangements are distorted and various factions are based on levels of skills, functional activities, and levels of status. The incentive system, assuming consistency, would be designed to reward technical innovation, with less capability to reward marketing and administrative improvements. This appears reasonable since house accounts ensure a sufficient level of business activity, and administrative paper work is perceived as incidental to the technical activities. Because individual sales are large but infrequent, you believe that salespeople are compensated with straight salaries and, as warranted, provided with nonfinancial symbols of success.

You, as investigator, reason further that some means have been developed to resolve conflicts among the three leaders and to provide seasoned advice concerning the welfare of the firm. Checking a step ahead, you find that a senior consultant, well versed in the industry, acts as an outside advisor. He attends the weekly "executive meeting" held each Tuesday evening, an activity that has become ritualized. There should be few problems with bureaucratic rigidities because of the youth of ATL and its continuing need for abrupt change.

Leadership Traits

The managers of ATL are young but experienced in the technical phases of the firm's operation. The partner-manager in charge of the laboratory is twenty-nine, the sales manager thirty-eight, and the chief engineer thirty-two years of age. Each might be termed an "entrepreneurial type" in that each accepts high risks for high returns, is hardworking and technically competent, and is emotionally as well as intellectually involved in the firm and its fate. They are directly concerned with every major testing job and accept the responsibility for its final approval. The managers realize that each testing job places unique stresses on the firm by requiring different techniques, equipment, work force, decisions, speed, and relationships with customers. In addition, they are prepared to react quickly to major testing projects that may come in with little or no warning.

They recognize that the future of ATL is largely determined by the activities of other businesses, to which their firm must be prepared to respond. Notwithstanding, the firm's leaders are competent, ambitious, and eager to take advantage of all reasonable business opportunities.

From these personal traits of ATL's leadership, you reason further that the firm might understandably be overmanaged in the technical areas to the neglect of nontechnical matters. In addition, you may expect to find authority in the laboratory relatively centralized, with narrow spans of management. And you may conclude that although planning is at best tenuous, ATL is destined to grow as far as its market potential permits.

A SYNTHESIS: THE PERSONALITY OF ATL

You now have a set of original assumptions about the types of responses this company is likely to make to certain strategic variables. Through personal observation of ATL's work place, processes, and subsystems, you can either verify them as valid or reject them as unsupported. As groups of reinforced assumptions are gathered, a composite of ATL's character can be drawn:

> ATL is an aggressive, viable company with undertones of an impersonal attitude toward its employees. Its authority centers are tightly held at the top in the technical areas. Though the organization is designed along functional lines, ATL accords elite treatment to its engineers and technicians. As a consequence, an informal but sanctioned status hierarchy distorts the levels of formal groupings. Divisions of labor are tentative so that roles can be changed as major projects impose unforeseen stresses on the firm. Spans of management are narrow because of tightly held authority arising from the highly technical nature of the work and the use of temporary personnel. Delegative processes and communications often are facilitated outside of

formal arrangements. Control is assiduously applied in the testing area while carelessly imposed over other arenas of activities. Incentive systems reward innovation, flexibility, and adaptability to task technical demands. The patterns of leadership are often autocratic because of the urgency of projects, the burden of responsibility for project approval, the concentration of technical competence, and the inability or unwillingness to delegate authority, thereby hindering the development of subordinates. ATL is subjected to wide variation in its volume of work, causing erratic patterns of behavior; however, its personality suggests that adaptation, conflict, and change are basic traits required and adopted for its survival.

Though a rough portrait, this appraisal of ATL's character can explain why internal processes and subsystems are established as they are and, in sum, lead to a better understanding of the firm's behavior. Having delineated these features, you can also get a better "feel" for the types of ideas and people that are compatible to ATL's unique personality. You will have a deeper appreciation for the subtleties that give the enterprise its distinct atmosphere, for its philosophy, and for the way it incorporates these aspects into its mode of operation.

Refining the Study of Organization Character

The foregoing analysis of ATL provides only a crude estimate, or first approximation, of its personality. Nevertheless, its results seem superior to studies that reveal only descriptive information, or explanations of only fragments of an organization.

To refine the accuracy of your view of forces shaping organization character, thereby sharpening its focus, you may proceed to study not only the factual environment as you perceive it, but also to interpret the situation as it is perceived by the leaders of the firm. To do so, you must identify managers' positions. These are the people whose influence counts, people whose attitudes are reflected throughout the enterprise. These men and women should be interviewed in depth to ascertain their appraisal of the operating situation. This refined search should probe for their evaluations in the following way: (1) Seek their definition of the local competitive environment and the challenges facing the company; (2) review the firm's history with them, paying particular attention to strategies employed and the careers of its leaders; (3) identify the goals, tactics, and biases of these people and of the enterprise. From these *interpretations*, you can again analyze cause-effect relationships and grasp the personality as an integrated whole. Again, this can be accomplished not by adding up all the parts to get a total, but rather by extracting the common denominators, which represent a fairly consistent set of behavior patterns imposed on the organization.

Organizational behavior is the net sum of responses to forces as the leaders of the organization perceive these forces and as they evaluate them to search for appropriate responses. Thus, this analysis of the *refined personality* may not square exactly with the original *estimated personality* because of differing perceptions and interpretations. You may find some areas emphasized and others needlessly slighted; or a firm working at cross-purposes with itself; or other inconsistencies stemming from leaders' differing definitions of the situation.

There is a major advantage to refining an inquiry in this way. Often discrepancies surface between the reality and the perception of forces that require reactions. As a result, management responds in a rational way, but to events as it interprets events. Thus, disparities can grow between the organization's patterns of behavior and demands from its environments. A student of organization character can frequently assist leaders to redefine their appraisal of the situation so that they can react more appropriately, and thus be more effective. Leaders try to adapt their responses to their interpretations of the operating situation. By guiding managers to a more accurate assessment of their operating world, an analyst can be a means of harmonizing organizational arrangements with the environment.

Use of the Organization Character Analysis

Though a valuable way of thinking about organizations, the concept of organization character should be applied prudently:

1. The student of organizations, given the current state of knowledge, should be satisfied with a *general* explanation that lacks scientific precision.
2. The analyst *must see the need* for understanding a firm's personality, realizing that it is required to explain behavior as well as to understand the ideas and people compatible with the organization.
3. The investigator should avoid criticizing organizational arrangements until able to explain the reasons for their existence and view them in the context of other related activities.
4. The student should also be willing, temporarily, to abandon approaches that give only fragmented understanding. When one has gained an overall comprehension, narrowed, specific studies can be invaluable, particularly since at that point detailed findings can be made more meaningful by a holistic awareness of the organization.

If these caveats are observed, the student has an effective analytical tool to better understand social institutions. The approach may seem unconventional, but the student of organizations needs unusual means to explain social phenomena. As Professor Larrabee observed, the social scientist can learn methods of study from his counterpart in the physical sciences:

> The biochemist did not conclude, because the methods used in the analysis of simple inorganic compounds would not work in dealing with complex organic substances, that therefore no adequate methods were possible. . . . On the contrary, they (sic) went ahead to invent new organic methods as well as new techniques for the understanding of organic part-whole relationships.[11]

SUMMARY

In this chapter, we have reviewed the concept of organization character. Though complex, the analysis provides insights into organizational behavior. An enterprise's character is studied by analyzing the impact of variables that influence its total development and behavior. To a degree, the concept serves to knit classical and neoclassical organization theory into a cohesive analytical whole explaining the dynamics of an enterprise.

Organization character is important to a student because it explains the enterprise's unique behavior. Further, the personality influences a firm's tolerance for certain modes of operation and determines the types of people who can effectively function within the atmosphere created by that character. And finally, such organizational studies emphasize the influence of behavioral aspects on the structure of an organization.

The analytical model for understanding organization character was presented, together with a brief analysis of one organization. We found that through a study of the forces converging on an organization—the industry setting, the local external environment, cultural aspects, and leadership traits—its character can be estimated. Once the analyst becomes aware of its overall character, the image can be refined through analyses of the perceptions of leaders and through more specific investigations, all relating back to the total functioning organization.

There are barriers in using this approach to study organizations. They are the same as those blocking any approach to explain complex systems of activities. Notwithstanding, the approach provides a more comprehensive awareness of organizational realities than do internalized studies limited to either structural arrangements or dynamic interaction.

DISCUSSION QUESTIONS

1. Why is an appraisal of an organization's character valuable to a student of organizations? To a job applicant? To an employee? To the principal leader? To an outside consultant? To the public relations director of the enterprise?

2. What are the hazards of using the organization character analysis?

3. How does the idea of organization character relate to other organization theories: classical, neoclassical, social systems, and the conceptual overview?

4. Why is it difficult for an insider to analyze the character of the organization? Why can't an insider do a better analysis? Or, is there a benefit, a "stranger value," to being an outsider?

5. Capturing a likeness of the character of an organization provides only a rough estimate of reality. The approximation lacks precision. What are the costs of applying the organization character approach? The benefits? And the other options available to us?

6. Study a specific small organization that is now unfamiliar to you. Use the converging analysis shown in Figure 9-4. What did you discover in your exploration? How much time did you invest on site?

10

A Composite View of Organizations

To realize any relations, even if they are correct, is not decisive; what is decisive is that they must be the relations structurally required in view of the whole, arising, conceived, used as parts in their function in the structure. And this holds equally for all operations of traditional logic when used in genuine thought processes.

Max Wertheimer[1]

To this point we have viewed human organizations in various ways to understand that each has a number of distinct though related dimensions. We have also examined each dimension, from simple elements to complex character, to develop a more complete awareness of the behavior of an organization. In doing so, we intentionally fragmented the on-going organization to examine its parts, stripped it of certain intricacies that unduly complicate understanding. Now let's put it all back together.

We are now ready to portray a composite view of the parts of organizations discussed earlier. Each view—elements, types, needs, life cycle, anatomy, authority bonds, culture, and character—can be now seen in relationship to the others and to the overall behavior of an organization. Further, distinction between descriptive teachings (how things are) and normative guidelines (how things should be) will be made, so that the reader can identify frameworks designed for descriptive, normative, explanatory, and evaluative purposes.

Obviously, the first goal of understanding organizations is to develop a comprehensive awareness of them. But beyond intellectual enrichment, organizational understanding is commonly of some practical use. Hence, at the end of this chapter, we will consider its most important objectives. We will weigh the value of such study in diagnosing organizational efficiency and effectiveness, predicting organizational behavior, and determining appropriate leadership patterns.

REVIEW AND SYNTHESIS OF ORGANIZATIONAL PERSPECTIVES

A composite view can be best gained through an illustration, coupled with explanation. Figure 10-1, "Composite of Organizational Perspectives," shows the development of the models presented previously. The arabic numerals indicate the chapters in which each viewpoint was presented. Under each title the reader will find certain traits listed that are characteristic of that particular viewpoint. The models of organization behavior begin with observing a simple organization and progress through various stages to end with an analysis of a specific organization. Now let us briefly reconsider the nature of the various perspectives as they relate to each other and as they contribute toward explanation of the behavior of a specific enterprise.

We initially viewed an organization as a *social system* in Chapter 1, "Role of Organizations." It presented a *simplex model.* We found that an organization forms when two or more people coordinate their activities toward a common goal or goals. We further observed certain traits common to all human social systems. Organizations are *social inventions* of man. They are in part designed by people, in contrast to natural systems such as astronomy, physics, and chemistry. Thus, they are *imperfect*—the consequence of *partly designed arrangements* and *partly random responses.* Though social systems are distinguished from natural systems, they are artificial only to the extent that they are products of people's inventiveness. They are the result of a spontaneous human penchant to aspire toward goals beyond the reach of any particular person. Hence, *social systems are determined not by Nature but by human nature.*

Social systems, like most organic structures, are *open systems* that exchange resources, including information, with their environments. They are marked by a high degree of openness; people elect to join or leave the institution. A social system is *stable yet viable.* Stability is assured when activities are governed to remain within defined limits; viability, when processes permit reactions to environmental changes. Organizations thus exist in a state of *dynamic equilibrium,* or moving balance.

To maintain an appropriate degree of change and stability, a representative sample of activities and output is fed back into the system so that succeeding activities can be controlled. The feedback mechanism is artificial and commonly termed *servomechanism.* This ser-

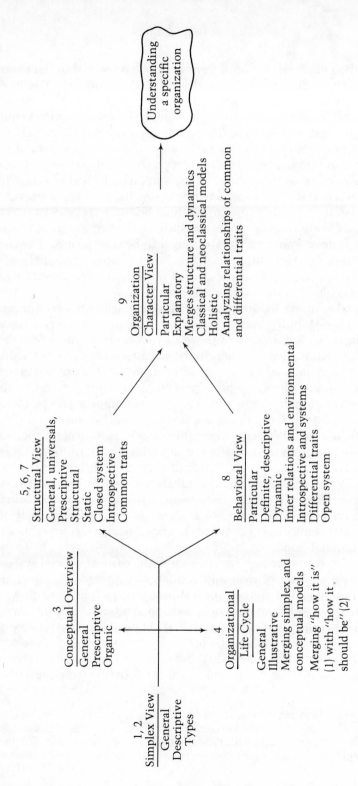

FIGURE 10–1. Composite of Organizational Perspectives (Arabic numerals indicate relevant chapters)

vomechanism provides feedback from both behavior within the enterprise and events outside it. Internal feedback is required to achieve stability, efficiency, and orderliness. External feedback enables the system to react to changing environmental forces, thus maintaining viability. The process is analogous to that in human physiology in which the body's communications network facilitates stability and adaptability. Motor coordination and posture control represent internal feedback that has a decisive effect on the stability of the human biological system. The changing external stimuli such as temperature, light, and pressures call forth homeostatic mechanisms to produce bodily change. Social systems usually demonstrate modest adaptive behavior compared with that of the human system. Organizations can be transformed dramatically and quickly. More often, however, they change grudgingly and slowly. This fact is indeed at the core of our dilemma in maintaining sound yet flexible institutional arrangements.

Artificial systems are designed to fill basic needs and perform crucial functions—stability, viability, communications, divisions of labor, and coordination—analogous to those carried on by natural systems. These functions require the common structures and schemes we discussed in Chapters 5, 6, and 7. Though social systems are contrived, they share some of the same basic properties of natural systems. An organization of human beings, however, is more complex, less predictable, and more mystical than most aspects of natural systems.

Viewed as a social system, an organization is a group of people, but one structured by roles. The roles are integrated by authority, status, communications, control, and rewards to direct them toward enterprise goals. This way of thinking about organizations raises two important points: First, the need for integrating in order to attain objectives brings on a need for central direction, or leadership. As with biological organisms, some central agent, must make the critical decisions requisite to organizational cohesiveness, coordination, and viability. In social structures a leader is such an agent. Second, the parts of a social system are not made up only of men and women but, more accurately, are comprised of men and women with mutually dependent roles. As a consequence, the behavior of a social system is often more continuous and predictable than that of an individual. Thus, we are better able to describe, analyze, and explain the behavior of a system of individuals than the behavior of the individual persons who comprise a system. There is an organizational continuity, which William Haines describes in this way:

> The social organization maintains its role structure amid a flow of constantly changing individual persons occupying these roles. Men are continually hired, fired, promoted, and demoted. They join and resign. They are born and they die. The organizations potentially, at least, go on forever.[2]

The word *potentially* is important here. It leads us to consider the conditions that impede an extended life span. Further, it leads us to examine the traits of an organization required to ensure long-run success.

Chapter 2, "Types of Organizations," dealt with classifying organizations as to their fundamental purpose, social or economic. As such, it merely defined the types of activities pursued through organized efforts—a simplified viewpoint.

Chapter 3, "Needs of Organizations," departed from the typical avenue for discussion of organizations. It introduced a new view *based upon the simplex model*. It encouraged the reader to picture a *conceptual overview* of an organization by considering an *idealized model*. It asserted that a sound organization is a *goal-seeking social system* that should be *internally consistent* and *environmentally consonant*. Like the discussion of social systems in Chapter 1, the model is for general use. Unlike the descriptive discussion in Chapter 1, the conceptual model is *prescriptive* in nature. The presentation encourages the reader to reconceive his or her image of an enterprise and to consider *its* needs.

The conceptual viewpoint was presented at that point to broaden the reader's frame of reference to the overall organization, to introduce the organic nature of organizations. This broadened perspective served to avoid premature concentration on the internal affairs of enterprises.

Often, people believe that they have a useful, comprehensive view of an organization because they are participants in one. Though accurate, their view is not comprehensive; it is narrowly introspective because of their position in the organization. As a consequence, they have a narrowed, if not slanted, view of the enterprise. It is somewhat like a person's describing a cup and saucer while looking out from the bottom of the cup. Though the image described is neither inaccurate nor intentionally distorted, it simply does not encompass the total object. In part, the mission of Chapter 3 was to urge the reader, for once, to hold the cup and saucer at arm's length—to separate the organization from the reader as a student of organization—so as to be in a position to view the system as a whole.

The second objective of presenting the conceptual model in Chapter 3 was to provide a template of idealized organizational design against which observations of actual organization behavior could be compared, contrasted, and evaluated. With the conceptual overview as a guide, observations of variations can be identified. Evaluations then can be made and recommendations for improvements advanced. The conceptual model also holds important implications for both appropriate organization and leadership behavior. Therefore, we will return to it later in this chapter.

Chapter 4, "Life Cycle of an Organization," also swung the reader's attention off the usual path by which organization study is approached.

It portrayed a hypothetical organization as it moved along a time continuum marked by changes in environmental forces and internal culture. Its progress over an intentionally accelerated life cycle—formation, maturity, old age and, in this instance, demise—was described. This was done to *merge the simplex view of behavior and the conceptual model of behavior to show the relationships* between "how things are" and "how things should be." The example described features of behavior, both functional and malfunctional, that could occur in any enterprise. Thus, lessons from this study apply *generally* to all organizations.

In Chapter 5, "Structure of Organizations," we returned to the usual path for studying organizational behavior. Our attention was focused for the first time exclusively on the inner workings of an organization; we surveyed *classical thought,* which deals largely with the structure and subsystems basic to all forms of organizations. These common aspects include the fundamental structure to facilitate specialization, reintegration of specialized activities, direction, and control. Classical teachings, we found, concentrate on organizational components that in unison produce balance or equilibrium. The teachings are meant to be universal guidelines for general application in all organizations. They are prescriptive in that they tell the way people should be organized. Indeed, they encourage searches for the "one best way." Classical teachings are of inestimable value in producing technical and economic efficiencies within an enterprise, but this application is narrowly limited by the uniqueness of specific organizations. They provide invaluable aids to understand the structure of an organization, but with little attention devoted to its unique cultures.

Chapter 6, "Anatomy of Organizations," concentrated on drawing the structural components together into a formal, unified hierarchy. Basic organizing principles were presented and analyzed; these included spans of management, unity of management, functional foremanship, the scalar principle, and line/staff relationships. These are all *common aspects,* of concern to early traditional thinkers, who gave prescriptions of how organizations should be organized for general use. In this, they were widely concerned with the static structure that produced stability and efficiency within the organization.

Chapter 7, "Subsystems of Organizations," introduced the basic integrating elements of organizations. As with structural and anatomical arrangements that were examined in earlier chapters, elementary ways to bring on cohesiveness absorbed classical thinkers. They enunciated principles that serve as elements common to all organized endeavor, and the prescriptions for their design took on the tone of dogma for general application. Subsystems to disseminate authority, communications, incentives, and control were viewed as essential mechanisms to interlock, interrelate, and adjust individuals and subunits into a single unit in pursuit of overall goals. Though crude, these subsystems of influence, among others, interweave the fabric of human interaction. They produce structured relationships.

Chapter 8, "Culture of Organizations," dealt with organization behavior from a conventional viewpoint, but it departed in many significant ways from the structural view. It both narrowed concentration to the *inner workings* of an organization and viewed an organization in total as a dependent entity in a changing environment. Studies of the inner workings of social systems render descriptive information on what is occurring. They apply to particular organizations, with their main thrust aimed at discovering distinguishing aspects such as informal arrangements, leadership patterns, and traditional traits that temper or change structural arrangements. These studies encompass events and activities that explain the dynamics of human interaction. In a word, they are directed at finding the behavioral nature of an organization.

The illustration of the "Conceptual Overview of an Organization," Figure 10-2, marks the progress of the study from Chapter 1 through Chapter 8. The number of the chapter in which each discussion took place appears next to the feature shown. Attributes of the model in parentheses are of a structural nature, studied mostly by early contributors to organizational thought. Other features are behavioral in nature, either internal or external to the organization, and were the object of later studies by behavioralists and systems analysts.

The standpoint taken in Chapter 9, "Character of an Organization," is somewhat unorthodox in organizational studies. Yet it provides a framework though which structural and behavioral observations can be merged to explain the behavior of a specific organization. Let us stress that explanation is on a different plane of knowing than either that of prescription or description. The model presented in Chapter 9 provides an analytical framework within which to set observations so that overall explanations are brought out. First, the approach can provide an analysis of the relationships between structure and dynamics. Second, and closely related, it can produce a keen awareness of an organization's behavior by evaluating the impact of differential forces on structures and subsystems common to all organizations. Thus, the use of this analytical model provides a sketch of "real" behavior, including the "what" and "why." Most importantly, this sort of examination forces us, once again, to broaden our frame of reference from the internal view to a holistic overview of an organization. This broadened outlook is required to make a comprehensive evaluation of any given institution.

So over the course of the book, we have looked at organizations from various vantage points to better understand them—simplistically, structurally, dynamically, analytically. Consider now, how these perspectives can benefit a member of an organization.

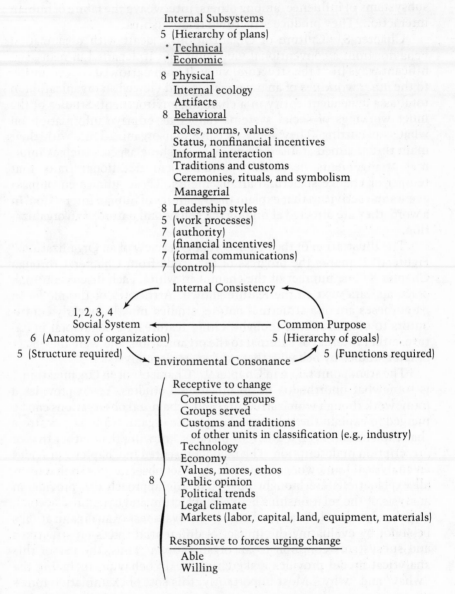

Internal Subsystems

5 (Hierarchy of plans)
* Technical
* Economic
8 Physical
　Internal ecology
　Artifacts
8 Behavioral
　Roles, norms, values
　Status, nonfinancial incentives
　Informal interaction
　Traditions and customs
　Ceremonies, rituals, and symbolism
　Managerial
8 Leadership styles
5 (work processes)
7 (authority)
7 (financial incentives)
7 (formal communications)
7 (control)

Internal Consistency

1, 2, 3, 4
Social System　　　　　　　　　　　Common Purpose
6 (Anatomy of organization)　　　　5 (Hierarchy of goals)
5 (Structure required)　　　　　　　　5 (Functions required)
Environmental Consonance

Receptive to change
　Constituent groups
　Groups served
　Customs and traditions
　　of other units in classification (e.g., industry)
　Technology
　Economy
　Values, mores, ethos
8　Public opinion
　Political trends
　Legal climate
　Markets (labor, capital, land, equipment, materials)

Responsive to forces urging change
　Able
　Willing

(Features in parentheses are structural in nature; other features are behavioral and systemic.)
*Not discussed in text.

FIGURE 10–2.　Conceptual Overview of an Organization

THE VALUE OF COMPOSITE VIEWS

Now what does it all mean? How can composite views of organizational perspectives be of value? Examining organizations from different vantage points, as we have said, can lead to a greater awareness and a keener appreciation for these complex social contrivances. This is the primary objective of the type of analysis presented here. But knowing alone is not generally the final disposition of findings. The object of most knowledge is the solution of problems. And, from a composite perspective, an analytical framework is developed for the purpose of dealing with them. Problems in human organizations generally grow out of current operating practices, anticipating future responses to pressures, or the roles and responsibilities of leadership. Understanding the character of a specific organization as it relates to the conceptual model of sound behavior can be an invaluable method of analyzing and solving such problems.

Let us now briefly evaluate the applicability of the composite of organizational perspectives to the four problem areas depicted in Figure 10-3: organizational understanding, organizational appraisal, prediction of organization behavior, and an approach to a theory of leadership.

Organizational Understanding

The major goal of the composite of organizational perspectives shown in Figure 10-1 and the conceptual overview shown in Figure 10-2 is to provide guidelines for a comprehensive understanding, an overall awareness of the microsociety in which, presumably, most people are functioning and contributing.

Cultural sophistication *is* important. As with an enlightened citizen in the broader society, activities and events take on greater, often new, meanings when one can evaluate observations. So it is with the sophisticated person in a complex organization. Such an individual understands that organizations, like individuals, have needs. A person can analyze patterns of behavior to find the reasons behind them and, in finding underlying causes, can develop new vistas for appreciating institutionalized processes. The result is cultural awareness. In turn, the aware citizen in an "enterprise society" can be more tolerant of operational idiosyncracies, of knowing their causes; he or she can: Understand why structural arrangements are required; predetermine the compatibility of new ideas and innovations with the character of the enterprise; accurately assess patterns of activities and behavior that fit the cultural patterns of the institution; and can more precisely evaluate the types of people who could identify with the culture, as well as those who might be misfits.

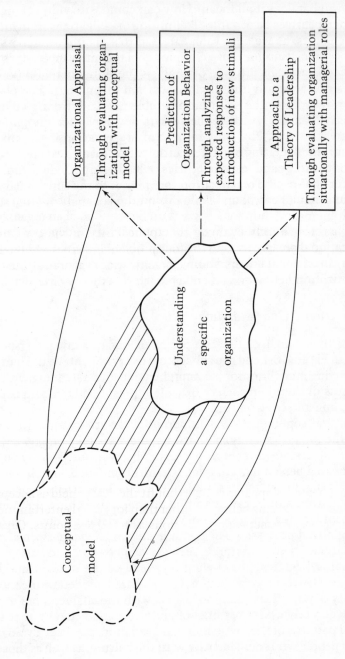

FIGURE 10–3. Inferences from the Composite of Organization Perspectives

Consider, by contrast, the plight of the organizationally naïve individual. This person would feel subjected to arbitrarily imposed constraints; would chafe under seemingly unexplainable structural and cultural peculiarities, or inconsistencies; would have recommendations rejected because they are ill-timed or ill-fitted to the organization; might attempt to emulate the role and behavior of others but without understanding why certain behavior is appropriate or inappropriate; and would be ill-equipped to evaluate the various types of persons whose efforts would enhance the enterprise. The naïve person is culturally deprived of the chance to mesh his or her potential contribution into the main stream of complex organized activities—is culturally disadvantaged, at least when compared with an individual versed in organizational realities.

A composite of organizational perspectives can provide basic insights into social endeavor. It can extend the candle of awareness as a guide to enlarge the horizons of one's understanding of an organization. Though lighting a candle often only emphasizes the depth of darkness rather than fully illuminating a subject, awareness of the murky unknowns of organization behavior is the first and perhaps the most basic lesson. Knowing what one does not know is, after all, one mark of an educated individual.

Organizational Appraisal

In appraising something or someone, we make decisions concerning such qualities as rightness or wrongness, appropriateness or inappropriateness, congruence or irrelevance, strength or weakness. To make such judgments, we must have mental (cognitive) sets of accepted behavior against which we relate the events we observe for comparisons (fits) and contrasts (misfits). For instance, if a person makes a derogatory judgment about the behavior of a president in a certain situation, we must assume that the detractor possesses a model of expectations of presidential behavior under the circumstances involved. In this example, the actual behavior apparently does not fit the model held as acceptable. The object of observing behavior, other than for casual entertainment, is lost unless we have sets of expectations as reference points. Organizations are appraised—effective or ineffective, efficient or inefficient—based upon observations of actual behavior measured against some model of sound conduct.

In this book we have introduced a model to act as one cognitive set—the conceptual overview—to serve as a template for idealized organizational behavior. If a sound enterprise strives for a high degree of internal consistency and environmental consonance, then these requirements may be used as a basis upon which an analyst's actual observations and understanding of an organization are built. When processes, structures, subsystems, events, and activities square with the model, the ideal model fits the observed data; and the appraiser can simply document this finding as a part of the "organizational checkup." When deviations are found, particularly gross ones, the analyst can recommend remedies to bring the behavior of the organization more closely in line with the model of acceptable behavior. Let us stress that the "treatment" can now be tailored to fit the conceptual model *and* the unique personality of the enterprise because the analyst has gained comprehensive perspective—a feel—for both the organization's character and the organizational ideal.

Predicting Organization Behavior

With our current knowledge, predicting organization behavior is highly conjectural. And the composite of organization discussed here provides no sure cure for improving our deficiencies as forecasters. As we have attempted to show throughout this work, a human organization is immensely complex. It is woven of numerous mutually dependent events and processes. Though critical to an analysis, they cannot be quantified or even numerically ranked as to their relative influence. Hence, forecasting models used today can provide only a rough sketch, or approximation, of future operating realities. All that we can now hope for is a crude portrait of organization behavior.

Certain basic predictive capabilities can be safely asserted from studies of a composite of a specific organization. First, structured, collective behavior is more predictable than self-determined, individual behavior. Second, decisions are more apt to be rational when they are subjected to review by others, particularly if the reviewers are persons from whom the decision maker seeks esteem (either as individuals or reference groups). And third, most organizations react to changing environmental conditions. Hence, the same analytical approach may be used to predict behavior as is used to explain organization character. That is, to estimate the changing behavior of any complicated structure, including human organizations, one probes into the system at its most predictable point or points. In turn, one assumes rational responses to changing forces calling for general reactions, but with a minimum of random reaction.

As a corollary, to predict shifts in the national economy, one evaluates the influence of a change in a highly predictable economic indicator, while holding other sectors constant. An economist may evaluate the impact of an increase in the supply of money, the influence of new capital investment, or the effect of government spending on the system. The condition of constancy is then released to predict the influence of the change on each of the flows (subsystems) that are individually and mutually affected. It is then possible to estimate the net impact of the change of the factor on the total system. In forecasting macroeconomic behavior, the analyst would not usually be concerned with such aspects as the economic behavior of autonomous units, household inventories, or perhaps the foreign sector, because these elements are highly sensitive to random variations. Nor would an economic forecaster be concerned with the changing institutional structure in making short-run predictions. Rather, the analyst would study the influence of flows and stocks of money on the existing structure.

In a similar way, to predict the behavior of a social enterprise, an analyst breaks into the organization model to anticipate the most reasonably predictable behavior. Though lacking the larger number of events to increase the chances of accuracy enjoyed by an economic analyst, one can predict organization behavior within an acceptable range of certainty. The organizational analyst attempts to evaluate the impact of such changes as a new environmental force, new leadership, or changed goals on the organization. After considering the influence of a determinant on organization behavior, and holding related functions and subsystems constant, the analyst releases other related variables to estimate the net impact of a change on the total system. In making an initial estimate of future behavior, the organizational analyst would not deal with minute detail or major anatomical aspects of the organization structure. The investigator would instead estimate the short-run influence on the existing structure of changing critical external and internal determinants of behavior.

For example, consider a study to predict the behavior of a company that is found to be a polluter of water, air, or land. Before external concern mounts to an uproar, the firm attempts to neutralize adverse opinion by pacifying environmentalist groups and others at the forefront of discontent, lobbying for protective legislation, and advertising the firm's great contribution to the local economy. But, in spite of these efforts to nullify threats to its present operation, public opinion bristles. Then political figures respond, also pressuring for reform. Lawsuits are threatened. Environmental forces—public opinion, political sentiments, and threats of legal action—arise and impinge upon the firm, forcing it to take remedial action.

With a composite portrait of the firm, the analyst infers that it will respond grudgingly to external pressures, with corrective measures that will only be compromises to impede regulatory legislation. Further, the investigator predicts that high incentives will be given to employees for suggestions to remedy the problems, together with stringent penalties for violations of antipollution procedures. This tack, it is thought, will encourage employees to believe in the sincerity of the firm's efforts to resolve its ecological problems. The analyst also predicts an increase in public relations activities to persuade the firm's public that its efforts are genuine.

The predicted strategy includes initial changes in subsystems for certain control and incentives as well as increased activity in public, political, and industry relations coupled with a finer division of labor in these areas. At this point, it is reasoned that other systems and structures will remain undisturbed.

This evaluation leads from an environmental force inward to its impact upon leaders and customary modes of behavior, aspects that are generally highly predictable. The analysis then moves to the redesign of common arrangements, internal systems and structure. At this point in the investigation, the impact of these initial changes can be estimated on related systems such as communications and authority centers. Finally, the net sum of responses can be foretold as the final statement of change predicted for the firm. Observations of actual change will then substantiate or refine initial predictions.

On the other hand, the study may lead to a very different conclusion. The analyst may learn that historically the leaders of the company have resisted external pressures for change. It may be that the firm has actually programmed responses to excuse its contamination of the environment; formed a bureaucratic maze of procedures to insulate itself from pressures urging change; and over the years has created a tradition for preserving the status quo. Knowing this, the analyst would reasonably predict that internal defenses would stiffen to resist growing pressures for change. But he or she would also recognize that these conditions cause rigidities within that lead to serious discords between the company and its environment.

Though a crude predictive tool, the approach appears to be superior to other techniques available. The accuracy of the forecast is enhanced by knowledge of the critical variables that shape organization behavior as well as perception of the intervening forces (leadership and tradition) that filter inputs and reactions. With intensive study and refinements of our knowledge of complex organization, we may then formulate a general theory of leadership.

APPROACH TO A GENERAL THEORY OF LEADERSHIP

There is no general theory of leadership—no coherent, comprehensive, and consistent body of scientific principles that is universally agreed upon by authorities to form the foundation for a science. This void frustrates the professionalism of management and impedes the orderly development of programs to educate leaders. It stifles the establishment of guidelines for behavior by leaders to ensure organizational efficiency and effectiveness. It is known, however, that leaders are functionally needed in all organizations. Indeed, to Chester I. Barnard's way of thinking, ". . . executive organization develops out of the need for the organization to coordinate its parts. These specialized functions," to the scholar Barnard, "grow out of the organization's need for communication and coordination."[3] It is known that leaders are needed to facilitate certain processes, to direct the efforts of people toward enterprise goals in an orderly manner. And, it is known that for an institution to fulfill its function through those processes, its leaders play a prescribed role. The leader's role often must include varied (at times, paradoxical) dimensions of system regulator, change agent, mediator, trustee, and catalyst for action.[4] Varied behavior is necessary to meet the many diverse expectations from constituent and support groups. Though we know that leadership and its processes are functionally required by all organizations, and that to fulfill its processes certain role behavior is required, no general theory has yet evolved to provide universal guidelines which, if followed, constitute sound leadership.

Yet, the underpinnings of a general theory are here, if we recast and reevaluate the notions we commonly accept about the activity of leadership. Let us think it through. An organization of people functionally requires the role behavior of leaders, as a consequence, certain processes carried through by them. This is true to the extent that if formalized arrangements are not provided to appoint leaders, some will nonetheless arise in response to informal interaction and a sensing that certain functions must be fulfilled. Coming to this conclusion in a different way, all systems—physical, biological, chemical, economic—require a catalyst, or force, to generate ordered activity. Organizations are systems. The catalyst that causes orderly motion in organizations is the delegation of authority by leaders so that other persons throughout the hierarchy can make decisions and take action toward enterprise goals. So leadership is needed.

If leadership is effective, its patterns and processes as well as the role of the leader will be to fulfill the needs of the particular organization during his or her tenure. Indeed, leaders fail when they merely use organizations to fulfill their own needs to the neglect of those of the endeavor. Leaders succeed when they recognize that the fulfillment of their needs is rooted in organizational success. Thus, they serve in behalf of the organization as their means to self-fulfillment. Each organization requires its unique balance of stability (internal consistencies maintained by system regulators) and change (environmental consonance induced by change agents). Hence, a general theory of management must be related to a general theory of organizations, because the effectiveness or ineffectiveness of leaders is intimately tied to the needs of the organization.

As an example, the measure of sound leadership in a certain enterprise at a given time may be not its growth or efficiency, but rather the leader's skill in implementing changes considered critical to the survival of the organization. By contrast, the needs of that same enterprise during a succeeding era could be measurable growth and increased internal efficiencies. In both instances, the mark of sound leadership is its ability to fulfill the role and responsibilities required by the immediate needs of the organization. Thus, it would appear that any theory developed to provide scientific principles for leaders must be inextricably anchored in a theory of the behavior of organizations. After all, superior leadership effectively stems from a leader's ability to respond to the situation and thereby provide appropriate guidance to that particular endeavor. Churchill, Lincoln, and Napoleon all had that ability. As a result, recent teachings on "contingency theory" have grown in popularity, encouraging us to recognize that leadership is sound only when it responds to demands in the context of the leadership setting.[5] This contingency idea is an extension and refinement of earlier teachings on the situational,[6] or zeitgeist, theories.[7] They are all built on the logic of structural/functional requirements. In this instance, the operating situation imposes functional requirements filled structurally by leaders.[8]

Problems commonly arise concerning the "proper" roles and responsibilities of leaders in various positions throughout organizations. Difficulties of this type are very common in rapidly changing enterprises. They are also found in slowly changing organizations where new demands on leadership have evolved but have not prompted critical self-evaluation. Under either circumstance, patterns of leadership can easily become inappropriate—hence, ineffectual.

For instance, an enterprise may have moved into a period of activity in which rigid compliance with directions and unquestioning reliance on higher authority are mandatory. Some leaders may cling to a benevolently permissive pattern suitable to an earlier time when operations were more relaxed because of less stringent environmental or internal pressures. A need for a change, furthermore, may occur in any type of organization. Imagine, for instance, a medical team managing a clinic under normal circumstances. Then picture the group being called into action to deal with a disaster in which many people are injured. The demands imposed by the more urgent situation would force the patterns of leadership to change.

Valid patterns or styles of leadership are functionally related to the demands of the operating situation, thereby appropriate. As suggested earlier, a leadership pattern that works well under one set of circumstances may appear incongruous, if not ludicrous, in another situation. For instance, the qualities expected of, and demonstrated by, the leader of an athletic team would be generally inappropriate if applied unaltered to a string ensemble. Though both organizations require leaders, the nature of the setting—subordinates, interaction, culture, and environmental demands—has changed. In turn, these changes exert pressures on a leader to redefine his or her approach if the new needs of the total endeavor and the new expectations of subordinates are to be fulfilled.

To most of us, it is axiomatic that a theory of effective leadership *should* come from realistic responses to an appraisal of the unique demands imposed by the institutional situation. Further, some of us recognize that a major source of managerial obsolescence lies in clinging to some pattern of leadership that worked in one setting but is totally ineffective in a changed one. And one thing that is certain is change. Thus, if a pattern of leadership is rooted in a certain attitude of a leader rather than a frank, objective appraisal of the needs dictated by the situation, the behavior it engenders may be inappropriate. Indeed, appropriate behavior would occur only by chance.

There are those who believe a pattern of leadership that seems to work well for a person should endure, and that one should alter the situation the pattern is intended to govern to make it consistent with that approach to leadership. Though the benefits of doing so are clear, making substantive changes in the operating situation is usually impractical for a number of reasons. First, most leaders fall heir to a unit with certain innate demands, a heritage, and a corps of various types of people. Second, the situation is dominated by systems of activities and processes beyond the control of middle and lower managers. And third, even leaders over the entire operation find that the internal culture of an enterprise is influenced by uncontrollable external forces which, in part, shape the situation. Thus, it is more realistic and practical to consider the situation as a given in the short run, and as such, one which demands that leaders tailor their leadership approach to it. This modification is very difficult, for both situations and people are more unbending than one would expect.

A theory of leadership based on situation or contingency, can be derived for a particular organization by initially analyzing a composite of the enterprise's character, or personality. In turn, this portrait of the system's behavior, together with an evaluation of its mission, can be compared and contrasted with the ideal conceptual model. In this way, it is possible to ascertain necessary systems of management such as orientation, authority, compensation, incentives, and control, as well as the necessary or proper mix of varied leadership patterns to provide for different functional needs. It will be found that the organization requires certain behavioral patterns in various positions of leadership if internal consistency and environmental consonance are to be maintained. Conflict, cooperation, or appeasement; motivation or dissuasion; integration or differentiation; aggressiveness or passiveness; competition or collectivism; innovation or conformity; and leadership patterns from dictatorial to participative-developmental to permissive—*all* are needed in varying degrees by leaders in different situations within a complex organization. The behavioral patterns required by the organization form the foundation from which a theory of leadership *for that particular enterprise* can be developed. These organizational requirements form the functional necessities for leaders and usher in theoretical patterns of appropriate behavior.

All complex organizations need people who are innovative if not imaginative, as well as people who conform. Though the eternal problem of freedom versus conformity will be left to the philosophers, a blend of diverse individual talents is required to provide an organization with balanced change. Today leaders often do not know the different types of individual behavior required for sound organizational activity. In the absence of this knowledge to assess individual contribution, but saddled with the responsibility for judging it, leaders resort to sometimes bizarre standards. As management scientist Leonard Sayles puts it:

> Not knowing how to assess Jones's contribution to effective management, we evolve irrational fetishes and taboos. The striped tie, the ivy league suit, the sheepskin, the appropriate tone of voice, automobile, wife, and home location, even the testing programs designed to exclude all but the "safe" pedestrian types: these are all manifestations of *imperfect knowledge* about how to evaluate an employee. They are *not* the inevitable products of life in a large organization.[9]

Sayles concludes, that superstitions such as "likeness is goodness" are similar to the behavior of a primitive tribe that does not understand meteorology and the occurrence of rainstorms. Their rain dances do not fall into disrepute until they develop comprehension. Understanding, in the case of organizational strength, will develop when we admit that fixed patterns of thought, family, race, backgrounds, religion, interests, do not a sound enterprise make. Diversity, not uniformity, of talents is required for complex organizational activities and responsibilities. Indeed, give us a complex organization of "look alikes" and we will have a good example of a weak organization, because certain activities and responsibilities will be ill-handled, mishandled, or not handled at all.

Further, subsystems of organizations—structural, physical, cultural, and sociopsychological—are often also designed to encourage undue degrees of conformity, because leaders are not as aware of the need for change as they are of the need for stability and efficiency. Hence, when one relates the members of such an organization to their operating assignments and its goals, the structure and subsystems simply do not fit the situation. The organization has become somewhat like an Elizabethan house in a modern neighborhood. Inept appraisals of the appropriateness of human contributions to different functions spawn stifling conformity and conservatism, leading the way to institutional obsolescence.

A complex organization requires a cast of performers to play out the roles required by the enterprise's functional needs. Consider a charitable institution, for instance. It must generate financial support to maintain itself, respond to changing needs so as to continue to justify itself, and provide services to constituent clients—the impoverished; physically, mentally, or culturally; the disabled or others in some way ill-fated. The leaders conducting the major groups of activities growing out of the institution's functional needs may be as diverse as Figure 10-4 indicates. Though diverse roles played in unison are required, their *combined* behavior meets the needs of the organization. Each leader fills a common role as the person responsible for planning, organizing, directing, and controlling activities for which he or she is directly accountable. But each also plays a unique part in filling the organization's needs for resources, stability, change, and contribution (services). By understanding both dimensions of role behavior, we move toward a general theory of leadership.

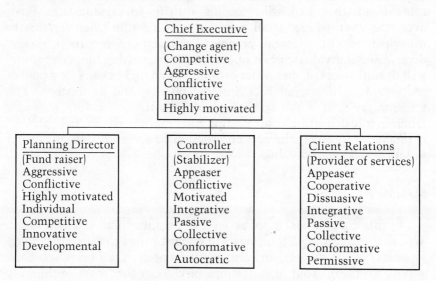

FIGURE 10–4. Varied Leaders in a Charitable Organization

If change is the object of a leader's efforts, behavioral patterns needed by the organization are estimated (expected) and then related to the actual patterns (observed). Deviations can then be spotted so that reorientation or other remedial steps can be taken. The process is prescriptive rather than preventive. It identifies appropriate behavior instead of merely correcting sources of ambiguity.

To anticipate changes in organizational needs that require new patterns of leadership behavior, an analyst would again weigh the patterns of leadership as suggested by the conceptual model (expected) against those in effect (observed). But in addition, the analyst could simulate certain desirable changes in the conceptual model—the goals, the structure of the social system, the design of the internal subsystems, or some combination of these elements—to predetermine changes required between the configuration of the current and future conceptual models (anticipative). Once this was done, the analyst would relate actual leadership behavior to anticipated needs for future leadership patterns so that possible deviations could be foreseen and programs designed to alter patterns that might become inappropriate and ineffectual. Often, programs to modify behavioral patterns include efforts to help leaders rethink situational demands, to "role play" under current and future conditions, and to encourage leaders to reappraise role relationships through increased sensitivity to new ways to interacting.[10]

It may seem paradoxical to say that, on one hand, role behavior is required that will fit into a particular organizational culture, and on the other hand, that look-alike leaders stultify an organization. First, everyone, everywhere, at all times, assumes a role when relating to other persons. But, second, complex organizations require a broadly diverse and individuated cast of players. Thus, casting for persons who will fit multifaceted, dissimilar organizational niches calls for a pool of individuals with varied backgrounds, talents, and aspirations. The growing problem is not one of role differentiation; rather, it is one wherein role definition is so exacting and pronounced that the "player" is unable to interpret the part and therein to accommodate his or her uniqueness as an individual.

SUMMARY

In this chapter, a composite view of organizations was developed. We synthesized the various views of organizations to illustrate the relatedness of the models, and also to differentiate their purposes. Each way of thinking about organizations produces other ways of thinking about them: either descriptive, prescriptive, explanative, or evaluative. In essence, we found that to this point we have considered organizations from various vantage points, or frames of reference, to better understand them. We have pondered an organization as a simple social system and as a more complex arrangement; we have examined its life cycle, its structure, its anatomy, its cohesive elements, its culture, its personality. We have also developed one conceptual model for comparative purposes.

In concert, the models presented open up a number of ways organizations can be studied. First, the major value in such exercises is that evaluations from several viewpoints give one a more comprehensive awareness of the nature of organizations. Second, the use of the composite and conceptual models offers a practical, theoretical framework for diagnosis. Third, the composite model can be used as a crude device to forecast reasonable responses to forces for change. And last, a composite of organizational perspectives can serve as the foundation upon which a general contingency theory of leadership can be built. In a word, the organizational models presented here form an analytical framework to bring about comprehension, analysis, prediction, and effectiveness.

Nonetheless, there are major barriers confronting leaders who attempt to bring their enterprises in line with the ideal conceptual model of efficient and effective behavior. The difficulties innate in maintaining a stable yet viable enterprise in turn carry trenchant implications for leaders throughout an enterprise. Chapter 11 will deal with certain of these implications for leadership in managing organizations.

DISCUSSION QUESTIONS

1. "To realize any relations," Max Wertheimer concludes, "even if they are correct, is not decisive . . ." Why is his conclusion especially pertinent to understanding organizations?

2. Why are various organizational perspectives required? Why not begin with the total overview—organization character?

3. Why aren't organizations explained entirely by the logic of structural answers to functional necessities to reach goals?

4. What benefits can be gained from comparing and contrasting the conceptual model with the defined character of a specific organization?

5. What is the relationship between organization theory and an approach to a general theory of leadership?

11

Organizations and Leadership

We must teach men and women how to renew the organizations and institutions of which they are a part. And in order to do that we are going to have to give far more thought to the principles underlying the rise and fall of organizations than we have given to date.

John W. Gardner[1]

To this point we have considered various ways of thinking about organizations. Let us now weigh the implications of these findings for leaders of organizations and of the subunits within them. The following passages are somewhat *prescriptive* in nature. That is, they are *guidelines* for leaders based upon our knowledge of organization theory. They provide lessons to be applied in general—within all types of institutions and for application by leaders at all levels.

The composite of organization theory was presented in Chapter 10 to provide a synthesized perspective of organization behavior, a portrait of the way an organization behaves. It was pointed out that, among other benefits, this overview could be related to the conceptual model of idealized behavior to detect points of agreement and divergence. Stated another way, the composite of "how things are" and the conceptual model of "how things should be" could be compared for evaluative and, in turn, remedial purposes. We find that in a vast number of organizations, congruity is lacking between external forces and the behavior of the institution. Further, we find that nearly all enterprises are afflicted with some degree and type of internal ambiguity.

Why are these conditions permitted to occur and become chronic? Why should actual behavior depart from idealized behavior, when the latter is compatible with institutional needs? After all, social organizations are largely artificial, contrived and formed by human beings. Why aren't they reformed? If it becomes apparent that a social structure has developed wasteful frictions within, or pursues goals that have grown obsolete, or has become unsuitable to its goals in the eyes of those it serves, why aren't responsible corrective actions taken? Could it be that no one is "listening" to the forces pleading for reform? In sum, why are social institutions permitted to become wasteful—economically, ecologically, humanistically—as well as outdated—insensitive, apathetic, lethargic—when weighed against the needs of the broader society they serve? It is to these difficult yet crucially important questions that we now turn.

This chapter presents certain of the conditions that drain organizational strength thereby shortening the life span for countless enterprises. We will also consider the strengths leaders must demonstrate to design and manage strong, sound enterprises.

ATTRIBUTES OF LEADERSHIP

Attributes, as used here, are those qualities required by leaders to fulfill their function in maintaining the organization. Leadership refers to those men and women who hold positions of authority over subordinate workers. The traits of leadership recommended are limited to those that are essential to preserve organizational strength and are indicated as desirable by the conceptual model.

The reader may wish to refer again to the conceptual model. For your convenience, it is reproduced in Figure 11-1. You will observe that it is now depicted in its final, fully developed form. Common and structural arrangements of the social system remain unaltered, but elements that must be considered to achieve internal consistency and environmental consonance have been detailed and classified. Internal elements that in unison will reconcile to human interaction are now divided into four major classifications: structural, physical, cultural, and sociopsychological arrangements. Technology, economics, and physical ecology have been added to complete the model, though they are beyond the scope of this book. External elements that act as change catalysts have been shown to indicate the diverse forces to which receptivity and responses are required.

By reviewing the conceptual model, the reader can develop a full appreciation for the complexity of maintaining that delicate balance required for efficiency and effectiveness. Further, it is hoped that through reappraisal one can sense the major barriers to efficient organization design and reformation that are frequently put up by leaders. Such shortcomings as organizational introspection, irrationality, bias, and narrowed or distorted perspectives all can lead to paralysis or inap-

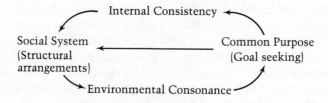

Structural and Subsystems

Authority, financial compensation and incentives,
work processes, formal communications, hierarchy
of plans, control, role of leadership, and microeconomics

Physical Arrangements

Human ecology, economics, and technology

Cultural Arrangements

Tradition, customs, rituals, ceremonies,
symbolism, and heritage

Sociopsychological Arrangements

Informal interaction and communications, roles,
norms, values, status, and leadership patterns

Internal Consistency

Social System
(Structural
arrangements)

Common Purpose
(Goal seeking)

Environmental Consonance

Receptive to Change

Constituent group expectations; needs of groups
served, customs and traditions of industry, or
other structure; technology; economy; values,
mores, ethos, and public opinion

Responsive to Forces Urging Change

Able
Willing

FIGURE 11–1. Conceptual Overview of an Organization.

propriate action. Let us consider now the leadership traits required to overcome these common threats to organizational health.

Conceptual Overview

One serious source of difficulties in organizations is leaders' inability to attain a comprehensive grasp, a conceptual overview, of their own enterprise. When myopia, or component-thinking, occurs at any level, it leads to a number of unfortunate consequences. *First, imbalances are created.* As we know, a major change in any one area of an organization reverberates throughout to related units and activities. In the absence of a conceptual overview, leaders tend to see their particular areas as fragments of the whole effort, when in fact they are all intimately integrated parts. *Second, impractical decisions are made.* Without a feel for the culture and direction of the overall enterprise, recommendations and decisions are made that, while not actually *incorrect,* are out of phase with the operating situation. They simply do not fit. *Third, unity of purpose is thwarted.* Leaders are unable to relate their efforts and those of their subordinates to the overall goals of the enterprise. A narrowed view restricts leaders' ability to grasp the relevance of the contribution of their units—to understand the "why" of work. And this tunnel vision frustrates the leaders' capability to link the purpose of their subordinates' efforts to the overall purpose of the enterprise. *And fourth, leaders' responsibilities to subordinates cannot be fulfilled.* Most people look to their leaders for guidance in matters beyond their skill, experience, authority, or perceptual scope. Though such matters often require technical or behavioral counsel, they frequently call for answers whose implications are broader than the unit immediately affected. As a consequence, any leader's skill in fulfilling responsibilities to dependents in the system will be sharply curtailed by an unduly introspective or circumscribed view. The leader will be less effective if unable to place the efforts, activities, and aspirations of subordinates into the context of the broader enterprise. And since this ability is generally expected by both superiors and subordinates, it deserves cultivation.

A view that is so narrowed that relevant information is screened out is inadequate for informed decisions and actions. Indeed, to some of us the most important characteristic of a leader is this ability to "sense the whole," as well as the harmony (or disharmony) of the parts contributing to the whole. One must "feel the infinite complexity known as the organization."[2] To leaders in middle and lower positions, this means gaining an awareness of the overall personality of the enterprise; leaders in upper levels must augment this with a grasp of the total relevant external situation.

For example, consider the plight of a first-level leader who is eager to mesh with the undertaking and contribute but attempts to do so without an awareness of the overall organization and its mission. In Phase One, this supervisor might begin to discover inconsistencies within his or her section, and between that unit and others. A new leader with a fresh outlook would very likely be more sensitive to unusual behavior patterns than a seasoned veteran who has grown to accept certain frictions and frustrations as the normal state of affairs. Sensing need for changes in the unit, the new head makes them and then submits a series of suggestions to superiors in the belief that they would improve interunit relationships. Next, the leader sets the unit's goals with subordinates, knowing that management by objectives gives direction, substance, and commitment to endeavors. And, finally, this supervisor attempts to relate the efforts of unit personnel to the broader effort by explaining the reasons for procedures governing quantity, quality, time use, and costs.

In Phase Two, a number of unfortunate and demoralizing incidents befall this well-meaning, but misguided supervisor. In rapid succession, it becomes apparent that the changes made within the unit are incompatible with procedures in related units. Each of the suggestions submitted falls on seemingly deaf ears, bringing responses such as "We tried that once . . . ," or "Our competitor tried that . . . ," or "That simply doesn't fit our operation." Next, the new leader finds that though the goals adopted within the unit are admirable, they do not mesh with higher goals of the enterprise. And then the eager newcomer learns that the reasons for the operating procedures are very different from what he or she had told the employees . . . and they know it. The supervisor is now faced with the embarrassing chore of returning to the people to undo the errors. What a degrading experience, particularly when a new chief needs to develop mutual respect with the members of the unit. Each of the errors was caused by the leader's inability to gain an awareness of the overall enterprise—the myopia that robs one of "sensing the whole."

Inadequate, narrowed outlooks are caused by a number of conditions. Among them, specialization of various kinds, and the absence of an analytical framework for examining an organization are at the forefront. Specialization by definition pre-empts generalization, preventing a broad overview of an organization.

Narrowed concentration is the fruit of formal education, professional interests, and authority levels. Consider, first, the collegiate program of the typical student preparing for a career of contribution to organized effort. Academic exposure to administrative sciences is confined to fragments of an enterprise's activities and functions. Candidates for leadership are expected to choose a specific study from such areas as engineering, computer technology, economics, political science, finance, and marketing. Ostensibly, concentration brings on a higher degree of expertise by making the activity easier to learn, or perhaps, to teach. Whatever the rationale, the view of organized effort is directed to one narrow sphere of activity, often to the exclusion of kindred events and the overall enterprise. Yet these other activities have an intensely intimate relationship. The result is that the relevant gestalt, which is the organization, is lost. The perspective is even further constricted if the student is preparing for leadership in a particular type of institution—business, military, public, medical, educational. The viewpoint of a fragment of activity in a specialized type and culture of an organization is the one cultivated.

Second, the candidate for leadership would understandably seek a position using the skills gained in a specific area of professional interest and education. Commonly, such a person would be placed initially in a position to learn some part of the work in a certain functional area. A new employee, for instance, in social work might be assigned to a youth club, at the grass-roots level, to counsel girls on skill interests. Thus, the scope of the budding leader would be refocused now even more narrowly on a part of a part of the overall endeavor, that is, helping young people to grow culturally, psychologically, and physically.

Third, leaders' scope is limited by the viewpoint attendant on their particular level of authority. For instance, the outlook of a first-level leader over a unit of clerks is confined to the function of clerical activities, as well as to the lower authority levels of the enterprise. On the other hand, a budget coordinator as a staff assistant to a controller may enjoy the benefit of "seeing" the long downward hierarchy of organization, but that perspective is limited to a single, highly specialized activity. Indeed, it is only the view from the top that permits one to gain an overall perspective *automatically*. Subordinated individuals in more specialized functions gain an appreciation for the overview of the organization only through their active efforts to learn it.

And fourth, alas, it is true that some leaders in higher authority positions are unwilling or unable to help a person in a lower position to understand the broader field influencing his or her area of responsibilities. In discussing this issue with a friend and colleague, he told me of the following experience:

> My first job in banking was to work as a trainee in what was called the Collateral-Discount Department. This was a very important department dealing with customers who had large sums invested in 90-day notes with the bank. My job was to keep track of their collateral, its value, inventory, and so forth. During the year of my training assignments, I asked my supervisor discerning questions to better become aware of the overall picture: bank policies and strategies, open-market operations of the Federal Reserve, the influence of the supply of money on lending policies, and so on. The supervisor would usually respond by telling me that it was not my job to worry about those broader issues; that I should confine my interest to activities within the department.[3]

The superior intentionally restricted the growth of the trainee by such narrowness. The former trainee concluded, "It was almost like telling me that I wasn't really interested in those things; or if I was, I shouldn't be." Sensing a need to know but being kept from knowing leads to frustration and naïveté. So we see that a conceptual overview of an organization is thwarted by varied types of specialization, yet an overall awareness is crucial to enlightened leadership. What is the resolution to this dilemma? Leaders must actively pursue a sufficiently broad frame of reference to cultivate the conceptual skills required to play the total role of leader. And this requirement leads us to the final roadblock to organizational sophistication—the lack of an analytical framework.

An analytical framework is essential to organizational understanding. In its absence, the complexities of organized life appear to defy comprehension. Hence, when we couple these two facts—specialization diminishes understanding, and only active application of an analytical framework permits a conceptual overview—it is small wonder that leadership often suffers from incomplete comprehension.

Using the analytical framework to determine the personality of an organization, any participant can develop a more complete overview of the venture. Though some peculiarities will doubtless remain unexplained due to limited data or the cultural immunity of an insider to subtle clues, a broadened view can be achieved. In turn, it can explain the reasons behind enterprise behavior such as cultural limitations, vital goals, sensitive areas, taboos, or priorities. When this approach is put to use, any leader will become more effective through developing the ability to discern the appropriateness of behavior as it is related to the enterprise's unique functional and cultural requirements.

Unity of Purpose

The entire scheme of all aspects of a social system is anchored in its purpose as perceived and shared by its members. Goals lead to the structural/functional and situational design of an organization. They act as the rallying point around which initial cohesiveness and integration can be established. Lack of agreement on goals, or failure to relate sub-goals clearly to the overall objectives of an organization, results in wasteful conflict, confusion, and frustration. There are three major causes of a loss of common purpose: The first is differing perceptions by key leaders; the second is emphasis on the *substance* of tasks exclusively, ignoring their place in the attainment of goals; and the third is pursuit of individual goals to the neglect or jeopardy of organizational goals.

Leaders' differing perceptions. It is common to find that leaders in sensitive positions define the mission of their common enterprise in different terms. This often results when each leader heads a specific functional activity such as production, marketing, and finance in a business enterprise. The head of each major unit develops a conditioned way of "seeing" the operating situation. As a consequence, responses to the fundamental question, "What business are you in?" when put to managers of a publishing firm may elicit widely diverse views. The president may envision the central goal as securing a marketing niche in institutions of higher learning with a list of superior texts in narrowly defined subject areas. The vice-president of production may define the primary objective as mass production of high quality books; the vice-president of finance, as rapidly turning inventories and the adoption of works with complementary life cycles in the market place. And the vice-president of marketing may believe that the firm is in the broad field of written communications and should sell to whatever markets are available to it.

Varying definitions of an organization's purpose are understandable. We see things differently from different frames of reference. And, perceptual divergences occur from executive suites down to foremen stations. Further, organizations usually reward people for performing in their specialty area without concern for the overall mission. Rewards, of course, reinforce behavior and perceptions. But if such dissimilar conceptions of purpose are permitted, they will surely lead to internal inconsistencies because subsystems that influence employee behavior in each major unit are largely a product of individual managers' assessments of the overall objectives and their respective units' parts in their attainment. Inconsistencies need not result within the individual departments, but ambiguities will surely arise when the subunits are related to the overall enterprise.

Ignoring task's relations to goals. Common purpose can also be lost when participants in an organization are not informed about the relationship of their roles, activities, and contributions to the overall objectives. Though detailed operating procedures, coupled with compensations for performance, persuade workers to act as required, bureaucratic techniques fail to tell them why their activities are important in reaching the enterprise's broader objectives. This common omission— the "why" of tasks—often causes employees to feel lack of identity with organizational goals. As a consequence, not only does the work become meaningless, but conflicts flare up from unnecessary fragmentation, isolation, and vested interests in what seems to workers to be unrelated bits of performance considered to be ends unto themselves. Nothing could be further from the truth, nor as damaging to unity of purpose and organizational cohesiveness.

The "why" of activities is often not fathomed because of the structuring required to attain specialization. The "why" of human effort is sometimes unanswered because it is overshadowed by communications from higher authorities to make certain that the "what," "when," and "how" of activities are executed to increase leaders' sense of security that things are under control (often under control, but also far under potential performance.)

Focusing on common goals. Next, leaders need a comprehensive awareness of the organization's hierarchy, the hierarchies of plans (including goals and incentives), and the relationships among these institutionalized hierarchies. With these rankings firmly grasped, leaders are in a position to know how the activities of their respective units fit into the contextual hierarchy of the enterprise. Such broadened understanding permits an explanation of the reasons for expectations such as activities, procedures, goals, and behavior. The leaders can now also isolate inconsistencies.

And last, the leader should be emotionally prepared to develop sub-ordinates through orientation and counseling leading toward their increased involvement in the enterprise. An inappropriate temperament among leaders often is the Achilles' heel to ensuring unity of purpose. After all, why keep subordinates informed? An informed employee can be more self-sufficient, -reliant, -governing, and -fulfilling in his/her work. Now, the notion of creating such self-sufficiency in workers is a threatening spectre to leaders who are insecure. It means that to gain subordinate identification, (basic to participation, involvement, and dedication) the leaders will lose employee dependency, use of authority, unquestioning compliance, and indeed, the decreased need for their functions as leaders. What an ominous threat to some! A leader viewing his role in such an emotional context would impede not only employee awareness but also unity of purpose.

A misguided leader, however, would harbor the desire to keep sub-ordinates uninformed, and thus dependent. A supervisor who clings to the idea that leaders must manage the people in their organizations, or subunits, would hold subordinates subservient through ignorance. Yet organizations do include leaders who pursue this strategy. It is a popular misconception that leaders manage people. Leaders manage organizational arrangements so that people can manage their activities and achievements toward enterprise goals. As Barnard observed:

> You put a man in charge of an organization and your worst difficulty is that he thinks he has to tell everybody what to do. And that's almost fatal if it's carried far enough.[4]

Leaders do facilitate, or make possible, the processes of planning, organizing, directing, and controlling because these are required for integrated, coordinated effort. This does not mean that leaders must do the tasks related to these processes. Rather, leaders must *facilitate* their being done by others. Subordinates can be valuable, if not invaluable, in making sound recommendations for the design of activities. However, for them to do so, managers must inform them on the common pursuit, and enlighten them as to the relationship of their parts to the broader endeavor.

Others contend that the overall mission of an enterprise is thwarted because the needs of individual participants are unfulfilled through the attainment of overall goals. To them, some tenuous set of goals that are compatible to many participants is evolved out of general conflict and compromise. The most important cause of a loss of common purpose, to these theorists, is that different people in the organization want and expect different things from the organization. Whatever may be the process of identifying overall goals, once established they become basic and indispensable to all else that goes on in an organization.

Environmental Consonance

All micro-social systems, called organizations, exist because they fulfill some need in the broader social system, the society. As discussed earlier, each organization is sanctioned by some social justification. Certain organizations, called businesses, must also justify their activities economically. In both instances, however, an organization must continue to fulfill its social commitment *in an often rapidly changing environment.* Changes such as constituency expectations demand some appropriate response if an institution is to survive.

It seems that humanity has learned its lessons well in accommodating major tasks through the formation of complex structures of activities by people. Yet for reforming social arrangements once they are established and institutionalized, we have only marginal skills. Hence, in all types of human endeavor some organizations cling to outmoded goals, formal organization structures, and internal subsystems until they are grossly insensitive to environmental demands. Either "earthquake changes" of revolutionary impact are required, or the endeavor goes under when more responsive enterprises arise to fill the void.

Now let's consider the major causes of environmental ambiguity that can lead to organizational obsolescence and try to illuminate conditions that impede environmental consonance. Why would a leader permit the status quo to prevail when the enterprise is admittedly a product of a fluid field of forces? How can leaders remain unaware of cues suggesting change when the enterprise has specialized "eyes and ears" to sense external shifts? And why, once the need for change is identified, would an organization be unable to react in a rational way within a reasonable period of time?

First, as an enterprise becomes mature (more significantly here, secure), its leaders often tend to redirect attention from the external environment, with which they are now in harmony, to internal matters. Leaders turn their attention inward to achieve efficiencies that have been foregone until the enterprise is assured of support from outside. They internalize to develop consistencies within the system for efficiency. But in so doing, they may grow unduly concerned with internal operations (ethnocentric, or inner-directed) to the neglect of sensing external changes (outer-directed). Or, as some might express it in pondering primitive people, they become "their cave" directed rather than "other cave" oriented.

Second, specialization within an organization causes the heads of various functional units to "tune in" to specific types of information from the environment. Data that in concert could be used to reshape goals, policies, and strategies is thus fragmented and chaotic. For example, an organization is a vehicle for sensing external forces. But it must screen out seemingly irrelevant information if it is to avoid a clogged communications subsystem—"organization arteriosclerosis." The organization must then strike a compromise between what data are received and what are rejected. Thus, as John Howard observes, "organization perceptions involve only parts of the environment, [and] these perceptions may be biased even before they experience the modifying action of the organization and that of the executive's frame of reference."[5]

The selection of environmental data will be biased by the receivers' particular needs for information. For example, picture a typical business enterprise. It has receptors to information from outside the firm in marketing research, sales, finance, personnel, purchasing, industrial engineering, and of course the president. Its formalized receptors, or sensing capabilities, can be viewed as in Figure 11-2. Each sensing position under the president is attuned to certain outside information to guide its particular area of decision making and action. But the sources and the nature of the data to which each is attuned are vastly different. In general, marketing research is designed to "listen" to data from present and potential markets, sales to product markets and competition, finance to money markets, personnel to labor markets, purchasing to raw material markets, and industrial engineering to capital equipment markets, including changing technology. As a consequence, data that should in total serve as "corporate intelligence" are often fragmented and unrelated.

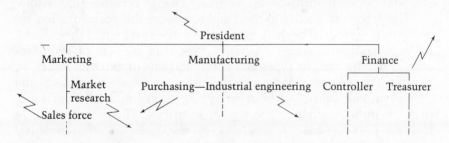

FIGURE 11-2. Typical Sensing Capabilities of a Company

Further, positions designed to sense relevant external forces tend to be dominantly, if not predominantly, attuned to economic aspects in the firm's environment. This predisposition causes a bias. It focuses attention on economic aspects to the neglect of other relevant environmental forces: forces that are more horizontal but will emerge to have economic influence in the future. A producer of home appliances, for instance, may be acutely aware of current market data but may screen out indicators of changing styles of living that could revolutionize product design and marketing. Effective leaders "listen" to social forces:

changes in constituent and support groups' life styles, values, social mores, feelings, and expectations. These are the forces that precede economic behavior for they are the determinants. As such, they give leaders advance notice of trends that will require appropriate organizational responses.

Ideally, a mature organization would develop communications systems at the interface between itself and its external environment. It might proceed along the following evolutionary path to build sensing systems: a system to gather composites of environmental data, and a system to analyze the impact of the data and advance alternatives for change. Instead, organizations often attempt to ameliorate forces requiring change. Their development takes on the path observed by Katz and Kahn:

> At Stage 1 certain characteristics of a human population and some common environmental problem interact to generate task demands and a primitive production structure to fulfill them. At Stage 2 devices for formulating and enforcing rules appear. An authority structure emerges and becomes the basis for managerial and maintenance subsystems. Stage 3 sees the further elaboration of supportive systems at the organizational boundaries— structures for procurement, disposal, and institutional relations.[6]

Organizations can be debilitated if they insulate themselves from forces requiring changes. Further, if they perceive only parts of the environment—and generally these are only those forces having immediate economic impact—evolutionary change becomes impossible.

Third, leaders' ability to react and to change their organization appropriately is limited by their capacity to make sense out of their world. An organization develops programs. Programs are sets of responses called forth by various types and configurations of external forces, or stimuli. The programs offer routine solutions to common problems and thereby provide control without paralyzing the organization with issues that rise unnecessarily to the top for solutions. The organization, as Howard puts it, has "a repertory of responses to environmental events."[7] If a problem, however, does not have a preprogrammed solution, it becomes awkward and risky to handle.

Leaders inherit an ongoing organization with its inherent structure of programs. They do not commonly design the organization or their own subunits, by some structural/functional or means/ends analysis. Usually the goals must be inferred rather than being explicit. And often, this inability to identify goals rests at the root of problems hampering organizations. People learn routines rather than goals. Because they think in terms of set procedures, they may not adjust appropriately to changing demands. Procedures, though necessary, tend to receive attention that should be devoted to goals. Though goals may change through internal bargaining, those that emerge may lack consonance with external conditions. Both environmental ambiguity and internal inconsistency can stem from such confusion over procedures and goals.

And fourth, people are reluctant to change. An organization's managers can be keenly aware of relevant external forces, analyze them accurately in concert, and effectively interpret their impact upon the enterprise and its people. Yet, their subordinates will be reluctant, if they don't actually refuse, to change. This tendency has been observed and variously explained throughout recorded history. It is caused in part by psychological, cultural, social and, at times, economic factors. But the tendency was placed squarely before us, with one explanation, by Machiavelli:

> That we cannot change at will is due to two causes: the one is the impossibility of resisting the natural bent of our characters; and the other is the difficulty of persuading ourselves, after having been accustomed to success by a certain mode of proceeding, that any other can succeed as well. It is this that causes the varying success of man; for the times change, but he does not change his mode of proceeding.[8]

In sum, environmental consonance is maintained by two elements: (1) leaders who recognize openly that their organizations are dependent entities shaped by forces from the broader environment and (2) the interaction of these forces with those that can be generated from within the organization. This recognition is fundamental to setting the stage for organizational viability. As John Beckett puts it:

> The person who reckons with those forces and assesses their power to influence one another under a variety of prospective circumstances is *the systems architect—the interpreter of the forces that prevail between the environment and the system.*[9]

The problems, of course, lie in understanding what forces act to exert influence on the organization, how to design programs appropriate to sense impending change, how to synthesize data and place them into context, how to recognize which external forces demand a response and which may be changed or ignored, and how to incorporate necessary changes.

As prerequisites, enlightened leaders will discipline themselves to cultivate an adequate perceptual framework to recognize forces from related environmental systems, and to effect changes where required. The benefits from such strong-mindedness will be fourfold. First, the inclination toward organizational introspection will be avoided so that leaders can be aware of environmental systems to which the survival of their enterprise is linked. Second, leaders will mitigate the tendency to heed only specialized, fragmented data from the environment, which are dominantly biased toward short-run, economic consequences. Third, the inclination to confuse routines, procedures, and methods with goals will be eliminated. And fourth, leaders will be intellectually and emotionally prepared to cope with change; to recognize its pervasiveness, its scope, its continuousness, and its cultural impact.

In this era of "permanent revolution," leaders must realize that no organization can be precisely designed and rigorously maintained like a machine to achieve *fixed* goals. Max Ways points this fact up to business leaders, and it is scarcely a less pointed lesson for leaders in other types of organizations:

> Today, the highest activities of management become a continuous process of decision about the nature of the business. Management's degree of excellence is still judged in part by its efficiency of operation, but much more by its ability to make decisions changing its product mix, its markets, its techniques of financing and selling. Initiative, flexibility, creativity, adaptability are the qualities now required.[10]

Indeed, as Ways asserts, the essential task of today's leaders is to become agents for change. Though goals (for example, the growth and integrity of the organization) may be relatively fixed, the means to reach them will change to meet the forces in the environment. Ways's view of the role of leadership doubtless will have a higher chance of materializing if leaders recognize the implications of the impact of social forces on their organizations and on their roles as leaders.

Environmental pressures from a more fluid society can thrust the purpose, or goals, of an organization into a state of flux. Further, changing demands can alter the internal dimensions of the organization. And in turn, either or both of these developments will affect the design and management of the internal subsystems of activities if internal consistency is to be preserved. The impact of outside forces might be illustrated schematically as in Figure 11-3. Arrows designate the sequences of changes. Changes reverberate throughout as one would expect a system to react when related to external systems.

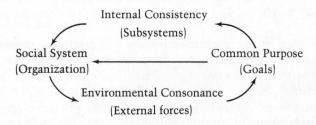

FIGURE 11–3. Sequential Changes From External Forces

The effects of reactive strategies are pervasive in that a chain reaction occurs from the top of the enterprise to the bottom. As such, it is as important for a first-level supervisor as it is for the head of the enterprise to understand the process of change and its impact. The leader over a small subunit of activity in an enterprise is also initiating changes, while maintaining a semblance of order and balance, as is the chief executive. *The difference is one of degree, rather than one of kind.* Thus, dealing with change to ensure accord with external forces is a universal function of leadership.

Internal Consistency

Effective leaders are adaptable so that they can cope with environmental change. But that single dimension of a leader's role (through which most changes enter our society) is not enough. Leaders are also looked to as agents of efficiency, as "systems regulators."[11] Efficiency comes as a result of ensuring internal consistency among goals, subsystems, and people.

Inconsistencies cause waste: technologically, procedurally, humanistically and, ultimately, economically. They permit such conditions as duplication, overlap, confusion, redundancy, voids, less-than-top performance, and demoralization to sap an enterprise of its strength and vitality. Yet they are present in some form or another in nearly every organization. For instance, in one organization, rewards do not square with goals; in another, authority blocks needed member involvement; and in yet another, nonmonetary symbols of achievement fail to support goals.

Leaders are aware of the debilitating effects of internal inconsistencies, but such ambiguities exist. Indeed, they continue to emerge. Let us now analyze certain of the major causes of internal inconsistencies. We should probe for answers to the following questions, answers which can provide guidelines for leadership. Why are wasteful ambivalences permitted to thrive within organizations? Why do they tend to persist even after they are isolated as the cause of inefficiencies? And how can leaders throughout an enterprise identify and challenge ambiguities that act to impede rather than to facilitate progress? Let us consider first the causes of internal inconsistencies and then move to an approach for leaders to bring on more balanced operations.

There are a number of causes for internal ambiguity, perhaps more than this small treatise can reasonably cover. It is well, however, to cite certain of the more common reasons, for by being aware of their nature, leaders can better understand and cope with inconsistencies as they find them.

The first major source of internal imbalance is confusion over major goals by leaders in influential positions. Misunderstandings over what is truly important, and the priority of goals, bring on illogical formations of the organization (specialization, groupings, spans of management, and so forth), as well as irrational design of subsystems of activities (authority, status, rewards, and symbolism).

Second, ambiguities spring from a situation wherein changes in goals, structure, and subsystems are made periodically over time, but without the benefit of a conceptual overview for a comprehensive reappraisal. As a consequence, a certain change may be made without consideration of its impact upon related activities. Conflicts, or at least miscalculations, are bound to result. For instance, consider the simple yet serious error brought on by a leader of salespeople who decided to alter procedures to assign a salesperson to the office on a rotating basis to handle an excessively heavy load of clerical work generated by reports for control. The leader announced the new procedure. It met with concern, distaste, and open resentment from the salesforce. The leader failed to recognize that the idea clashed with a number of related subsystems of influence. Rewards for selling, an activity which carried high status were on a pure, or straight, commission basis. And sales effectiveness customarily led to high individual autonomy. In one unprecedented decision, subordinates' income, status, and freedom were placed in jeopardy. Further, they had been told for years that their sales performance was their primary goal in the eyes of upper management. Now this action belied those words. Wasteful confusion and conflict ensued.

Third, unwanted conflicts often erupt because of divergences between leaders' needs and those of their organizations. As examples: Leaders may wish near-perfect performance when the economics within an enterprise suggest that something a bit less is prudent. They may wish to be kept continually and thoroughly informed although the volume of reports demanded hurts both production and morale. Or they may harbor insecurities about making errors to a degree that they burden subordinates and the system with much more data, than the import of the decision warrants. And on and on. Thus, inconsistent behavior within an organization often stems from conflicts between leaders' needs and the requirements from the operating setting.

Managers may also feel a need to preserve the status quo at a time when pressures for internal change or reform have grown intense. They may have acquired, quite unconsciously, vested interests in the pattern of present activities, enjoying the comfort of expertness, the security of established role behavior, and the continuity of established role relationships. In a word, leaders in such situations feel adequate—technically, psychologically, culturally. Nearly any substantive change will tear at the roots of their feelings of completeness. In a word, with change they will feel inadequate. Hence, it is quite natural for leaders to fight pressures requiring adjustments. People in other related positions may alter their behavior to conform to new demands, but if some superiors hold to past behavioral patterns—voids, overlaps, redundancies—confusion and conflict are bound to result. This is the dilemma faced by those who believe that reorganizations have been effected when the lines and boxes are changed on an organization chart. They are soon shocked to find that unless they have changed the perceptions of those people affected by the change, the organization runs the same as it did before the graphic alterations were made.

Fourth, when directives are introduced by specialized staffs—such as production planning, quality assurance, budgeting, collections, marketing coordination, work volume measurements, or service— but fulfilled by operating line units, such as, areas, divisions, and departments—conflicts often occur. Hence, if staff agencies are vying among each other for support from line forces for their particular program, imbalances or discontinuities can easily occur. This condition causes imbalances by an overemphasis on one phase of work to the detriment of other related phases. This is the type of inconsistent behavior that commonly arises out of multiple authority flows from varied staff specialists as well as line generalists.

Fifth, organizational traditions breed internal inconsistencies. This is particularly true when they block objectivity and critical reevaluation of arrangements—when they leave unchallenged, institutionalized customs that may be based on myth or outdated needs.

Organizations, as the seasoned expert quoted previously said, do develop "minor cults" and "major religions." These are patterns of activities that have been established over time and, after having been institutionalized, become sacrosanct as unquestioned procedures. For instance, operations research may have become a minor cult, while the concept of decentralization may have been dignified to the status of a major religion. These are rigid doctrines, or dogmas, that begin at some point as desirable activities or ways of thinking. They then become institutionalized as *the* way things are done. Often they lead to formalized units of people with vested interests in preserving them. The problem is that most ideas and behavior become inappropriate as operations are adjusted to meet changing demands.

"Piece-part" changes when other parts of the organization are affected represent a sixth and last frequent cause of internal inconsistency. Parts are adjusted at various times but rarely are related subsystems reappraised, redesigned, and readjusted to ensure congruent, synchronized interaction among them. In the absence of analysis with a sufficiently broadened perspective to include all relevant internal systems—economic, technical, and human—ambiguities will occur because internal arrangements are interdependent. Manipulation of a given part makes itself felt on related systems, whether their redesign has been planned or not.

SUMMARY

Let us review the lessons that organizational understanding holds for leaders. The major causes for internal inconsistencies stem from confusion over goals, insufficient perspective, conflicts between leaders' needs and those of their organization, imbalances brought on by specialized influence centers, unquestioned institutionalized traditions, and "piece-part" changes. These causes of inefficiency are eliminated by leaders who clearly define the mission of their organization: leaders who can set goals, rank them in importance, and communicate them (through hierarchies of goals, plans, and rewards) to the people who play the vital part in their attainment.

Discord that needlessly saps organizational strength is also eliminated by leaders who sense the overall *gestalt* of their organization, including its need for balanced development, and its structural, intellectual, moral, and cultural state. In this way, conflicting or cross purposes from such natural areas as individual versus organizational needs, specialists' versus generalists' efforts, and cultural tradition versus new ways of operating, can be appraised in light of goals and organizational means to reach them.

Enlightened leadership, whatever the level, is based upon the individual's ability to develop a mental framework, or set, in which events and activities are perceived and evaluated in relationship to the overall organization and to its goals. It is not easy. Procedures tend to obscure goals; detailed work takes precedence over conceptual reflection; component thinking commonly may impede systems thinking; artificial structures, subsystems, and procedures may assume positions of unquestioned durability; and symptoms of problems examined in reports may be accepted as the causes of problems. Far too often enlightened leadership becomes dimmed by specialized routinization.

Truly effective leaders first cultivate an awareness of the overall operation—its character and objectives. Second, they recognize the artificiality and momentary character of internal arrangements so that they can be analyzed, challenged, and changed. Third, competent leaders ask the right questions to probe beneath effects and symptoms and lay bare the real causes of internal inconsistencies. Fourth, they redesign structures and subsystems to purge them of ambiguities, but in such a way that the revisions will fit the character of the organization and serve as more congruent means to its goals. Fifth and last, aware leaders ask themselves, "What voices outside my organization have I avoided hearing?"

DISCUSSION QUESTIONS

1. In what ways is it difficult for a leader to make changes amid stability and create stability amid change? What does this do to the unit, section, department, division, or total organization under the leader's control?

2. What is the "delicate balance" between the stability required for efficiency and the viability necessary for survival? Consider here various enterprises—a manufacturer of plastic novelties, a manufacturer of furniture, and a manufacturer of wooden pencils.

3. What would probably be the feelings of a first-level leader who perceives her or his responsibility as a system stabilizer for efficiency's sake, but is assigned to a job shop in a printing organization. Now, contemplate the feelings of a first-level leader who sees his responsibility as a change agent, but is assigned to a clerical unit in a federal bureau.

4. Why do leaders compete within an organization, at times to the point of counterproductive conflict, rather than cooperating toward enterprise goals and against outside competitors?

5. Why is organizational renewal so difficult? (As a metaphor, why is individual self-renewal so very difficult?)

12

Perspectives for Leaders

A major problem inherent in it [the study of organization and leadership] is that one must accept a concept of relativity that is tremendously complex and . . . leaves one with little firm ground upon which to stand. Absolutes vanish, and events and happenings have to be explained in relation to other aspects of the situation.

William B. Wolf[1]

The essence of a liberal education is man's understanding of the systems of which he is a part.

Jay W. Forester[2]

In Chapter 11, we considered the relationships of the needs of organizations to attributes required by their leaders. In this chapter, we contemplate various ways of thinking and approaches to education through which a leader can acquire the attributes needed for effectiveness. We encourage the reader to take a number of vantage points opening up new perspectives, or slants, on the nature of leadership.

A fundamental belief underlies this discussion. It is that leadership, if sound, is functionally related to the needs of the organization and its members. Leadership is largely situational; it is a response to the demands of the operating unit including, of course, its members. Put another way, leadership is contingent upon the nature of the organization. Inept leadership becomes evident when leaders lose sight of the organizational contingencies that govern expected behavior and are unwilling or unable to respond appropriately to the operating situation.

In addition, a leader's chances for success are improved when organizational relationships are perceived more realistically. Once one grasps organizations in different terms, the need for certain leadership skills can be recognized, based upon one's interests in the organized efforts. After identifying needs for learning, we will present a number of avenues for gaining the relevant leadership skills.

RELATIVITY AND LEADERSHIP

Strong leaders cultivate a high tolerance for relativity and a low need for absolutism. By this we mean that men and women occupying positions of responsibility in organizations develop an acceptance of facts (intellectually and emotionally), not for their own value but as they relate to other events, activities, constellations of activities, and the overall organization. Effective leaders suppress the tendency to require complete, concrete, measurably perfect data of meaning only unto itself. Acceptance of relativity is essential because evaluation of an event or other data may mean little until related to other events or data and to the total system (organization). This is the essence of systems thinking. And, since leaders are systems designers, catalysts, and regulators, acceptance of interdependent performance is basic if their thinking is to be sound.

It is generally conceded that an organization exists in a state of dynamic equilibrium. By this we mean a moving balance in a certain span of time and space. If the system fails to achieve balance, efficiencies elude us; if it is unable to assimilate changes, we cannot maintain its effectiveness in a changing environment. Expressed a bit differently, but without losing sight of the basic precept, we have been considering the nature of models similar to the one shown in Figure 12-1. But here, the reasons for maintaining internally consistent and environmentally consonant relationships is illustrated. We have entertained the idea that efficiency may emerge out of stability by cultivating internal consistency between goals, the people, and the institutionalized subsystems through which the people pursue the goals. We also considered the notion that organization effectiveness results from two major capabilities: (1) to cultivate a continuing surveillance over shifting environmental forces requiring organizational change, and (2) to preserve the ability of organization members to adapt to change.

Herein lies the basic need for understanding relationships of tandem activities. If these are misread leaders will not perceive the dual implication of their responsibilities, to foster continuity as well as to break it. Hence, an undiscerning manager may emphasize one aspect, stability, to the neglect of the other, viability, or vice versa.

For example, a first-level supervisor works dedicatedly for months to introduce efficiencies into a certain production process by specializing assignments, proceduralizing the tasks, and refining coordination. A

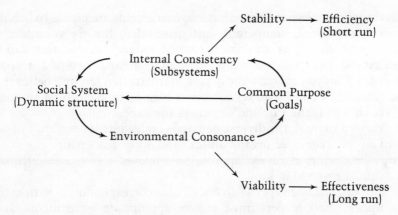

FIGURE 12–1. Relationships of the Conceptual Model to Efficiency and Effectiveness

stable, continuing, efficient process results. After this, the supervisor is asked to automate one segment of the process. Adopting the new technology is disruptive. It brings on discontinuities—in assignments, procedures, roles, status and role relationships, and coordination—within the section. The change is necessary, however, if the company is to benefit from improved technology. So the production supervisor now works again to achieve stability and continuity through bringing the unit into new balance.

Leaders should be aware of their two-dimensional responsibility to maintain continuity and also to create discontinuity. In the absence of such an awareness, each crucial aspect of the leader's role may not receive appropriate attention. Perhaps worse, a lack of understanding could make a leader feel that the forces stemming from the organization's need for change amidst continuity impose unreasonable, if not intolerable, expectations. It is best to recognize the paradox in the situation and its implications for leadership roles.

Most persons new to management labor under the sometimes mythical idea that their primary, if not exclusive, responsibility is efficiency. They want activities within their province to appear orderly, efficient, and "business-like when viewed by superiors, peers, or outsiders." Thus, threats to stability, change, become a villainous specter. Just about the time leaders have achieved order and efficiency, "they" introduce a new procedure causing disorder and inefficiency. It is little wonder that supervisors inclined to preserve the status quo feel that "someone up there" in the organization is determined to thwart their deep desire for efficiency; a subtle conspiracy is at work, they think, to disrupt stability and to frustrate them. Indeed, there are people in line management who spend their entire careers on the front lines of a losing battle to fight change and to defend traditional ways of doing things. The emotional casualties on those hapless battlefields are pitiful to behold. Sincere, dedicated, competent, but misguided, leaders volunteer to serve as unwitting psychological cannon fodder, because they fail to understand the true meaning of management's two-fold responsibilities. Can you imagine the degree of frustration felt by a believer in the "efficiency cult" who served, say, a high-fashion clothing producer where change is the rule and sameness the exception?

Viewed in total, the diverse demands on leaders are evidence of one of many paradoxes of organizations, and so of leadership. Nature is always enduring, always changing. As a related subsystem, organizations must respond in kind.

But, organizations per se do not change correspondingly with external forces; their leaders must induce appropriate adjustments. It is axiomatic that rational reactions do not automatically occur in social systems—people make them happen. Thus, programs to train and develop leaders, in some significant measure, are efforts to help leaders in varying positions, with varied responsibilities, to behave in ways appropriate to organizational efficiency and effectiveness, stability and viability.

Many positions of leadership in an organization are primarily concerned with *either* stability or viability. Though line leaders' positions require a balanced perspective, many staff specialists are *predominantly* involved in satisfying either one type of organizational need or the other—stability or viability.

For example, consider the major thrust of activities related to the following types of specialties:

Type of Staff Specialty	Organizational Need Satisfied
1. Quality control	stability
2. Research and development	viability
3. Production scheduling	stability
4. Marketing research	viability
5. Methods engineering	stability
6. Public relations	viability
7. Cost control	stability
8. Ecological adviser	viability
9. Operations research	stability
10. New technology; industrial engineering	viability

These are but a very limited array of specialized positions. Yet they provide examples of positions geared primarily to bringing on either organizational structuring or flexibility.

Leadership Training

Let us now consider certain types of leadership training and development activities.[3] Over the last fifty years or so, a number of important methods and techniques for managing an enterprise have been introduced. Many have proven successful and have been included as courses to develop leaders' skills. Review the following list of commonly accepted techniques:

1. PERT (Periodic Evaluation and Review Technique) and other critical path systems
2. Business gaming
3. Production scheduling
4. Environmental studies
5. Value analysis
6. Sensitivity or T-group labs
7. Long-range forecasting techniques
8. Situational theory
9. Time and motion studies
10. Decentralization; profit-center management
11. System design techniques
12. Creativity training: brain-storming, cybernetics
13. Operations research: linear programming, dynamic programming
14. Management grid training
15. Cost effectiveness analysis
16. Scanlon plan; other profit-sharing techniques
17. Decision theory: decision trees and allocation models
18. Motivation laboratories
19. Human factors engineering
20. Management philosophies

This partial list of techniques carries with it "a thrust in one of two directions—either toward greater order, systematization, routinization, and predictability, or toward greater openness, sharing, creativity, individual initiative,"[4] and consequential change: one effort to tighten an organization and make it more integrated and stable, the other to loosen it up and give it greater viability, flexibility, and adaptability. Arranged in one way, the training techniques with odd numbers relate to the skills required for organizational stability, and those with even numbers are designed to develop skills needed largely to bring on organizational viability.

Now let's try to tie it all together. It's apparent that seemingly conflicting functions are at work here. Further, because of their education, roles, and authority positions some people specialize in fulfilling the functions of either stability or viability. If this is true, it carries with it clear implications for those persons preparing themselves for leadership.

A person serving (or aspiring to serve) in a specialized staff position can analyze the major emphasis of its tasks and seek those skills required to fulfill them. For instance, a cost control supervisor, primarily concerned with internal consistency, efficiency, and stability, can benefit from studying value analysis, system design techniques, cost effectiveness analysis, and quantitative decision theory. A research and development analyst, by contrast, may reap more exposure to business gaming, environmental studies, and creativity training because the function of the position is directed toward sensitivity, environmental consonance, and viability.

A person in (or aspiring to) a generalized line management position can see that his or her unit will need both stability and viability. Hence, its head needs to be aware of the various leadership talents necessary to build a complex, efficient, effective, modern organization. Such a leader also needs to be aware of the talents and skills that may be available from specialized staff advisors. This individual will also be familiar with the diverse needs of the organization and the need for people to assume different responsibilities to fulfill those needs, and so develop various leadership skills.

The major problem with leadership development programs is that they are not designed to fill the individualized needs of leaders. Thus, they do not provide specialized training to those leaders requiring it. Training efforts are commonly far too general. Some top executive decides that, say, sensitivity training is "good" and everyone gets a dose, whether needed or not. As the relationship of organizational needs to the functions and roles of leaders in particular positions becomes more widely understood, some of the universally designed leadership development programs may become less popular because they are inappropriate and irrelevant.

Thoughtful students of organization and leadership recognize the relativity of organizational arrangements. In a complex system absolutes vanish, leaving one with the uneasy feeling of attempting to achieve delicate balances—balancing such characteristics, to mention a few, as:

Conflict, cooperation, and appeasement
Organizational needs and individual needs
Competition and cooperation
Conformity and nonconformity
Owners' goals and leaders' goals
Output and self-maintenance
Equity and debt
Quantity, quality, time use, and costs

Formal and informal interaction
Autocracy and participation
Empathy and objectivity
And on and on.

Leaders, in this sense, are involved in weighing trade-offs, not unlike those confronting political leaders in the broader society. There, balance hinges on the great societal issues such as power and moral integrity, freedom and control, individuality and codetermination, progress and security, centralized and decentralized authority, and contribution and equity. In the complex organization, dynamic equilibrium hinges on balancing these same issues plus many others.

The informed leader is aware of the issues, their relativity, and the need for balance. It is small wonder that often the decisions and actions of leaders seem conservative, if not downright cautious. It is not that leaders are conservative by nature. It is rather that the impact of their decisions and actions is often so broadly and deeply felt by others and involve such contradictions, that they must come up with a compromise to maintain institutional balance.

THE BALANCE BETWEEN STABILITY AND VIABILITY

An organization is continually changing. In a stable state, the system is whirring away within. In a viable state, as is here meant, the organization is responding also to requirements for change from outside. It's a matter of balance between the two types of movement. Here, a number of questions arise: How much stability and how much viability are required? What determines the degree of tolerance for gaining internal efficiencies? And what determines the degree of change required to avoid obsolescence? It seems clear that some organizations seem committed to basic stability, while others seek rapid change. Why the differences?

In an oversimplification, the rate of change for viability is dictated by those changes in the external environment. Leaders are basically reactive. They react, and organizations respond, to alterations in technology, economics, and social trends outside the enterprise. The rate of environmental change governs the degree of stability that is tolerated. If forces in a certain organization's external field are swirling along at a change rate of, say, 50 percent a year, its leaders can only expect to preserve a corresponding rate of 50 percent a year for internal stability, *if they are to maintain environmental consonance.*

As examples, consider first a municipal utility that provides water to a district where little growth and few changes are experienced. We estimate that changes occur over, say, a year at a rate of only 20 percent. The remaining 80 percent of the institution's operations are essentially unaffected by outside influences. Those operations unaffected by change, with their related subsystems, thus, *can* be refined to get higher efficiency. For contrast, consider now a firm that engineers and produces plastic products, a business of high growth, new technology, and rapid changes of product line. We estimate that 80 percent of the operations are in a state of induced flux, dictating changes within a year. Only 20 percent of the organization's activities are stable enough to bring on internal efficiencies. During other periods, or course, the utility may be faced with rapid changes, while the plastics firm moves into a period of more stability.

There are at least four lessons for leaders in this organizational phenomenon. First, here again leaders are confronted with trade-offs. Volatile changes cause disequilibrium and inefficiency. To maintain the environmental consonance required for survival, we must forsake some degrees of efficiency, in the short-run at least. Those leaders who want the cake of efficiency but also want to consume it by initiating repeated changes are bound to be dissatisfied, if not frustrated, by the performance of their units. They cannot have maximum equilibrium in the midst of disequilibrium.

Second, an external environment producing only few changes can permit leaders to appraise, analyze, and refine internal operations systemically and behaviorally. Greater efficiencies within can then be made. However, the opportunity for efficiencies from stability can also lead to bureaucratization that stifles innovation, ingenuity, and the human spirit. Often (once is too often) an enterprise permits slowly evolving environmental changes to usher in organizational rigor mortis, to the detriment of all associated with the enterprise.

Third, external conditions change at a varying pace over the life span of an organization. Leaders should be quick to recognize this fact and to respond to these changes so that the organized effort will be strengthened. As an example, during one phase in an organization's span of operation, leaders may be preoccupied with internal affairs because outside forces demand little attention. However, in any phase of the life span, leaders' attention may have to be diverted from internal arrangements to external pressures so that collective energies are marshalled for appropriate responses. While the object of leadership is to preserve stability amidst change and change amidst stability, fluctuations in these conditions can, over time, require differing responses. As the challenges confronting their enterprise change, leaders must alter their expectations concerning the level of efficiency as it relates to the level of change.

Fourth, the people and ideas that fit an organization in the throes of sweeping changes differ from those that are congenial with a staid one.

The nature of the external environment, as we have stated, influences the character of the organization. The character of the organization, in turn, affects the types of people and ideas that are compatible with it. Some persons and their ideas would square nicely with the operations of the water utility, used above for illustrative purposes. Other persons and their ideas would happily match the operations of the plastics manufacturer. But would the same person and ideas as comfortably fit both institutional settings? Probably not. A person must do some soulsearching if hoping to be affiliated with an organization in a mutually satisfying relationship.

The Leadership Role

Leaders, in this discussion, are those men and women who formally influence the behavior of other people and in turn influence the organization. They may do so any place from the top of an organization down to the first level of leadership, or in some specialized staff positions dispersed throughout the enterprise. The term *leader* has been used synonymously with labels such as administrator, executive, manager, supervisor, or foreman. *Role* herein means the part people play in organizations. The leadership role is thereby the organizational part played by those persons who formally influence the behavior of other people and, as a consequence, affect the organization's behavior.

Basic Organization Needs

A human organization is a system, and like all systems it must be regulated, governed, or managed. Physical and living systems are governed by laws of nature. The continuity of the moving balance of the solar system is regulated by certain laws of force, acceleration, and mass. The dynamic equilibrium of a forest, lake, or desert is governed by natural laws of survival wherein plant and animal populations are in balance but are also constantly subjected to changes in their physical and biotic environment. Disasters such as major forest fires or floods may throw physical and natural systems out of equilibrium, but natural laws reestablish stability at a new point of equilibrium. Human systems, called organizations, must also be managed so as to maintain their dynamic equilibrium. But unlike systems of nature, no laws automatically preserve an organization's continuity nor ensure its viability. Leaders are functionally required to establish order, to interpret forces necessitating change, to mediate between external forces and organization reaction, and to reestablish order at a new point of balance, or equilibrium. If they are effective, the system survives; if they are not, the system dies.

Now let us review the basic organization needs to attain a state of directed dynamic equilibrium:

1. Common purpose, or goals
2. Social system and subsystems (technical, behavioral, cultural, physical, procedural, economic)
3. Force to cause action (actually reaction, brought on by delegation and other influences)
4. Internal consistency (refine systems for efficiency)
5. Environmental consonance (redirect system, goals and internal composition for long run effectiveness)

The fulfillment of these organizational needs is the responsibility of leadership. Hence, organization needs point up the functions that must be facilitated by leaders, and the appropriate role required to do so. In turn, when one grasps the functional relationship between an organization and its leadership, one can easily go a step beyond to understand its implications for preparation for leadership.

Leadership Functions

First, leaders set, define, and communicate the purpose, goals, or ends of organizational effort. This is basic to integrated, coordinated, and directed activity, whether the organization is a shoe-shine stand or General Motors; a commune, a kibbutz, or an army. Purpose is communicated by action and symbolism as well as words. To be effective, purpose needs to be accepted by those contributing to its fulfillment. This means, as we have asserted earlier, that "it must be redefined in terms of specific objectives for specialized units."[5]

Second, leaders design (most commonly redesign) the overall social system and its subsystems of operating relationships to encourage participants to strive for their part in the organization's goals. All joint human endeavors require subsystems for orderly operations. As examples, John A. Beckett observes:

> Rock groups, dance bands, symphony orchestras, athletic teams, committees, governments, and innumerable others offer ample additional evidence that even in organizations that consist exclusively of people, management is achieved largely through the instrumentality of a *system* of operating relationships. . . . In the case of music and athletic groups, for example, it is the system that enables the activity to be operated through the development of individual skills and through exhaustive rehearsal and practice of the group.[6]

Leaders anticipate a variety of conditions and design the overall system and its related parts so that needed operating relationships can flourish.

Third, leaders act as catalysts to induce reactions that will propel the system toward its goals. Since a leader's influence is brought to bear on the total structure, he or she serves both as system catalyst and regulator. The sound leader cannot exert random force on the organization, or induce behavior in one part to the jeopardy of others, or expect results from individuals that the system will not tolerate. It would be somewhat like reversing gears in a forward moving car only to find that the car has been damaged because the mechanized system cannot adjust. To make corrections or changes, the entire fabric of operating relationships must be considered.

Leadership to Barnard, though vital to organization success, was quite different from the function described in classical thought:

> Leadership is the power of individuals to inspire cooperative personnel decisions by creating faith—faith in common understanding, faith in the probability of success, faith in the ultimate satisfaction of personal motives, faith in the integrity of objective authority, faith in the superiority of common purpose as a personal aim of those who partake in it.[7]

The role of leadership is thus, in part, one of a moral element through which faith is created for sustaining cooperation. Without it, "organizations do not survive,"[8] as we have historically observed.

Fourth, leaders design and redesign systems to bring about internal consistency. Systems largely do the managing. It is unrealistic to believe that leaders manage an organization. In truth, "the organization as a whole manages itself."[9] At the least, the subsystems manage stability, continuity, and control.

Fifth, and last, leaders interpret environmental forces; translate their impact upon the organization; design changes that appear appropriate to cope with the changing environment; and implement the changes through adjustments in goals, means, and subsystems of activity. An organization must adjust constantly to both internal and external forces. Leaders (or, more completely, the hierarchy of leaders) are the nerve center of the enterprise. Part of a leader's role is to sense the need to adjust and to initiate appropriate action.

In sum, a leader's role includes the traits of innovator to establish and communicate purpose, systems designer, leader or catalyst, systems regulator and boundary mediator, and agent for change.[10] We can now summarize the leader's role *as a functional requirement of the organization* (Table 12-1). It seems clear that the role of leadership is based upon the needs of an organization. Further, it seems apparent that as emphasis shifts from one organizational need to another, related changes must ensue in leaders' roles. That is, at one span of time in an organization's life cycle, internal consistency may be of paramount importance, causing leaders to stress systems redesign and regulation. During another time span, on the other hand, the threat of organizational obsolescence might cause leaders to emphasize their role as agents for change.

Let's turn now from the relationships between organizational needs and leadership roles to the implications of these *reciprocal elements* for preparing a person for leadership.

TABLE 12–1. Functional Relationships of Organization Needs to the Leadership Role

Basic Organization Needs	*Basic Aspects of the Leadership Role*
1. Common purpose	1. Establish and communicate purpose
2. Social system and subsystems	2. Design systems and subsystems
3. Catalyst to place system into motion and maintain cooperation	3. Give direction
4. Internal consistency	4. Systems regulator, boundary mediator, and stabilizer for efficiency
5. Environmental consonance	5. Sensing and change agent for viability and long-run effectiveness

BASIC LEADERSHIP SKILLS

Widely recognized authorities on leadership have, over the last seventy years or so, introduced a number of ways of thinking about the skills required by leaders. Each way of thinking has been handily (though, at times, untidily) capsulized as a "school of leadership." These schools include, among others, the process, scientific management, human relations, decision theory, and systems schools. Each way of thinking about preparation for the practice of leadership vies for support through devotees who hold up their chosen school as "the" approach to mastering the art of leadership. Earlier, it was scientific management; later, human relations; now, it is systems theory. Perhaps this single-mindedness is the price to be paid for honest dedication to a certain belief. Yet no single way of thinking prepares one to lead. The diversity of the processes, functions, and roles assumed by a leader demands multidimensional preparation.

Let's consider, a final time, basic organizational needs as they relate to the primary functions required of leaders. But this time, we'll extend the implications one step further to include the attendant skills they need (Table 12-2). You will note that to fulfill the functions required by an enterprise, leaders at all levels need various types of orientation. Leaders are prepared by exposure to such teachings as systems thinking; technical, behavioral, and conceptual skills; processes of leadership; principles of leadership, sound attitudinal frameworks; and situational analyses. No one teaching suffices, but rather all of them merge into the *composite of skills* essential for leading any organization.

Let us look more closely at each type of skill as preparation for leadership, and at its part in strengthening managers.

Systems thinking is the way in which a set of units is viewed and its relationships understood. The conceptual ability is invaluable to leaders because it enables them to establish realistic organizational goals; to design and refine internal systems supporting goal attainment; and to sense and adapt to relevant, inevitable changes in external forces. Though of indispensable value to a competent leader, the systems approach has not replaced or negated less comprehensive models. As Beckett puts it:

> All that can now be said is that the new insights have further exposed the inadequacy of old models, provided a different approach to conceptualizing organization, and made possible the creation of models which are highly useful in visualizing the larger whole and managing some of its lesser subsystems.[11]

Leaders need to comprehend the entire system pertinent to their organizations if they are going to be able to do anything constructive about improving them.

Processes thinking insists that leadership is a function through which planning, organizing, (sometimes) staffing, directing, controlling, and (earlier) coordinating are facilitated. This way of thinking is also valuable because, whether the processes are systematized or not, leaders must ensure that these functions are fulfilled throughout their organization. They may be facilitated through subordinates' procedures, automation, or other extensions of leadership, but, they must be fulfilled if leaders are to provide the design of systems, be catalysts to action, and

---

TABLE 12–2. Sequential Relationships of Functional Organization Needs to the Functions and Skills of Leaders

Basic Organization Needs	Basic Leadership Functions	Basic Leadership Skills
1. Common purpose	1. Establish and communicate purpose	1. Systems oriented, conceptual, situational
2. Design social system and subsystems	2. Design systems	2. Systems orientation. Processes and principles of leadership and technical skills
3. Catalyst for action	3. Direction	3. Behavioral, situational, attitudinal set
4. Internal consistency (refine system)	4. Boundary mediator. Systems regulator. Stability → efficiency	4. Conceptual, technical, behavioral, systems oriented
5. Environmental consonance (introduce change)	5. Environmental sensitivity. Change agent. Viability → effectiveness	5. Conceptual, technical, behavioral, systems oriented, situational

regulators of systems. These elements are crucial to organizational success.

The dangers in viewing leadership as a process is that it falsely segments the total activity and holds the fragments in a static state for evaluation. Often, when we do so to simplify an intricate activity, we fail to put the activity under investigation back together. As A. Sommerhoff admonished: "The properties of the wholes are apt to be lost in the process of fragmentation."[12] There is value in studying the *structure* of leadership, just as there is benefit in studying the structure of society, matter, thought, people, or organizations. It can be of real value, as long as we recognize clearly that we unrealistically atomize and hold inactive a system of action that is in reality a dynamic, on-going interrelated process. Nevertheless, the structural approach to the study of leadership gives one structure and classifications within which concepts and principles can be evaluated.

Principles are generally accepted guides to thought processes, decision making, and action. They can serve as a foundation for the design or redesign of an organization. They can also be useful as guides in forming subsystems for activities and influences such as authority and status, communications, rewards and negative sanctions, and controls. An awareness of leadership principles permits a leader to be more effective in framing and reframing internal systems. The principles also provide proven guidelines applicable to each of the processes of leadership.

Attitudinal sets. A sage woman once told me, "to discuss attitudinal sets is to make common sense difficult." Yet, a set of sound attitudes is so crucial to the success of a leader that the risk of making "common sense difficult" must be taken.

Though technical competence—in economics, technology, and physical layout—is required, leaders also need to develop appropriate attitudes. Rarely do they fail because of technical ineptness, but many fail because of poor attitudes toward themselves or others. Exposure to the following lines of thinking can help them reappraise and redefine their roles and approaches to human interaction:

Appreciation for human wants
Realistic role relationships with subordinates
Recognition of the weaknesses of authority (power)
Congruent superior/subordinate interaction
Awareness of preconditioning
Humility in communicating
Tolerance for mistakes, both one's own and others'
Courage to delegate
Empathy: objectivity and subjectivity
Self-awareness
Mediation of pressure

A realistic attitudinal set is immensely important to a leader's success. Indeed, relatively few persons fail as leaders because of intellectual ineptness or technical incompetency. Rather, emotional weaknesses often cause their downfall. A healthy attitude, by contrast, can provide a leader with the outlook essential to design and manage a sound, productive enterprise.

Situational awareness is the ability to sense changing forces in the operating situation that suggest modifications in behavior, if a leader is to be effective. This type of sensitivity provides a map for realistic, consistent leadership behavior. With such vision the leader is better able to construct practical objectives; design a workable social structure; provide needed leadership; nurture internally consistent subsystems; sense the necessity for, and implement, change. Without situational awareness, the leader becomes ineffective and the organization grows insensitive to changing demands and hence obsolete. Robert Tannenbaum and Warren Schmidt put the issue squarely before leaders in this way:

> The successful leader is one who is keenly aware of those forces which are most relevant to his behavior at a given time. He accurately understands himself, the individuals and group he is dealing with, and the company and broader social environment in which he operates. And certainly he is able to assess the present readiness for growth of his subordinates. But this sensitivity is not enough . . . The successful leader is one who is able to behave appropriately in the light of these perceptions.[13]

SUMMARY

Leaders are expected to possess and to demonstrate skills of a general nature. Such knowledge can be developed only through multidimensional approaches to studying leadership. No narrow school of thought or single discipline could possibly provide adequate preparation for the challenge of management. This is the price one pays for serving in a sensitive position in a complex organization. Though the skills needed to deal with such complexity are naturally sophisticated, they are intimately related to the role required by the leadership, which is in turn functionally contingent upon the needs of the organization.

Each approach, each school presented, casts some light on the meaning of leadership just as analyzing organizations from various viewpoints produces a bit more awareness of their complex nature. But, as with the study of organizations, a composite picture of leadership is valuable. It is drawn from an understanding of systems thinking; technical, behavioral, and conceptual skills; processes of leadership; principles of leadership; sound attitudes; and situational analyses. All of these teachings combine to arm a leader with the composite of skills required to comprehend the nature—and practice the art—of leadership.

DISCUSSION QUESTIONS

1. Why are a high tolerance for relativity and a corresponding low need for absolutes helpful to leaders?

2. Many positions of leadership in complex organizations are specialized in that some are primarily accountable for maintaining stable operations while others are essentially responsible for introducing change. Why might this be important if you were deciding on a career position and career path? (Consider your needs.) Once you have chosen an entry level position, what then are its implications for preparatory training?

3. Do systems encourage or discourage the development of leaders' individual skills and contribution? Defend your answer.

4. There are "schools of leadership" available to us that offer various ways of thinking about the activity. Why doesn't any one suffice to prepare a person for leadership?

5. Relate "basic organization needs" to "basic aspects of the leadership role." What are the implications of these functional relationships for a person preparing to lead?

Epilogue

People can shape their institutions to suit their purposes, provided that they are clear as to what those purposes are; and provided that they are not too gravely afflicted with the diseases of which institutions die—among them complacency, myopia, an unwillingness to choose, and an unwillingness on the part of individuals to lend themselves to any worthy common purpose.

John W. Gardner[1]

We come finally to certain philosophical reflections on *The Nature of Organizations*. On one hand, this book merely provides various positions from which its readers can view and study the human dimensions of organizations. The viewpoint taken within each chapter could be expanded to book length. Further, the technostructure, microeconomic system, inner ecology, physical artifacts, and other mechanistic traits of organization behavior outside the human aspect might be given attention. The primary mission of the book, however, is to open to the reader whole new vistas of thought displaying a social system from different perspectives. The effort is eclectic, a drawing together of a number of seemingly unrelated views on organization theory into groups, or classes of thought.

On the other hand, the book suggests knowledge beyond mere understanding of organizations. It introduces a conceptual model of idealized behavior by an organization against which actual behavior can be measured. It also specifies certain of the reasons for institutional inefficiency, inhumanity, and rigidity. Herein lies the basis for philosophical comment.

Sound organizations are crucial to a sound society. This is clearly apparent when one recognizes that intermediate institutions—those

211

between the individual and the state—are the means through which nearly all of society's needs for services, goods, efficiency, and progress are satisfied. It is less apparent, though also of critical importance, that organizations are also looked to for nonmaterial satisfactions. People identify various needs as their own and affiliate with a variety of organizations to satisfy them. One person, for instance, may be a member of a company, a church, a political party, a fraternity, an alumni/ae association, a charity, a community, and a family; differing human needs are taken to various intermediate organizations, which are specialized to satisfy them effectively. This phenomenon is the mainspring of pluralism; and pluralism, in turn, is a basic reality of the structure of modern society. But other more basic human needs are also fulfilled through organization; yearnings for belonging, recognition, and self-fulfillment are most commonly satisfied through interaction with other people in concerted efforts.

Organizations are indispensable in supplying humanity's and society's material and nonmaterial wants. It is this *essentialness* of organizations that draws criticism from artful enemies and candid friends of a pluralistic society. They censure large organizations as entities alien to the individual; they condemn the costs to society of institutional inefficiency and of methods used for institutional self-preservation; and, most vocally, they deplore the inability of establishments to adjust to changing expectations from both individuals and society. All these defects are perceived as the malignant beginnings of the ultimate demise of our social order. In large measure, the criticisms are valid.

Organizations are often an unnatural arena for people's activities. The necessity for conformity, dependency, codetermination, and underachievement can be oppressive. Humans, after all, are the most intelligent of all species and thereby can be the most individuated. A person's natural state, contrasted with say, that of social insects, is minimal compliance with roles, division of activities, and organization. The human being lacks the instincts for social control through which physical specialization and cooperation are developed for community in lower orders. Our natural inclination is toward individualism; however, we must learn the socializing processes necessary to organize if our material and nonmaterial needs are to be fulfilled. As Ralph Linton satirically reports, "We are, in fact, anthropoid apes trying to live like termites, and, as any philosophical observer can attest, not doing too well at it."[2]

Organizations can spawn mediocrity. They moderate roles, norms, values, behavior, and expectations to an average acceptable between superior and inferior contributors. By so doing, limits for tolerable behavior are set: Inferior performers move up into the limits, or are rejected; superior performers, if viewed as a threat to the establishment, either scale their performance downward into the acceptable range or are rejected. Deviations are intolerable. We once saw pools of people who for cultural, age, sex, physical, ethnic, or other reasons were considered inferior.

Now, with widespread affirmative action programs required by law to correct those ills, we see those who were shut out being pushed in, and this causes other sorts of problems. We see individuals who because of high intellect, unwillingness to conform, or other reasons are also unfit for institutional service. Individuals in the first category are confined to ghettoes or reservations; those in the second also retreat to ghettoes and reservations—but these refuges go by names like Caltech, Salk Institute, UC Berkeley, and Rand Corporation. And no affirmative action law can pry them loose. We are all familiar and sympathetic with the plight of those who cannot be assimilated into organizations because they are viewed as "socially inferior." Let's consider the cost of losing those persons with superior potential to strengthen organizations. Here, we lose valuable critics of organizational life. No discord can be heard within. No discontents to raise discerning questions. No saviors to provide templates for better ways to proceed.

When deviant thinking is rejected in organizations under a totalitarian state, higher authorities can ostensibly bring on improvements in subordinate enterprises. But in a democracy, when mediocre organizations cannot tolerate superior deviations, where are the ideas to come from for superior organizational arrangements?

Organizations at times magnify immoral leadership. Some observers are saying that people in organizations emulate the moral codes of their leaders, as children often do with parents. If leaders set an unethical course, subordinates will tend to follow it.

Organizations can be inefficient drains on society's resources. It is true that resources drawn from outside an organization are employed within for two major purposes: the first, to produce a good or service wanted by some group; the second, to produce the forces required to maintain and perpetuate the organization. Thus, although resources are wasted in this process, it is presumed they will be offset by the organizational efficiencies achieved through specialization, mechanization, and automation. But, are inefficiencies offset? Let's consider the example of a college. When first established it draws resources from the community in the form of land, buildings, funds, and people to teach students. As the college matures, however, its leaders discover that there are other activities required for institutional self-maintenance and protection. The school must cultivate support from civic leaders, politicians, trustees, alumni/ae, and students' parents. Further, it must build elaborate systems of activities and structures of authority to fulfill the needs for self-maintenance. As a consequence, substantial amounts of resources are diverted from teaching to administration. Some of the school's most gifted faculty are taken from the classroom to pursue the broader objectives; the ratio of students to teachers increases; teaching and counseling become less personal; energies of teachers are invested in nonteaching activities; parts of the school's physical facilities are assigned to impress favorably, or accommodate, outside interests; and so on. At times, these self-maintaining activities appear to be of greater importance to the leaders than the institution's primary mission: teaching students. Self-maintenance becomes preëminent. Though all organizations must invest in self-preservation, such activities can become prohibitively wasteful, both in the use of resources and in the diversion of resources to organizations that can ignore economic justification. Enterprises that must justify themselves economically are at least economically efficient when compared with competitors, productive, or not.

Organizations can be ineffective in meeting needs for change. Such rigidity is detrimental to their individual participants and to the broader society. Leaders of institutions who are enthralled by their own aura of institutional security are wary of change. Yet society is caught up in a permanent revolution—technological, sociological, ideological. Expectations of organizations are changing at a whirlwind rate. Certain examples underscore the broad-gauged impact of these changes: Subordinates in the Roman Catholic Church have become more outspoken in opposition to the Pope's authority, students have beleaguered college administrators, union members have voted down contracts recommended by their elected officials, consumers are alarmed at the relentless pursuit of profits by businesses that neglect their social responsibilities and a distrustful electorate has grown reluctant to delegate decisions to representative governments. People have lost faith in traditional institutionalized arrangements and are no longer calm or acquiescent. Their concern encompasses all classes of organizations—churches, schools, unions, business, and government. And the organization that stands unresponsive in the way of the quest for progress—unwilling or unable to bend—will be broken.

Continuing reform has become the necessary way of organizational life. We must learn to reform established institutions in an orderly way, as we have learned to form them, if we are to avoid perpetuating the legacy of past errors. If we cannot or do not willingly develop the necessary skills, organizations will fail to act on the legitimate aspirations of those upon whom their survival depends. Participants or constituencies will feel irritation, frustration, desperation and, ultimately, failure when they come face-to-face with their inability to influence those institutions that dominate most aspects of their lives. When the fabric of institutionalized society is inflexible, or when it chafes the human spirit, destructive forces are unleashed. The threat of open rebellion led British Prime Minister Edward Heath to make the following statement to the U.N. General Assembly during its twenty-fifth anniversary session: "It is a somber thought, but it may be that in the 1970s civil war, not war between the nations, will be the main danger we will face."[3] Heath's prediction of civil wars and civil disorders is now history. The need for reform throws a heavy burden of responsibility upon the leadership of organizations at all levels—a responsibility to discern the guidelines for reform and to facilitate its realization.

The needs for organizational reform will doubtless multiply as a function of the greater intensity of interdependence between institutions and individuals on the one side, and the perpetuation of current ideological trends through succeeding generations on the other. It seems reasonable to conclude that the impact of the emerging values has been scarcely felt by the mainstream of organizations; but in the words of the legendary showman, Al Jolson, "You ain't seen nothin' yet!"

ELEMENTS OF ORGANIZATIONS' RENEWAL

An organization can be self-destructive if its leaders permit ethnocentrism among its members. A self-bestowed status of superiority breeds lethargy, absolutism, cultural deprivation, and zealous defense of the status quo. *Unalterable structures, dependent for survival upon a dynamic system, are doomed to obsolescence and finally failure.*

Leaders need a new philosophy conducive to the process of institutional self-renewal. Just as man and woman, marriage, society, and state need to be continuingly regenerated, so do organizations. Let me suggest several elements of a philosophy to ensure organizational renewal.

There are two curious facts about those organizations that fail: First, it is obviously impossible to find one that wanted to fail; and second, there were ample warnings of impending danger, clearly discernible to observers, preceding trouble. Now if these observations are true, why do leaders permit their organizations to fail? The eminent scholar and dedicated statesman, John W. Gardner, provides the most plausible answer:

> Eyes that see not, ears that hear not, minds that deny the evidence before them. When organizations are not meeting the challenge of change, it is as a rule not because they can't solve their problems but because they won't see their problems; not because they don't know their faults, but because they rationalize them as virtues or necessities.[4]

The moral is undeniable, the implications clear. Critical, comprehensive, objective reappraisal is mandatory. If an organization—whatever its mission—is to meet the challenge of the times, to avoid "the rapid obsolescence that overtakes the somnolent today,"[5] it must ask itself some difficult, uncomfortable, at times embarrassing, questions.

Some questions that leaders must answer follow: Specifically, what is our mission? What are our three to five most important objectives ranked in order of importance? Are there implicit nonrational goals? Are these *goals* or *means* to the real goals? Do the goals mesh wiith external expectations and constraints? Are our resources, particularly our human resources, organized so that they support the goals as we have ranked them? Which of our policies, strategies, and procedures get in the way of our attaining the goals? Do our people know how their endeavors fit the overall objectives? What information from the environment that is needed for decisions is not received because we do not have a program to accommodate it? What have we been refusing to hear from our critics? What unproductive activities have we tolerated because we, or someone, have a vested interest in preserving them? And (perhaps) how much damage has been perpetrated against the best interests of the organization through the abuse of power by men and women in sensitive positions—abuses of basic rights as all forms of prejudice, inequity, capricious behavior, or arbitrary discipline?

These types of disturbing questions are needed to determine the areas requiring reform. Answers to such questions, though often startling, are required to analyze the ways in which organizational arrangements need renewal. It is probably unduly optimistic to believe that those inside an organization could pose such delicate questions, much less probe into sensitive corners for replies. Nevertheless, answers to such questions are basic in anticipating requirements for change. It is probably more reasonable to expect that leaders—knowing the limitations of insiders' views, yet realizing the need for objective reappraisal of an organization—will summon competent outsiders for comprehensive, unbiased counsel. It may be, for this reason, that planning committees of organizations will someday include not only insiders for their technical and economic capabilities, but also outsiders for their conceptual skills and comprehensive appreciation of other aspects— sociopsychological, historical, anthropological, and philosophical—of an organization's environment.

An organization can be a responsive and responsible means for carrying out the weighty endeavors required to fulfill human needs. To attain such noble ends, however, leaders must understand organizational problems. They must be sensitive to forces dictating change. And leaders must possess analytical frameworks through which problems can be evaluated and solved. With skillful leadership, we just may be able to move Drucker's prophesy from the future to the present:

> In the long view of history, it is for social innovations—and not technical ones—that America may be best remembered.[6]

Notes

CHAPTER 1

1. Walter Goldschmidt, *Comparative Functionalism* (Berkeley, California: University of California Press, 1966), p. 42.

2. Robert Seidenburg, *Past Historic Man* (Boston: Beacon Press, 1952), p. 1.

3. José Ortega y Gasset, *Las Rebellión de la Masses* (Publisher left anonymous at author's request, 1930); and Wilhelm Röpke, *Jesuits von Angebot und Nachfrage,* (unknown).

4. Burleigh B. Gardner and David G. Moore, *Human Relations in Industry* (Homewood, Illinois: Irwin Publishing Co., 1964), p. 16.

5. Peter F. Drucker, *America's Next Twenty Years* (New York: Harper and Brothers, 1955), pp. 15–16.

6. This definition is one of the central premises of Chester I. Barnard's classic book, *The Functions of the Executive* (Cambridge, Massachusetts: Harvard University Press, 1938), and will be used throughout this text since it has stood the challenge of time.

7. At this point, the common traits are introduced as static elements in organizations. In chapters that follow, the false condition of constancy will be eliminated so that the reader can consider the elements as related, dynamic subsystems of organizations.

8. Professor William B. Wolf studied the idea that organizations develop a unique character, or "personality," and reported the findings as "Organizational Constructs: An Approach to Understanding Organizations," in *Journal of the Academy of Management,* I (1958), 8. Now, the concept is widely recognized by authorities as a reality and referred to frequently, though there is little agreement on a generally accepted term for the phenomenon.

9. Daniel Katz and Robert L. Kahn, *The Social Psychology of Organizations* (New York: John Wiley and Sons, Inc., 1966).

10. Ancient Indian parable.

CHAPTER 2

1. Daniel Katz and Robert L. Kahn, *The Social Psychology of Organizations* (New York: John Wiley & Sons, Inc., 1966) p. 113.

CHAPTER 3

1. Robert Desman, organization behavioralist and associate in consulting. Interview on May 7, 1975 at Scottsdale, Arizona.

2. Thomas M. Ware, "An Executive's Viewpoint," *Operations Research*, VII (1959), 3–4.

CHAPTER 4

1. John A. Beckett, Management Dynamics: The New Synthesis (New York: McGraw-Hill Book Company, 1971) p. 147.

CHAPTER 5

1. William G. Scott, "Organization Theory: An Overview and an Appraisal," *Journal of the Academy of Management* (April, 1961), p. 8.

2. Some of the lasting contributions to the way we think about organizing came from Frederick W. Taylor, Henry L. Gantt, Frank and Lillian Gilbreth, Morris L. Cooke, Harrington Emerson, and Henri Fayol.

3. Keith Davis and Robert L. Bloomstrom, *Business And Its Environment* (New York: McGraw-Hill Book Company, 1966), p. 78.

4. Fayol, Henri, *Industrial and General Administration* (Geneva, Switzerland: International Management Institute, 1925). The book was originally written in French in 1908 and, upon presentation, was translated into English and German in 1925 by the Institute.

5. This is a part of an analysis that appeared earlier as an article written by the author entitled "The Myth Inherent in Responsibility Center Management," *MSU Business Topics*, (Spring 1972), pp. 49–58, and as a part of a collection of his essays entitled *Exploring Vital Elements of Organization and Management*, (Dubuque, Iowa: Kendall/Hunt Publishing Co., 1976).

6. Luther Gulick and L. Urwick, eds., *Papers on the Science of Administration* (New York: Institute of Public Administration, 1937).

7. Frederick W. Taylor, *The Principles of Scientific Management* (New York: Harper and Brothers, 1911), pp. 50–55.

8. Frederick W. Taylor, *Shop Management* (New York: Harper and Brothers, 1903) p. 58.

9. Henry L. Gantt, "Work, Wages, and Profits," *The Engineering Magazine Company*.

10. Wallace Clark, *The Gantt Chart* (New York: The Ronald Press, 1922).

11. Frank Gilbreth, *Bricklaying System* (New York: M. C. Clark Publishing Co., 1909).

12. Harrington Emerson, *The Twelve Principles of Efficiency* (New York: John R. Dunlop, 1911).

13. Morris L. Cooke, *Our Cities Awake* (New York: Doubleday, Doran and Co., 1918).

14. Fayol, *Op. cit.*

15. See C. Bertrand Thompson's *The Theory and Practice of Scientific Management* (Boston, Mass.: Mifflin Co., 1917).

CHAPTER 6

1. William B. Wolf, *Conversations with Chester I. Barnard* (Ithaca, N.Y.: ILR paperback No. 12, Cornell University, 1973) p. 29.

2. Interview with William Patterson, Senior Consultant (Firm name withheld), Los Angeles, March 1967.

3. Sir Ian Hamilton, *The Soul and Body of an Army* (London: Edward Arnold and Company, 1921), p. 229.

4. V. A. Graicunas, "Relationship in Organization," in *Papers on the Science of Administration*, eds. Luther Gulick and L. Urwick (New York: Institute of Public Administration, 1937), pp. 181 ff.

5. James H. Healey, *Executive Coordination and Control* (New York: American Management Association, 1962), p. 77.

6. See William T. Greenwood, *Management and Organizational Behavior Theories* (Cincinnati, Ohio: South-Western Publishing Company, 1965); Harold Koontz and Cyril O'Donnell, *Principles of Management* (New York: McGraw-Hill Book Company, Inc., 1959); Justin G. Longenecker, *Principles of Management and Organizational Behavior* (Columbus, Ohio: Charles E. Merrill Books, Inc., 1964); William H. Newman, Charles E. Summer, and Kirby Warren, *The Process of Management* (Englewood Cliffs, New Jersey: Prentice-Hall, Inc., 1967); George R. Terry, *Principles of Management* (Homewood, Illinois: Richard D. Irwin, 1964).

7. Longenecker, *Principles of Management*, p. 180.

8. Ibid.

9. Greenwood, *Management Theories*, pp. 451–52.

10. Ibid.

11. J. C. Worthy, "Men, Management, and Organization," Proceedings of the Fifth Personnel Management and Industrial Relations Seminar (Los Angeles: October 1951).

12. George Filipetti, *Industrial Management in Transition* (Homewood, Illinois: Richard D. Irwin, Inc., 1953) p. 36.

13. Terry, *Principles of Management*, p. 397.

14. Ibid., p. 404.

15. Ibid., p. 394.

16. *Holy Bible*, King James Version, Exod., 19: 17–23.

17. Ibid., 19: 21.

CHAPTER 7

1. Chester I. Barnard, *Functions of the Executive* (Cambridge, Mass.: Harvard University Press, 1938), p. 137.

2. Claude A. Villee, *Biology* (W. B. Saunders Company: Philadelphia, 1962) chap. 21–26.

3. For study of other related subsystems, see Frank Baker, *Organizational Systems* (Homewood, Ill.: Richard D. Irwin, Inc., 1973) Section IV for a general orientation. For *communications subsystems*, see William T. Greenwood, *Decision Theory and Information Systems* (Cincinnati, Ohio: South-Western Publishing Company, 1969); Henry C. Lucas, Jr., *Computer Based Information Systems in Organizations* (Chicago, Ill.: Science Research Associates, Inc., 1973), chap. 14; Robert V. Head, *Manager's Guide to Management Information Systems* (Englewood Cliffs, N.J.: Prentice-Hall, Inc., 1972), chap. 6; William A. Bocchino, *Management Information Systems* (Englewood Cliffs, N.J.: Prentice-Hall, Inc., 1972), chap. 5; Fremont E. Kast and James E. Rosenzweig, *Organization and Management: A Systems Approach* (New York: McGraw-Hill Book Company, 1970), chaps. 12, 13, and 16; and Richard C. Huseman, Cal M. Logue, and Dwight L. Freshley, *Readings in Interpersonal and Organizational Communications* (Boston: Holbrook Press, Inc., 1974). For *incentive subsystems*, see David L. Cleland and William R. King, *Management: A Systems Approach* (New York: McGraw-Hill Book Company, 1972), Section five; and Rocco Carzo, Jr. and John W. Yanouzas, *Formal Organization: A Systems Approach* (Homewood, Ill.: Richard D. Irwin, Inc., 1967), chap. 15 (also chap. 8 on authority and control). For *control subsystems*, see Martin K. Starr, *System Management of Operations* (Englewood Cliffs, N.J.: Prentice-Hall, Inc., 1971); Richard A. Johnson, Fremont E. Kast, and James E. Rosenzweig, *The Theory and Management of Systems*. (New York: McGraw-Hill Book Company, 1973), chap. 4; Richard J. Hopeman, *Systems Analysis and Operations Management* (Columbus, Ohio: Charles E. Merrill Publishing Co., 1969), Part II; John Beishon and Geoff Peters, *Systems Behaviour* (London: Harper and Row, Publishers, 1972), chap. 7; Van Court Hare, Jr., *Systems Analysis: A Diagnostic Approach* (New York: Harcourt, Brace & World, Inc., 1967), chap. 5; John P. van Gigch, *Applied General Systems Theory* (New York: Harper and Row, Publishers, Inc., 1974), chaps. 15 and 16; David L. Cleland and William R. King, *Systems Analysis and Project Management* (New York: McGraw-Hill Book Company, 1968), chap. 11 (see also chap. 10 on authority); John A. Seiler, *Systems Analysis in Organizational Behavior* (Homewood, Ill.: Richard D. Irwin, Inc., 1967), chap. 5 on social control; and Koya Azumi and Jerald Hage, *Organizational Systems* (Lexington, Mass.: D. C. Heath and Company, 1972), Part 4, communications and control.

4. The following discussion is based on a paper by the author entitled "The Myth Inherent in Responsibility Center Management," in *MSU Business Topics* (Spring 1972), pp. 49–58. The term "responsibility center" refers to a unit

where a leader is held accountable for results related to managing either costs, revenues, or profit.

5. The momentum generated by these types of constraints is somewhat related to the situation of providing special reports to top management, as seen from the viewpoint of a first-level supervisor. A chief executive requests a report in two weeks. The subordinate, allowing a margin for review, error, and so forth, requests the data in ten days. The next lower subordinate cuts the followup to one week. The deadline is tightened as the request moves downward until it is received by the first-level superior, who must provide the information—and it was effectively needed yesterday.

6. E. Wight Bakke, *Bonds of Organizations,* 2nd ed. (New York: Archon Books, 1966), p. xix.

CHAPTER 8

1. E. Wight Bakke, *The Fusion Process.* An interim report (New Haven, Conn.:, 1952), Labor and Management Center, Yale University, p. 12.

2. Chris Argyris, *Diagnosing Human Relations in Organizations* (New Haven, Conn.: Yale University Press, 1956), p. 17.

3. Walter Goldschmidt, *Comparative Functionalism* (Berkeley, Calif.: University of California Press, 1966), p. 53.

4. For a more detailed discussion, see Robert Grandford Wright, *Mosaics of Organization Character* University of Cambridge Press Series. (New York: The Dunellen Company, 1975).

5. The consultants interviewed represent a total of 220 years of experience in analyzing organizations for twenty-five national and international consulting firms. Each consultant was experienced in "organization planning," that is, the analysis of organizations to determine their requirements for people to reach enterprise goals efficiently. As such, the type of assignment taken requires a comprehensive approach to analysis. Though the use of expert judgments does not rule out other approaches to understanding organizations, their opinions are both more credible than their negation and more valid than other feasible sources.

The consultants asked that their names and firms be kept confidential, because they were dealing with sensitive information about the culmination of their experiences with a host of anonymous, but real, clients. The condition was readily agreed upon to ensure openness and candor. You may be assured, however, that the respondents who contributed the vignettes that follow are successful, experienced professionals who serve well as expert authorities.

6. William G. Scott, "Organization Theory: An Overview and an Appraisal," *Journal of the Academy of Management,* IV, No. 1 (1961), p. 11.

7. It may be that when a leader wishes to act in a nonrational or irrational way for personal reasons, rather than for institutional reasons, the leader reconceives his or her "interpretations" of the operating situation and acts in a way that now appears congruent with the newly defined appraisal of the situation.

8. Scott, "Organization Theory," p. 15.

9. Ibid., p. 17.

CHAPTER 9

1. Saul W. Gellerman, *People, Problems, and Profits* (New York: McGraw-Hill Book Company, 1960), p. 74.
2. See Philip Selznick, "Foundations to the Theory of Organization," *American Sociological Review*, XIII (1948), 30; and Joseph W. McGuire, *Business and Society*, (New York: McGraw-Hill Book Company, 1963) pp. 160–163.
3. See Justin G. Longenecker, *Principles of Management and Organizational Behavior*, Columbus, Ohio: Charles E. Merrill Books, Inc., 1964) pp. 313–324.
4. See Robert Presthus, *The Organizational Society*, (New York: Alfred A. Knopf, Inc., 1962) pp. 94–95.
5. *Ibid.*
6. See Gellerman, *People, Problems, and Profits*, esp. Chapter 3.
7. Harold A. Larrabee, *Reliable Knowledge*, (Boston: Houghton Mifflin Company, 1964), p. 340.
8. These findings were provided by experts and were partially presented in Chapter 8.
9. See Larry Senn's *Organization Character As A Methodological Tool In The Analysis of Business Organizations.* (Unpublished doctoral dissertation, University of Southern California, 1970) pp. 240–245.
10. The organization used for illustrative purposes was explored and analyzed by the author.
11. Larrabee, *Reliable Knowledge*, p. 340.

CHAPTER 10

1. Max Wertheimer, *Productive Thinking* (New York: Harper and Brothers, 1945), p. 3.
2. William Wister Haines, *The Image*, (New York: Simon and Schuster, 1968), p. 27.
3. Chester I. Barnard, *The Functions of the Executive* (Cambridge, Mass.: Harvard University Press, 1938), p. 216.
4. There are those who believe that the catalyst to organizational dynamics comes from the individual motivations of the members of the enterprise. Individual motivations, however, do not lead to orderly interaction or motion. In fact, they will bring on disorderly interaction if they are not calibrated. Leaders are the persons in the positions necessary to facilitate orderly, coordinated interaction or motion.
5. Fred E. Fiedler, *A Theory of Leadership Effectiveness* (New York: McGraw-Hill Book Company, 1967), pp. 143–144.
6. R. Tannenbaum and W. H. Schmidt, "How to Choose a Leadership Pattern," *Harvard Business Review* XXXVI, No. 2, (1958), pp. 95–101.
7. William B. Wolf, *The Management of Personnel*, (San Francisco, Calif.: Wadsworth Publishing Company, Inc., 1961) among other of his writings.
8. This idea also applies to political leadership. See Walter Goldschmidt, *Comparative Functionalism* (Berkeley, Calif.: University of California Press, 1966).

9. Leonard R. Sayles, *Individualism and Big Business* (New York: McGraw-Hill Book Company, 1963), pp. 182–183.

10. These programs are called, "organization development," a name given to an approach whereby behavioral scientists seek to improve organizations through planned, systematic, long-range efforts focused on the enterprise's character and its human and social processes. See Wendell L. French and Cecil H. Bell, Jr., *Organization Development* (Englewood Cliffs, N.J.: Prentice-Hall, Inc., 1973).

CHAPTER 11

1. John W. Gardner, *No Easy Victories*, (New York: Harper & Row, Publishers, 1968). See especially Chapter VII, "The Life and Death of Institutions."

2. William B. Wolf, *How to Understand Management* (Los Angeles, Calif.: Lucas Brothers Publishers, 1968) p. 26.

3. Interview with Jack R. Dustman, Professor, Northern Arizona University, Flagstaff, Arizona, May 1975.

4. Chester I. Barnard, as reported by William B. Wolf in "Precepts for Managers: Interviews with Chester I. Barnard," *California Management Review*, VI, No. 1, (1963), p. 91.

5. John A. Howard, *Marketing: Executive and Buyer Behavior*, (New York: Columbia University Press, 1963), p. 29. See Chapter II, "Organization Theory and Marketing."

6. Daniel Katz and Robert L. Kahn, *The Social Psychology of Organizations*, (New York: John Wiley and Sons, Inc., 1966) p. 109.

7. Howard, *Marketing*, p. 33.

8. Nicolo Machiavelli, *The Prince*, translated with an introduction by W. W. Marriott (New York: Collier, 1938) p. 206.

9. John A. Beckett, *Management Dynamics: The New Synthesis* (New York: McGraw-Hill Book Company, 1971), p. 176.

10. Max Ways, "Tomorrow's Management: A More Adventuresome Life in a Free Form Organization," *Fortune*, (volume, issue unknown), p. 83.

11. Keith Davis and Robert L. Blomstrom, *Business and Its Environment* (New York: McGraw-Hill Book Company, 1966) p. 92.

CHAPTER 12

1. William B. Wolf, Management: Readings Toward a General Theory (Belmont, Calif.: Wadsworth Publishing Company, Inc., 1964) p. 326.

2. Jay W. Forrester, "The Structure Underlying Management Processes," Address to The Academy of Management. (Chicago, December 31, 1964)

3. Paul R. Lawrence and Jay W. Lorsch, *Organization and Environment: Managing Differentiation and Integration*, (Boston, Mass.: Division of Research, Graduate School of Business Administration, Harvard University, 1967), p. 160.

4. Lawrence and Lorsch *Organization and Environment*, p. 160–161.

5. Chester I. Barnard, as reported by William B. Wolf in *How to Understand Management* (Los Angeles, Calif: Lucas Brother Publishers, 1968) p. 27.

6. John A. Beckett, *Management Dynamics: The New Synthesis* (New York: McGraw-Hill Book Company, 1971), p. 138.

7. Chester I. Barnard, *The Functions of the Executive* (Cambridge, Mass.: Harvard University Press, 1938), p. 259.

8. Wolf, *How to Understand*, p. 27.

9. Barnard, *Functions of Executive*, p. 216.

10. Keith Davis and Robert L. Blomstrom *Business and Its Environment*, (New York: McGraw-Hill Book Company, 1966), pp. 92–93.

11. Beckett, *Management Dynamics*, p. 146.

12. *Ibid.*, p. 146.

13. Robert Tannenbaum and Warren Schmidt, "How to Choose a Leadership Pattern," *Harvard Business Review*, Mar.-Apr., 1958, p. 101.

EPILOGUE

1. John W. Gardner, *No Easy Victories* (New York: Harper and Row Publishers, 1968), p. 41.

2. Ralph Linton, *The Tree of Culture* (New York: Alfred A. Knopt, Inc., 1957), p. 57.

3. Edward Heath, *Provisional Verbatim Record of the 1881 Meeting of the U.N. General Assembly*, October 23, 1970, New York, pp. 31–43.

4. Gardner, *op. cit.*, p. 44.

5. *Ibid.*

6. Peter Drucker, *America's Next Twenty Years* (New York: Harper and Brothers, 1955), pp. 15–16.

Bibliography

Argyris, Chris. *Diagnosing Human Relations in Organizations.* New Haven, Conn., Yale University Press, 1956.

Azumi, Koya, and Jerald Hage. *Organizational Systems.* Lexington, Mass., D. C. Heath and Company, 1972.

Baker, Frank. *Organizational Systems.* Homewood, Ill., Richard D. Irwin, Inc., 1973.

Bakke, E. Wight. *Bonds of Organization.* New York, Anchor Books, 1966.

——— *The Fusion Process.* New Haven, Conn., Labor and Management Center, Yale University, 1952.

Barnard, Chester I. *The Functions of the Executive.* Cambridge, Mass., Harvard University Press, 1938.

Beckett, John A. *Management Dynamics: The New Synthesis.* New York, McGraw-Hill Book Company, 1971.

Beishon, John, and Geoff Peters. *Systems Behavior.* London, Harper & Row, Publishers, 1972.

Bocchino, William A. *Management Information Systems.* Englewood Cliffs, N.J., Prentice-Hall, Inc., 1972.

Carzo, Rocco, Jr., and John N. Yanouzas. *Formal Organization: A Systems Approach.* Homewood, Ill., Richard D. Irwin, Inc., 1967.

Clark, Wallace. *The Gantt Chart.* New York, The Ronald Press, 1922.

Cleland, David L., and William R. King. *Management: A Systems Approach.* New York, McGraw-Hill Book Company, 1972.

——— *Systems Analysis and Project Management.* New York, McGraw-Hill Book Company, 1968.

Combs, Arthur W., and Donld Snygg. *Individual Behavior,* rev. ed. New York, Harper & Brothers, 1959.

Cooke, Morris L. *Our Cities Awake.* New York, Doubleday, Doran and Co., 1918.

225

Davis, Keith, and Robert L. Bloomstrom. *Business and Its Environment.* New York, McGraw-Hill Book Company, 1966.

Drucker, Peter F. *America's Next Twenty Years.* New York, Harper & Brothers, 1955.

Emerson, Harrington. *The Twelve Principles of Efficiency.* New York, John R. Dunlop, 1911.

Fayol, Henri. *Industrial and General Administration.* Geneva, Switzerland, International Management Institute, 1925.

Fiedler, Fred E. *A Theory of Leadership Effectiveness.* New York, McGraw-Hill Book Company, 1967.

Filipetti, George. *Industrial Management in Transition.* Homewood, Ill., Richard D. Irwin, Inc., 1953.

French, Wendell L., and Cecil H. Bell, Jr. *Organizational Development.* Englewood Cliffs, N.J., Prentice-Hall, Inc., 1973.

Gantt, Henry L. "Works, Wages, and Profits." *The Engineering Magazine Company*, n.p.

Gardner, Burleigh B., and David G. Moore. *Human Relations in Industry.* Homewood, Ill., Richard D. Irwin, Inc., 1964.

Gardner, John W. *No Easy Victories.* New York, Harper & Row, 1968.

Gellerman, Saul W. *People, Problems, and Profits.* New York, McGraw-Hill Book Company, 1960.

Gilbreth, Frank. *Bricklaying System.* New York, M. C. Clark Publishing Co., 1909.

Goldschmidt, Walter. *Comparative Functionalism.* Berkeley, Calif., University of California Press, 1951.

Graicunas, V. A. "Relationship in Organization." In *Papers on the Science of Administration*, edited by Luther Gulick and L. Urwick. New York, Institute of Public Administration, 1937.

Greenwood, William T. *Decision Theory and Information Systems.* Cincinnati, Ohio, Southwestern Publishing Company, 1969.

—— *Management and Organizational Behavior Theories.* Cincinnati, Ohio, Southwestern Publishing Company, 1965.

Gulick, L., and L. Urwick, eds. *Papers on the Science of Administration.* New York, Institute of Public Administration, 1937.

Haines, William Wister. *The Image.* New York, Simon & Schuster, 1968.

Hamilton, Ian, *The Soul and Body of an Army.* London, Edward Arnold and Company, 1921.

Hare, Van Court, Jr. *Systems Analysis: A Diagnostic Approach.* New York, Harcourt, Brace & World, Inc., 1967.

Head, Robert V. *Manager's Guide to Management Information Systems.* Englewood Cliffs, N.J., Prentice-Hall, Inc., 1972.

Healey, James H. *Executive Coordination and Control.* New York, American Management Association, 1962.

Heath, Edward. Provisional Verbation. Record of the 1881 Meeting of the United Nations General Assembly, October 23, 1970, New York.

Holy Bible, King James Version, Book of Exodus.

Hopeman, Richard J. *Systems Analysis and Operations Management.* Columbus, Ohio, Charles E. Merrill Publishing Co., 1969.

Howard, John A. *Marketing: Executive and Buyer Behavior.* New York, Columbia University Press, 1963.

Huseman, Richard C., Cal M. Logue, and Dwight L. Freshley. *Readings in Interpersonal and Organizational Communications.* Boston, Holbrook Press, Inc., 1974.

Johnson, Richard A., Fremont E. Kast, and James E. Rosenzweig. *The Theory and Management of Systems.* New York, McGraw-Hill Book Company, 1973.

Kast, Fremont E. and James E. Rosenzweig. *Organization and Management: A Systems Approach.* New York, McGraw-Hill Book Company, 1970.

Katz, Daniel, and Robert L. Kahn. *The Social Psychology of Organizations.* New York, John Wiley and Sons, Inc., 1966.

Koontz, Harold, and Cyril O'Donnell. *Principles of Management.* New York, McGraw-Hill Book Company, 1959.

Larrabee, Harold A. *Reliable Knowledge.* Boston, Houghton Mifflin Company, 1964.

Lawrence, Paul R., and Jay W. Lorsch. *Organization and Environment: Managing Differentiation and Integration.* Boston, Mass., Harvard University, 1967.

Linton, Ralph. *The Tree of Culture.* New York, Alfred A. Knopf, Inc., 1957.

Longenecker, Justin G. *Principles of Management and Organizational Behavior.* Columbus, Ohio, Charles E. Merrill Books, Inc., 1964.

Lucas, Henry C., Jr. *Computer Based Information Systems in Organizations.* Chicago, Ill., Science Research Associates, Inc., 1973.

Machiavelli, Nicolo. *The Prince.* Translated by W. W. Marriott. New York, Collier, 1938.

McGuire, Joseph W. *Business and Society.* New York, McGraw-Hill Book Company, 1963.

Newman, William H., Charles E. Summer, and Kirby Warren. *The Process of Management.* Englewood Cliffs, N.J., Prentice-Hall, Inc., 1967.

Ortega y Gasset, Juan. *Las Rebellion de la Masses.* Publisher left anonymous at author's request, 1930.

Presthus, Robert. *The Organizational Society.* New York, Alfred A. Knopf, Inc., 1962.

Ropke, Wilhelm. *Jesuits von Angebot und Nachfrage.* Undisclosed.

Sayles, Leonard R. *Individualism and Big Business.* New York, McGraw-Hill Book Company, 1963.

Scott, William G. "Organizational Theory: An Overview and an Appraisal." *Journal of the Academy of Management* 4 (April, 1961), p. 11.

Selznick, Philip. "Foundations to the Theory of Organization." *American Sociological Review* XIII (February, 1948), p. 30.

Seidenburg, Robert. *Past Historic Man.* Boston, Beacon Press, 1952.

Seiler, John A. *Systems Analysis in Organizational Behavior.* Homewood, Ill., Richard D. Irwin, Inc., 1967.

Senn, Larry. "Organization Character As a Methodological Tool In The Analysis of Business Organizations." Unpublished doctoral dissertation, University of Southern California, 1968.

Starr, Martin K. *System Management of Operations.* Englewood Cliffs, N.J., Prentice-Hall, Inc., 1971.

Tannenbaum, R., and W. H. Schmidt. "How to Choose a Leadership Pattern." *Harvard Business Review* 36 (March-April, 1958), pp. 95–101.

Taylor, Frederick W. *The Principles of Scientific Management.* New York, Harper & Brothers, 1911.

――― *Shop Management.* New York, Harper & Brothers, 1903.

Terry, George R. *Principles of Management.* Homewood, Ill., Richard D. Irwin, Inc., 1964.

Thompson, C. Bertrand. *The Theory and Practice of Scientific Management.* Boston, Mifflin Co., 1917.

van Gigch, John P. *Applied General Systems Theory.* New York, Harper & Row, 1974.

Villee, Claude A. *Biology.* Philadelphia, Pa., W. B. Saunders Company, 1962.

Ware, Thomas M. "An Executive's Viewpoint." *Operational Research* VII (1959), pp. 3–4.

Wertheimer, Max. *Productive Thinking.* New York, Harper & Brothers, 1945.

Wolf, William B. *Conversations with Chester I. Barnard.* Ithaca, N.Y., Cornell, 1973.

――― *How to Understand Management.* Los Angeles, Cal., Lucas Brothers, 1968.

――― *The Management of Personnel.* San Francisco, Cal., Wadsworth Publishing Company, Inc., 1961.

――― *Management: Readings Toward a General Theory.* Belmont, Cal., Wadsworth Publishing Company, Inc., 1964.

――― "Organizational Constructs: An Approach to Understanding Organizations." *Journal of the Academy of Management* I (April, 1958), p. 8.

――― "Precepts for Managers: Interviews with Chester I. Barnard." *California Management Review* VI (Fall, 1963), p. 91.

Worthy, J. C. "Men, Management, and Organization." Proceedings of the Fifth Personnel Management and Industrial Relations Seminar: October, 1951.

Wright, Robert Grandford. *Exploring Vital Elements of Organization and Management.* Dubuque, Iowa, Kendall/Hunt Publishing Company, 1975.

――― *Mosaics of Organizational Character.* New York, The Dunellen Company, University of Cambridge Press Series, 1975.

Index